HEALTH POLICY REFORM IN CHINA

A Comparative Perspective

Series on Contemporary China   (ISSN: 1793-0847)

Series Editors: Joseph Fewsmith *(Boston University)*
Zheng Yongnian *(East Asian Institute, National University of Singapore)*

Published*

**To view the complete list of the published volumes in the series, please visit:
http://www.worldscientific.com/series/scc

Series on Contemporary China – Vol. 36

HEALTH POLICY REFORM IN CHINA

A Comparative Perspective

Jiwei Qian

East Asian Institute, National University of Singapore, Singapore

Åke Blomqvist

Carleton University, Canada & C.D. Howe Institute, Canada

World Scientific

NEW JERSEY · LONDON · SINGAPORE · BEIJING · SHANGHAI · HONG KONG · TAIPEI · CHENNAI

Published by

World Scientific Publishing Co. Pte. Ltd.

5 Toh Tuck Link, Singapore 596224

USA office: 27 Warren Street, Suite 401-402, Hackensack, NJ 07601

UK office: 57 Shelton Street, Covent Garden, London WC2H 9HE

Library of Congress Cataloging-in-Publication Data
Qian, Jiwei, 1976–   , author.
  Health policy reform in China : a comparative perspective / Jiwei Qian, Åke Blomqvist.
    p. ; cm. -- (Series on contemporary China ; vol. 36)
  Includes bibliographical references and index.
  ISBN 978-9814425889 (hardcover : alk. paper) -- ISBN 9814425885 (hardcover : alk. paper)
  I. Blomqvist, Åke, 1941–   , author. II. Title. III. Series: Series on contemporary China ; v. 36.
  [DNLM: 1. Health Care Reform--methods--China. 2. Delivery of Health Care--China.
3. Economics, Medical--China. WA 530 JC6]
  RA410.55.C6
  338.4'736210951--dc23

                                                      2014025127

British Library Cataloguing-in-Publication Data
A catalogue record for this book is available from the British Library.

In-house Editor: Yvonne Tan

Typeset by Stallion Press
Email: enquiries@stallionpress.com

Printed in Singapore

ABOUT THE AUTHORS

Jiwei Qian is a research fellow in East Asian Institute, National University of Singapore. After obtaining a B.Sc. in Computer Science from Fudan University, China, he switched his field of study to Economics and travelled to the U.K. where he earned an M.Sc. in Development Economics from the School of Oriental and African Studies, University of London. He developed an interest in health economics while a graduate student in the Department of Economics at the National University of Singapore from where he received his PhD in 2010 after writing a dissertation on health policy in China. His subsequent research on Chinese health and social policy has been published in journals such as *The China Quarterly, Journal of Mental Health Policy and Economics, Singapore Economic Review,* and *East Asian Policy,* and as contributions to several books and conference proceedings.

Dr. Qian's current research interests include health economics, political economy and development economics. Most recently, he has been working on a project dealing with social policy reform in China.

Åke Blomqvist, a native of Sweden, received his PhD from Princeton University in 1971. He taught at the University of Western Ontario in Canada until 2002 when he moved to the National University of Singapore as Professor and Head of Economics. In 2009 he moved to Beijing to take up a position in the Center for Human Capital and Labor Economics Research at the Central University of Finance and Economics. Since 2011 he has resided in Ottawa, Canada where he is an Adjunct Research Professor in the Department of Economics,

Carleton University. He also is Health Policy Scholar in the C.D. Howe Institute, Toronto, Canada.

Blomqvist's two principal areas of research have been economics of developing countries, and economics of social policy, particularly in health care. His work in development economics included stints of teaching and research in West Africa, Pakistan, and India. In recent years, his research has focused on health policy and health system reform in China and Canada, and together with his graduate students and other co-authors he has published articles, book chapters, and reports, on these topics.

CONTENTS

PART I
INTRODUCTION

Chapter 1

HEALTH POLICY IN CHINA: INTRODUCTION AND BACKGROUND

1. Introduction

Government policy toward the health care system has played an important part in the process of modernizing China's economy and society that began with the founding of the People's Republic in 1949.

At the end of its first three decades, the government could point to its health policy as a comparative success, with some justification. Although the attempt to manage the economy at large through comprehensive central planning ultimately proved unsuccessful and was substantially abandoned around 1980, the health care system that was organized during the period of the centrally planned economy represented a vast improvement in comparison with what had gone before it.[1]

By the 1980s, the system of health care funding in China was such that almost everyone had access to at least a basic standard of care, at little or no out-of-pocket cost. In the countryside, most of the population belonged to an agricultural commune, and every member of a commune had access to basic primary care as well as (on referral) hospital care, at low out-of-pocket charges. In urban areas, workers and their dependents, as well as retirees, also had access to subsidized care through their employer (the government or a state-owned enterprise

---

[1]Duckett (2010, Chapter 2) describes China's health care system in the 1950–1980 period. Banister (1987) also discusses its contribution to declining mortality before the 1980s.

(SOE)). As in rural areas, user charges were strictly controlled at low levels, and most of the funding of health service providers came either from the employers or as direct state subsidies; hospitals were owned either by the state or by large SOEs. In rural areas, primary-care providers were paid by the commune, and hospitals were funded by a mix of state and local subsidies and fee payments from the Cooperative Medical Schemes to which commune members belonged.

One important consequence of the strengthening of the health care system during this period was a great improvement in the standards of public health. Not surprisingly, great emphasis was put on improving population health through measures such as control of infectious disease via improved sanitation, vaccination campaigns, and so on.[2] These developments were accompanied by dramatic improvements in the basic indicators of population health. For example, between the first half of the 1950s and the mid-1980s, average life expectancy at birth in China rose from around 40 years to 65 years. History offers few examples of such a large population undergoing as rapid and sustained a decrease in mortality as China did during that period. While other factors, such as improved food security after the famine during the Great Leap Forward, also were part of the reason for this transformation, it can nevertheless be taken as evidence that the health care system that had been established by the 1980s functioned remarkably well, producing population health indicators that were very good for a country at the low level of per capita income that China then had. As Figure 1 shows, life expectancy in China in recent decades has consistently been much higher than in India, and relatively close to that in Europe even though China's per capita income is still much lower than the European average.

In the three decades since the early 1980s, the most dramatic development in China has of course been the remarkable success of the new approach to economic management that was started under Deng Xiaoping after Mao's death.[3] But China's health care system has also continued to undergo dramatic changes, along with society

---

[2]Again, see Banister (1987).
[3]A comprehensive recent discussion is in Vogel (2011).

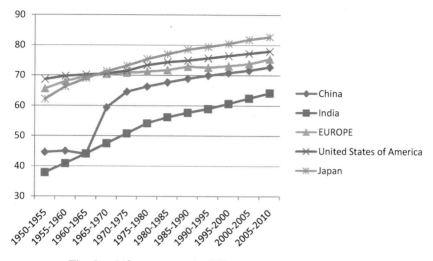

Fig. 1. Life expectancy in different countries, 1950–2010.

Source: United Nations, Department of Economic and Social Affairs, Population Division (2011), *World Population Prospects*.

at large. As the economy has grown and more resources have become available, the standards of medical care provided in some large hospitals in large Chinese cities are now similar to those in the world's high-income countries. Although the economy has been growing rapidly, health expenditures have grown even faster: between 1980 and 2010, the fraction of China's GDP that was devoted to health care grew from about 3.2% to over 5% (Figure 2).

But while the resources spent on health care have been rising rapidly and the standards of care may have been rising on average, as more modern and advanced drugs and treatment methods have come into use, they have not done so for all population groups. For a large proportion of China's citizens, access to medical care may currently be worse than it was several decades ago. At the same time, those people who *are* able to get medical care when they are seriously ill now often have to pay large amounts out of their own pocket, and the fear of large medical bills is one reason often cited in the press for the Chinese population's extraordinarily high savings rates. Generally speaking, dissatisfaction with the health care system in China today

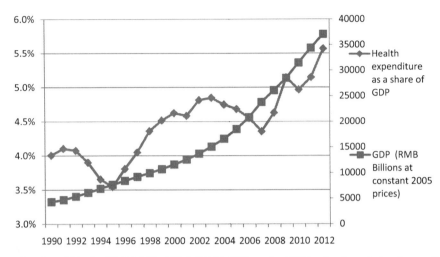

Fig. 2. China's GDP 1990–2012 (RMB Billions in 2005 prices), and the share of health expenditure in GDP.

Source: China Statistical Yearbook, various years.

ranks much more highly among citizens' concerns than it did three decades ago. In part, this of course reflects the remarkable success that China has had in raising the general standard of living of the population and lifting large numbers of people out of poverty. But while the economic policies that have been pursued to accomplish this have been enormously successful in most sectors, there are many who believe that in health care, they have made the system worse, not better, in important respects.[4]

---

[4]A substantial English-language literature now exists on the recent history of China's health care system and health policy. A detailed account from the late 1990s is Economist Intelligence Unit (1998). A very readable short summary of debates about Chinese health reform in the 1990s and early 2000s is Blumenthal and Hsiao (2005). A very detailed and careful set of Chinese-language papers on recent history and policy proposals is Ge *et al.* (2007). Blomqvist and Qian (2008) assess the reform proposals in an international comparative perspective, and in the year 2009, both *Health Economics* and *China Economic Review* published special issues about the reform process. Qian and Blomqvist (forthcoming) review recent developments of health reform in China since 2009. Duckett (2010) also reviews the history of health policy and how it has been affected by politics. Many papers and reports focusing on more specialized topics have also been published. For rural health care, an exceptionally detailed early account is in

2. The Health Care System Since the 1980s: Decentralization, Deregulation, and Reduced Subsidies

As China began moving away from the earlier centrally planned system of economic management toward a market-based one in the 1980s, three kinds of measures were implemented that deeply affected the population's access to health care. First, the commune model of organizing agricultural production was replaced by the "Household Responsibility System" under which land is allocated to individual families, and production and marketing decisions are decentralized to the family level. Second, many SOEs were privatized, reorganized, or even closed down. Third, responsibility for tax collection and funding of many kinds of government activity was to a large extent decentralized from the state to local levels of government.[5] These developments were to have profound effects, directly and indirectly, on the health care system.

2.1. *Reduced subsidies and higher patient charges*

As part of the fiscal decentralization process, state subsidies to hospitals were greatly reduced. While this was partially offset by increased subsidies from local governments, most hospitals nevertheless saw a large net decline in the government funding they received (especially in poorer regions where local government revenue was limited). To compensate, they were encouraged to find ways of generating more revenue from sources such as patient fees or markups on the drugs they provided.

Asian Development Bank (2002); more recently the World Bank has reviewed the rural system's progress in Wagstaff *et al.* (2009). Liu (2002) has a good early description of the background and design of the basic urban plans that cover employees; additional detail is in Liu, Nolan, and Wen (2004). For an account of public perceptions regarding these plans, see Wong, Tang, and Lo (2007).

[5] Here and in the rest of the book, we follow the convention of using "state" to refer to the central government, while "local government" refers to the provincial and lower levels.

While the state continued to maintain control over the fees charged for common ("basic") services and standard drugs, hospitals had more freedom in setting their own charges for various kinds of non-basic procedures (often those involving diagnosis or treatment with advanced equipment) and newer drugs. With reduced government subsidies and increased hospital autonomy, it became common for hospitals to compensate their doctors through a system of bonuses that were tied to hospitals' net revenue, which in turn depended partly on the amounts of money they were able to generate from patient charges and markups on the drugs they prescribed and sold. Indirectly, therefore, many doctors had an incentive to treat, and collect revenue from, a large number of patients, and to take into account the impact on the hospitals' revenue when making choices with respect to how to treat a patient with a given medical condition.

This shift in incentives on physicians may be part of the reason for the increase in the acquisition and high utilization of certain types of advanced medical equipment for which hospitals could charge high patient fees, and for the increasing rate of prescriptions of new drugs on which hospitals could charge high markups. These new patterns of medical care and drug prescriptions partly explain the very large increases that took place in the average cost per treatment or hospitalization episode during the late 1980s and 1990s.[6]

2.2. *Collapse of the rural Cooperative Medical Schemes*

At the same time that new treatment and prescription patterns raised the cost of each illness episode, there was an increase in the share of health care costs that individuals had to pay out-of-pocket. Prior to the 1980s, the fees charged by township and county hospitals for treating patients from rural areas were to a large extent paid for collectively, either by

---

[6]Data from *Chinese Health Statistical Yearbook* (various years) show that the average medical expense per in-patient episode rose from about 1,700 to 3,100 Yuan between 1995 and 2000, and to as much as 4,700 Yuan in 2006. (There was little or no general price inflation over this period.) In 2011, the average medical expense per in-patient episode rose to 6,600 Yuan.

the commune-sponsored Cooperative Medical Scheme to which all commune members belonged, or (for those with low income) from the village's collective welfare fund. Moreover, communes arranged and paid for most of the local primary care and pharmaceuticals that residents utilized. Since almost the entire rural population belonged to a local commune, this system came close to providing universal coverage, albeit for a relatively low level of care.

In the early 1980s, however, the system of communes was disbanded as agricultural production was reorganized on the basis of the "Household Responsibility System". While local government took over some of the functions that the communes had had, the state tried to maintain a low level of taxation on farmers and placed restrictions on local officials' taxation powers. An important decision was to interpret compulsory membership fees in a Cooperative Medical Scheme (CMS) as a tax, so that these schemes could only continue if farmers were willing to enroll on a voluntary basis. In most cases they were not, and most CMS plans collapsed. At the low point in the 1990s, only some 6.6% of the rural population belonged to a CMS; the remaining 87.3% were completely uninsured and had to pay the full cost of any medical care and drugs out of their own pocket (see Table 1).[7]

Table 1. Extent of health insurance coverage (percent of the respective populations).

	Urban			Rural		
	2003	1998	1993	2003	1998	1993
BHI	30.4	N/A	N/A	1.5	N/A	N/A
GIS/LIS	8.6	38.9	66.41	0.3	1.7	3.41
CMS	6.6	2.7	1.62	9.5	6.6	9.81
Other social insurance	2.2	10.9	4.44	1.2	3.0	2.34
Private insurance	5.6	3.3	0.25	8.3	1.4	0.33
No insurance	44.8	44.1	27.28	79.0	87.3	84.11

Source: National Survey on Health Service in 1993, 1998, 2003, Ministry of Health (2004, 2006).
Note: BHI and GIS/LIS are insurance schemes that primarily cover urban workers.

---

[7]An extensive review of the situation in the rural-area health care sector is in Asian Development Bank (2002).

2.3. *Reduced insurance coverage in urban areas*

In the urban areas, too, the proportion of health care that patients had to pay out-of-pocket increased, as many workers and their dependents became uninsured. Under the earlier system, most urban residents were insured either under the Government Insurance Scheme (GIS) which covered government employees and their dependents, or under the Labor Insurance Scheme (LIS) which covered workers in SOEs and (with reduced benefits) their dependents. But through the 1990s, there was a substantial reduction in the proportion of residents covered by these plans. Part of the reason for this was the trend toward privatization and increased financial autonomy for State-Owned Enterprises (SOEs).[8]

SOEs scheduled for privatization resisted taking over the responsibility of paying for the health care of current and (especially) retired workers and their dependents, and loss-making SOEs that could no longer count on having their deficits covered by the state sometimes chose to reduce their expenditures by no longer paying for the health care of these groups; some loss-making SOEs were even closed. As a result, the percentage of urban residents with health insurance coverage declined rapidly through the 1980s and especially in the 1990s. By 1998, it was estimated that as many as 44% of urban residents were without health insurance (see the row labelled "No insurance" in Table 1). This statistic probably understates the problem, as it most likely is based on the number of registered urban residents. But after 1980, China also has seen an increasing inflow of migrant workers from the countryside to the cities. These workers typically were not covered by the LIS under which SOE employees were covered, and may not be completely accounted for in the population base used in the estimate of the uninsured share of the population.

2.4. *Summary: A surging economy, worsening health care*

The switch toward economic policies based on market mechanisms that began in the late 1970s was based on the expectation that in a modern

---

[8]Further details on the decline of health insurance in urban areas during this period can be found in Gu (2010).

economy, voluntary transactions in competitive markets at prices freely agreed between buyers and sellers are likely to be more successful in raising productivity and incomes than a model of centrally planned allocation of economic resources. In accordance with this principle, the authority to decide what to produce and what inputs to purchase was decentralized to producing units such as families in the farm sector and individual enterprises of various sizes in other sectors. The incentives on producers to respond to market signals were enhanced by withdrawing subsidies from many loss-making enterprises, and by allowing those who were able to make a profit to keep much of it for re-investment in the firm or for increasing the pay and benefits of managers and employees.

In general, the policy was of course spectacularly successful, particularly in the agricultural sector and in manufacturing, whose production has increased by enough to not only satisfy the increased demand in the domestic market, but also to transform China into the world's dominant manufacturing exporter. The rapid growth in productivity in these sectors has led to large increases in the real incomes for the majority of China's citizens, especially in the large urban and coastal regions where the export-led economic expansion has had the greatest impact.[9]

But while the market-based approach has been successful in the economy at large, the evidence discussed earlier suggests that in health care, it has been much less so. While the total amounts that are spent on health care have increased faster than other spending, the access to health care for seriously ill people is no better than it was in an earlier era. Indeed, for the reasons discussed above, the incidence of untreated illness may be higher today than it was 30 years ago, as sick people forego treatment for fear that it will be very costly. Instances

---

[9]An often cited measure of the success of China's economic policy since 1980 is the large number of people who have been raised out of poverty as a result of the country's economic growth. For example, *The Economist*, June 1–7, 2013, quotes the astounding figure of 680 million for the reduction in the number of Chinese citizens whose income fell below a poverty line of $1.25 per day (in 2005 U.S. dollars, adjusted for purchasing power) over the period 1981–2010. Also see World Bank (2009).

of waste, in the form of treatment in cases where it is not needed but which is supplied because it raises providers' income, are frequently cited. Expensive forms of medication are often chosen over cheaper ones because hospitals benefit from the higher markups that they can charge on them, or because doctors can charge a fee when drugs are given through injections rather than by mouth.

Thus, in contrast to the case in most other sectors, the shift to a more market-based incentive system in health care has not led to higher productivity, only to substantially higher costs and more waste of resources. While the increased spending on health care has raised the incomes of doctors and other health care workers, and of producers of other health sector inputs such as drugs or medical equipment, the lagging productivity and waste in the health care sector has implicitly acted as a drag on the real incomes of the population as a whole. Why is it that the model that has worked so well in most other sectors has not done so in health care?

3. Do Market Mechanisms Work in Health Care?

While the Western literature on economics in general tends to be sympathetic to a market-oriented approach as an instrument to determine the allocation of society's resources, the literature on the economics of health care often is not. In particular, three interrelated ideas have been stressed in support of the view that markets typically will not perform well in the health care sector, so that there is a strong case for the government to intervene and actively manage both the financing and the production of health care.

The first is that some health services have the characteristics of public goods; an appropriate level of production of such goods will only occur if they are subsidized or provided by the government. The second is that the sick patients who appear on the demand side in the market for most health services cannot be looked at in the same way as the buyers who appear on the demand side in the market for other goods and services, even if attention is restricted to health services that are private goods. The third is that in a well-functioning health care system, consumers must not just have access to health services when they are sick, but also to health *insurance*, because they may get sick in the future. A market-oriented health care system, therefore, must not only produce health services efficiently, but must also give consumers access to health insurance on reasonable terms. However, even the evidence from countries with active private insurance markets suggests that without extensive government regulation, these markets do not function well.[10] We discuss these three ideas in more detail in the following.

3.1. *Some health services are public goods*

One clear reason why voluntary transactions in private markets will not ensure that sufficient resources are allocated to certain kinds of health services is that some of them have what economic theory refers to as spillover effects. Spillover effects exist for health services that yield benefits not just to the person who receives them, but to others in the community as well. The most important cases of this kind are treatment and prevention of contagious disease: If a person receives services that prevents or cures a contagious disease, these services benefit not just the person who receives them, but also other members of the community as the risk that they will contract the disease is reduced.[11]

In a voluntary transaction where individual patients have to pay the full cost of these services in the market, their decision whether or not to get such services will typically depend on a comparison of the cost with the expected benefits to the buyers themselves; unless individuals are particularly civic-minded, they will not give sufficient weight to the benefits to others when they make these decisions. For goods and services with spillover effects — public goods, in the terminology of economic theory — government must take the initiative to subsidize them, or provide them to consumers for free, in order for enough of them to be produced.

---

[10]These three ideas, especially the last two, are discussed extensively in three major surveys of health economics that currently exist: Culyer and Newhouse (2000), Glied and Smith (2011), and Pauly, McGuire, and Barros (2012).

[11]Both Culyer and Newhouse (2000) and Glied and Smith (2011) have chapters on infectious disease.

In high-income countries, policies to ensure that health services with significant spillover effects are adequately supplied are typically enforced by public health departments at the local level, although they may work together with providers of regular health services, such as primary-care doctors or nurses. Examples of tasks for which public health departments are responsible include administration and supervision of immunization programs for children and adults, and programs to prevent and contain various types of epidemics such as different types of influenza or sexually transmitted diseases. Their responsibilities can also include enforcement of rules relating to environmental factors that indirectly influence population health, even though they do not involve health services, strictly defined. For example, they may be the agencies that ensure high standards of cleanliness of food handling in restaurants and stores, and the quality of the water that citizens use and the air they breathe. All of these activities are organized and paid for by the government, since they would not be undertaken on an adequate scale through voluntary market transactions.

But while the work of public health departments is a critical component of the system that promotes population health everywhere, in high-income countries the resources that they use are very small in comparison with the amounts spent on regular health services. By far, the largest amount of health sector resources is accounted for by the provision of health services (and drugs) to deal with illness that is not contagious. While such services and drugs can be very valuable to the patients who receive them, they do not have significant spillover effects that benefit the community at large. Thus, while there may be other reasons why markets may not work well in the health care system at large, as further discussed in the next subsections, most health services are not public goods in the sense that this term is used in economic analysis: because they do not have significant spillover benefits, they are private goods.

In the early stages of the economic reform era in the 1980s, China was still a low-income country, and the per capita spending on health care was quite low as well. At that time, the share of health care resources that were used to deal with contagious disease and public health services with public-goods characteristics was large relative to the total: Spending on health services that were private goods and were directed at non-contagious disease was relatively limited. When the policy of reduced subsidies and greater reliance on revenues raised from sales in the market was extended to producers of health services such as urban and rural health clinics and hospitals, an unintended consequence was a reduction in some of the public health activities (such as immunization programs and control of various kinds of infectious disease) for which many of the providers had been responsible.[12] As we will further discuss in later chapters, subsidies and other government policies to ensure that these functions are properly discharged should be an important element of future Chinese health policy, even if market transactions are allowed to play a greater role in the provision of private health services for which spillover effects to the community are less important than they are for services that are properly classified in the public health domain.

3.2. *Patients as buyers of health services: Information asymmetry and competition*

The ability of buyers to benefit from being able to obtain a good or service through a voluntary purchase in the marketplace is obviously better when they have good information in advance about the characteristics of what they are buying, and how it will benefit them once they have bought it. Even if one focuses on services that are private goods without significant spillover effects, it is clear that in markets for health services (and drugs), patients usually do not have very good information. Beyond knowing that they are sick, the average person cannot diagnose what his or her problem is, nor do patients have the training and expertise to tell what drugs or treatment methods are available to deal with their problems, or how likely it is that they will get well. The doctors who treat them (the sellers), in contrast, have much better information about these things than the buyers do, and may be tempted to use this information asymmetry to their advantage. The bargaining power of buyers of health services is also

---

[12]The other example in China is mental healthcare. See Qian (2012b).

inherently weakened by the fact that most diagnostic and treatment services must be provided with the patient being present, and that the nature of the complete treatment process cannot be negotiated in advance.

The information asymmetry and the personal nature of health services also reduce the effectiveness of competition between sellers as a way of strengthening the ability of patients to benefit from access to health services in the market. In markets where buyers know exactly what they want or need in advance, and where it is easy to specify the exact characteristics of the good or service that is being purchased, buyers can easily compare the offers of competing sellers and choose the offer that they know in advance is their best option. In the health services market, in contrast, getting offers from more than one provider is likely costly and cumbersome as it might require the patient to be seen personally by each potential provider, and in any case may not be worth it since the typical patient does not have the technical expertise to properly compare the quality of the service that different providers are likely to offer, or different approaches to dealing with their particular problems.

The idea that the information asymmetry between patients and providers and the special characteristics of health services put patients, as buyers of health services, in a particularly weak and vulnerable position in their relationship with the sellers of these services, has been a central one in much of the economic analysis of the health care sector. Predictions based on this analysis suggest that unless the market is regulated or controlled in some way, the weakness of competition among sellers is likely to result both in prices of health services that are high relative to the cost of producing them, and possibly in an oversupply of many kinds of health services. The latter effect is especially likely to occur if new producers (doctors and hospitals) are allowed to enter the market without restrictions, and if there is an insurance system that reduces the out-of-pocket costs that patients face when they utilize health services, as discussed below. The high cost of health care in the U.S., where relatively unregulated private markets play a larger role in the health care system than in any other high-income country, is often seen as evidence that supports these predictions.

3.3. *Risk pooling and private insurance markets*

A third reason why voluntary transactions in private markets may not perform well in regulating the use of economic resources in the health care sector is that a well-functioning health care system must not only supply health services at reasonable cost, but must also respond to citizens' demand for risk pooling. This demand arises because the incidence of various health problems, and hence the need for possibly expensive health services, is both highly variable and unpredictable.

Many individuals are lucky in the sense that they go through life with only relatively minor and uncomplicated health problems that can be treated without using large amounts of health services. But a minority of individuals are less lucky and are afflicted by serious kinds of illness that require large amounts of ongoing treatment and medication in order for them to survive or to avoid severe pain and disability. For some, the demand for expensive health care will be concentrated toward the end of their lives if they suffer from painful and disabling conditions for a long time before they die.

The demand for risk-pooling arises because, on average, people in the community will be better off if at least part of the health care costs is paid for out of a common pool, rather than out-of-pocket by the individuals who are unlucky enough to experience serious ill-health, or their families. In retrospect, those who have contributed to the pool but have not had high health care costs are worse off than they would have been without pooling, but their losses are small in comparison with the gains to those who have had serious health problems and have been able to access health care that they otherwise would not have been able to afford, or that would have impoverished them and their families.

Risk-pooling arrangements, under which a substantial part of the cost of health care is paid for collectively, can be thought of as responding to a community's desire for equity in the distribution of economic resources, since it implies a redistribution from those who are better off in the sense of not requiring costly health care, to those who are unlucky enough to do so. However, risk pooling can also be justified on efficiency grounds. If it is not known in advance who will have serious health problems and require expensive care, risk-averse individuals will be willing to contribute to a risk-pooling arrangement that guarantees them access to health services and reduces the risk of financial disaster, even though they know that in retrospect they may not need this protection.

In a system where health services are heavily subsidized or directly supplied by the community, as in China before the 1980s, there is implicit risk pooling since individuals only pay a relatively small share of the cost of their health care out of their own pockets, with the rest being shared among all members of the community. When the degree of government subsidization is reduced, as it was through the 1980s and 1990s, the degree of risk pooling will also tend to be reduced, unless the reduction in implicit risk pooling through government is offset by an expansion in the amount of explicit risk pooling through the market for health insurance.

In theory, insurance-based risk pooling can be supplied in private competitive markets even if there is little or no government regulation or subsidy. Since risk-averse individuals are willing to pay for insurance if it is available in the market, private firms can make a profit by offering insurance contracts under which they agree to pay for all or part of the health care that plan members use, in exchange for premiums that they charge everyone who belongs to the plan. As in other markets, the cost to the consumers (in the form of the insurance premiums they must pay) will be influenced by the extent of competition among sellers (different insurance plans); if the market is sufficiently competitive, the premiums will be just high enough to pay for the cost of the care that plan members use, as well as the costs incurred in setting up and administering the plans.

However, as has been extensively discussed in the economics literature, private unregulated insurance markets generally, and in health insurance specifically, are unlikely to be very competitive. Moreover, administration and marketing costs can be quite high. Entry into the insurance market can also be costly and difficult, especially in a health care system that is in transition so that there is little statistical information that can be used to estimate the expected cost of the health care that plan members will be using under a new plan.

A particularly difficult problem in offering new plans in a market in which private insurance is not well-established is that of "adverse selection". This term refers to the tendency for the demand for insurance to be especially strong among individuals who know themselves to be at high risk for future health problems that will require expensive services. But if most of those who sign up for private insurance plans are in this category, the plans will have to charge high premiums in order to cover their expected costs; these high premiums, in turn, will make the plans unattractive to average individuals, limiting the profitability of offering them in the market.[13]

Given these problems, it is perhaps not surprising that the development of private health insurance in China was quite limited in the 1980s and 1990s, even though the extent of government risk pooling was dramatically reduced during those decades. As has been extensively documented, the result was that the policy of reduced subsidization of the production of health services and the increased role of charges on patients as a source of revenue for providers led to a dramatic increase in the population's exposure to illness-related financial risk, and even precluded large population groups from access to urgently needed care. It was these developments, perhaps more than anything else, that led many observers to characterize the application of market-based principles to the health care sector as a failure. Moreover, as we will further discuss in Chapter 3, the question of how to strengthen the degree of risk pooling remains a central issue in the debate regarding China's future health policy, with some favoring an expansion of the system of social health insurance as the best option, and others advocating a return to implicit risk pooling through increased direct government subsidies to providers of primary care and hospital care.

---

[13]The classic statement of the adverse selection problem in insurance is in Rothschild and Stiglitz (1976). There is ample evidence that it is especially likely to be present in health insurance markets in particular, and that attempts by private insurers to guard against it through "risk selection" are a major reason why private insurance markets tend to be both inefficient and inequitable.

4. Conclusion and the Way Forward

Given the developments in China's health care system in the 1980s and
1990s, it is not surprising that health policy and health system reform
have become increasingly important topics in the Chinese debate
over economic and social policy in recent years. China's experience
has confirmed the prediction from the health economics literature
that largely unregulated private markets will not perform well as an
instrument for governing resource use in the health care sector. In
retrospect, policymakers may wish that they had taken a somewhat more
gradual approach in decentralizing the management of the health care
sector and putting pressure on providers to raise more of their revenue
from patients.

At the same time, one should not underestimate the difficulties
and resistance the reformers faced in bringing about a dramatic
restructuring of the economic system as a whole, and how, under the
circumstances, they may have been reluctant to make exceptions to the
general principle of dismantling the system of comprehensive central
planning in any individual sector.[14] The process of reform was highly
controversial, and there were influential conservative forces both in the
bureaucracy and in the academic world who believed that the reduced
influence of the state in the economy went too far and should be at least
partially reversed. In health care, the opposition to reform continues
to be strong, in part because the current public dissatisfaction with the
health care system can be unfavorably contrasted with the way it was
managed in China in earlier decades, and also because those who favor a
more interventionist role for the state can point to an extensive Western
literature which elaborates on the likelihood of various forms of market
failure in health care. Today, even those who are strong supporters
of the policy of economic liberalization in general recognize that the
state must at least take a more active regulatory role in the health
sector.

---

[14]Interestingly, former Premier Zhu Rongji is reported to have said, some time after
leaving office, that health policy was one area in which he felt somewhat dissatisfied
with the outcome of the reform efforts.

But while there may now be widespread agreement that health care is a sector in which the tendencies toward various forms of market failure justify a more activist role for government than elsewhere, there is much less agreement on what form that role should take.

One major conclusion of the review of Chinese health policy since the late 1990s that we provide in this book is that its future directions are highly uncertain. The major policy initiatives that have been taken so far, seen as a whole, constitute somewhat of a stand-off between the forces on the new left who favor a return to a system of heavy direct subsidies and public management of health services providers, on one side, and liberals who believe that government intervention should focus on financing and regulatory measures, whilst allowing markets and competition to continue playing a major role in governing the production of health services and drugs, on the other.

4.1. *The rest of the book*

The rest of the book is organized as follows. In Chapter 2, we attempt to place our discussion of recent Chinese health policy in an international comparative framework, by reviewing developments that have led to health system reform becoming a major preoccupation of governments and the policy debate in most major countries in the world. As a background to our later recommendations for policy directions in China, we identify two countries in which there exist clear and consistent models that guide the ongoing reform process, namely the United Kingdom and Holland, and explain why elements of these models may be adapted and applied to a future Chinese system.

In Chapter 2, we also describe the health care systems in two other countries whose economies have been successful in the past, the U.S.A. and Japan, and explain why we believe the systems in those countries have fewer useful lessons for China than the U.K. and Holland, even though their economic performance in general has been very good. One conclusion we draw from considering the experience of health system reform in other countries is that it is a process that is very controversial everywhere, and which to a large extent is dominated by the actions of politically powerful special interest groups. China is not likely to be an exception to this pattern, and effective reform can only be accomplished if the political leadership succeeds in containing and limiting the influence of these interest groups.

In the following four chapters we then go on to consider the major developments and initiatives that have featured in Chinese health policy since the late 1990s. Chapter 3 discusses the strengthening of the social insurance system that began in the late 1990s, while Chapters 4, 5, and 6 deal with the three additional pillars of health system reform that were cornerstones of the 2009 health policy announcement by the State Council: establishing a network of basic (primary) care clinics throughout China's rural and urban areas, reforming the system whereby public hospitals are managed, and implementing a new national drug policy. In each case, we analyze the approach that China has attempted to use in the light of relevant principles from the Western literature on health economics and general economics, and draw on examples from other countries.

In Part III, we broaden the analysis somewhat and consider how health policy in China relates to two major trends that have become prominent in the more general debate about the future of China's economy. The first is the gradual re-orientation of economic policy from an almost exclusive emphasis on the objective of economic growth, toward more focus on the target of universal economic security and a more equal distribution of real income. Although economic analysis of income distribution policy typically focuses either on measures that affect the labor market (from which most people derive most of their income), or on the incidence of a country's tax-transfer system, we argue that in a middle-income country like China, policies to broaden the access to good health care potentially constitute one of the most effective instruments for raising the welfare of the poor, and hence contributes to increased equality in real income, broadly defined.[15] We discuss these issues in Chapter 7.

---

[15] Another area of social policy that also can have a powerful effect on the distribution of real income is education.

The second major trend is that toward increased decentralization of responsibility for the expenditure side of China's system of public finance, under which responsibility for the implementation of health policy in China now rests principally with governments at the local level. As we discuss in Chapter 8, while decentralized management of health policy has the desirable property of allowing the system to adapt to local conditions in a more flexible way, the incentives to which local officials and political decision-makers are subject may make it difficult to implement principles regarding health policy that have been formulated by the state. The fiscal pressures that local governments are subject to under China's present system of central-local revenue sharing and expenditure responsibilities may reinforce this tendency, which must be taken into account if central initiatives to use the health care system as an indirect instrument for promoting a more equal distribution of real income are to be successful.

In the last two chapters, finally, we summarize what we see as the main future problems that China's health policy makers must address. In Chapter 9, we consider how the current social insurance system can be strengthened and integrated with the initiatives to reform primary care, hospital management, and regulation of the pharmaceutical sector, to attain the goal of creating a system that provides universal insurance coverage and access to efficiently produced care of high quality. The basic model that we consider in this chapter is inspired by the U.K. example that we describe in Chapter 2, with appropriate modifications to the Chinese context. While markets and competition can play a significant role in promoting efficiency in the production of health services under this model, on the financing side it is dominated by the social insurance system, with only limited competition from private insurance.

In Chapter 10, we go further and consider an approach under which markets and competition play a significant role not just in the production of health services, but also on the insurance side. The scenario we consider in this chapter is inspired by the model that is serving as the guidepost for the reforms that have been underway for a number of years in Holland, as also discussed in Chapter 2. In Chapter 10, we also briefly discuss a policy issue that is of fundamental importance no matter which model is used on the financing side, namely how to regulate and manage the training of doctors and other health personnel in such a way as to promote cost-effective patterns of high-quality care based on choosing from the most advanced technology available anywhere in the world.

Chapter 2

HEALTH SYSTEMS
AND HEALTH REFORM:
INTERNATIONAL MODELS

1. Introduction

In China, the restructuring of the health care system since the 1980s can be interpreted as part and parcel of the more general transformation of the economy that has been taking place in the last three decades. But reform of the health care system has also been actively debated and pursued in many countries in recent years, not just in economies like China that are undergoing transition from an earlier era of central planning. In this chapter, we discuss the evolution of the health care systems and health policy in selected countries whose experience contains lessons of potential relevance for the way Chinese health policy should respond to the kinds of market failures that were discussed in Chapter 1. Specifically, we focus on two interrelated sets of questions.

First, while government policy in most countries has been much more interventionist in health care than in most other sectors of the economy, the types of interventions that have been used, and the institutional design of the health care system, have been very different from country to country. Can we identify one or more countries whose policies could serve as models for the system China wants to build for the future?

Second, the experience with health care reform in many countries has been very difficult in the sense that it has generated a great deal of controversy, to the point that the process of health policy reform almost appears to have come to a standstill. In discussing why reforms of economic policy have been difficult to accomplish in other sectors, economists have often focused on identifying the entrenched ("vested") interests that stand to lose from particular reforms, and how they can engage in political and other actions to slow down or block reforms that are in the broader public interest. What vested interests are powerful in the health care systems in various countries, and how have they been able to affect the health reform process?

A concept related to vested interests is that of "regulatory capture", referring to situations where government officials and political decision-makers in charge of regulating an industry gradually come to identify with the interests of those who have a stake in existing policies. To what extent is this concept relevant in health care? Based on the experience in other countries, will a form of regulatory capture be an important factor in future health policy in China, and will the influence of vested interests make health system reform increasingly controversial and difficult to implement in China as well? Alternatively, will China's system of government prove more capable of actually implementing a consistent set of health policies and regulation than governments in, for example, the U.S., Holland, or Canada?

Finally, in the Appendix to Chapter 2, we briefly consider an important reason why health policy has had such a central place in the debate over economic and social reform in so many countries: the fact that health care spending has grown much faster than the economy as a whole. What are the underlying forces that explain this pattern? The data in Chapter 1 show that spending on health care has grown much faster than other components of GDP in China as well, though its share still remains lower than that in advanced countries. Should future policy in China focus on cost containment so as to avoid spending as much on health care as today's rich countries, or are there good economic reasons for health care to gradually make use of an even larger share of total resources than it does currently?

2. Alternative Models of Health System Management

While most countries' health systems are similar in that costs are rising faster than GDP, they are currently very different in other ways, both with respect to the way health care is financed, and with respect to the way the production of health services is organized. On the financing side, most health care in many countries (the U.K., Japan) is paid for by the government, either out of general revenue or through compulsory social insurance, while in others a substantial share comes from private sources, either in the form of patient out-of-pocket payments (China since the 1990s) or from private insurance (the U.S., Switzerland, Holland since 2006).

With respect to health services production, there are large differences among countries in the relative importance of primary care and higher-level (hospital and specialist) care, and in the methods used to govern the relationship between primary care and the rest of the system. Different methods are also used to reimburse providers. In many countries, doctors are typically paid on the basis of fee-for-service in primary care (Canada, Japan) and in hospitals (Canada, the U.S.), while in others they are paid predominantly via capitation in primary care (the U.K., in some U.S. managed care plans) or via salary in hospitals (the U.K., Japan, China).

If technology and tastes are similar across countries, these very different models cannot all be optimal. In the rest of this chapter, we therefore consider two questions. First, is there anything like a consensus in health economics today as to what the characteristics of a good system are? Second, if it is indeed possible to identify a set of characteristics that a good system should have, why is it that countries do not seem to be moving very fast toward models with these characteristics?

2.1. *Features of an equitable and efficient health care system*

The honest answer to the first question probably is that at present there is no real consensus in the health economics community on the issue of whether there is one particular model of health system organization that would be the most efficient one for all countries. In reality, the debate on health system reform in most countries concerns relatively small incremental changes to the existing system, with no clear view of where the process will ultimately lead. China is an exception to this pattern: the drastic reorganization of the management of economic resources in general, starting in the early 1980s, was extended to the health care system which was dramatically revamped in the 1980s and 1990s. However, while the issue of health system reform in China is hotly debated at present, not only by local economists and political decision-makers but also by health economists from various countries in the West, the question of what model will be used as the guidepost for the construction of China's future health care system is far from settled, as we noted in Chapter 1.[1]

In this chapter, we nevertheless try to identify two somewhat different models that we think many health economists from all over the world would accept as reasonable approaches to constructing a health care system that satisfies the fundamental objectives that most societies want their systems to reach. One such objective concerns equity. Specifically, most people probably would agree that a good model of health system organization would have to have arrangements to provide adequate risk pooling in the sense that every citizen should be guaranteed access to needed health services in case of serious illness, even if they do not have the resources to pay for them on their own. Moreover, the financing of health care should not discriminate against those with adverse family health histories or previous illness experience (as it would in a system in which risk pooling was mostly through unregulated private insurance).

In some countries, many people tend to define the equity objective in a more demanding way, so as to include the requirement that every sick person should always be treated the same way, regardless of economic status.[2] This is somewhat different from the principle that everyone who is seriously ill should always have access to "needed"

---

[1] Recent surveys of the health policy debate in China, such as the special issues of *Health Economics* edited by Yip, Wagstaff, and Hsiao (2009), and in *China Economic Review* edited by Fleisher, Blomqvist, and Tan (2009), give an indication of the wide range of views that it still includes; see also Yip and Hsiao (2008, 2009).

[2] Recent surveys on the concept and measurement of equity in health care are in Olsen (2011) and van Doorslaer and van Ourti (2011).

care, since there is no hard and fast definition of what is meant by that phrase. In any case, a principle that says that a person's economic status should not be allowed to influence the way he or she is treated when ill, certainly is not a realistic one in a country such as China where current income inequality is very high. Nor, it could be argued, is it realistic or even desirable in a future world where technological progress has created an even wider range of treatment options, some very expensive, than exist now. In these circumstances, the concept of equity must be defined pragmatically, as a specification of a minimum level of care that every citizen should be entitled to when ill, regardless of economic circumstances.

A second criterion that a well-functioning health care system clearly must satisfy is to address the issue of overcoming the consequences of the specific characteristics of the market for health services, including the prevalence of third-party payment and the patient–provider information asymmetry, that have been such important parts of the health economics literature in the past. Most health economists today probably would agree that in order to do so, a good system should not just emphasize demand-side incentives on patients (such as high out-of-pocket payments for health services and drugs), but also the supply-side incentives that are inherent in different ways of reimbursing doctors and hospitals. The relevant incentive structure must strike an appropriate balance between the conflicting objectives of cost control and the population's health status, and there must also be mechanisms for rapid and accurate evaluation of new drugs and technology.

The two models that we would propose as candidates for the role of good systems in these respects are somewhat idealized versions of, first, the one that has gradually been evolving in the U.K. over the past several decades, and second, the one that is envisaged under the rules that were adopted in the Netherlands in 2006. We will sketch the basic features of these systems in the next two subsections; later in Chapters 9 and 10, we return to the question of how the principles underlying them can be incorporated as elements in China's future system of financing and organizing the production of health care.

2.2. The U.K. system

In the U.K., the equity objective is largely satisfied because every U.K. resident is automatically covered by the National Health Service (NHS) which provides the same comprehensive coverage for everyone, at zero or low out-of-pocket charges. While people with high income are free to seek privately provided care on their own, this is apparently not considered in the U.K. as implying a significant departure from the equity objective, as long as the standard of care provided under the NHS is sufficiently high.

With respect to the efficiency objective, the U.K. system has long had strong supply-side incentives affecting the provision of primary care via the use of rostering and capitation (further explained below). Over time, the reforms that began in the early 1980s have also introduced various forms of financial incentives on primary-care doctors (referred to in the U.K. as General Practitioners, or GPs) in their role as gatekeepers with respect to patients' access to specialist and secondary care, and with respect to their use of prescription drugs. Over time, it is also likely that there will be increased use of supply-side incentives in the provision of specialist and hospital care, under the system of "Practice-Based Commissioning" that is currently being developed. (One of the first steps in the reforms that were begun by the Thatcher government in the 1980s was to make hospitals more dependent on revenue that they could earn under contracts with GPs and other "purchasing" agencies involved in the process of channeling patients to different hospitals.) In recent years, the NHS has also been strengthening its system of technology evaluation, through the National Institute of Clinical Excellence (NICE), which has become somewhat of a model for similar institutions elsewhere in the world.[3]

Under the rostering-capitation system that is at the heart of the NHS model, each resident of the U.K. must, in order to be entitled to any of the benefits of the NHS, be registered with one (and only one)

---

[3]Flood (2000) is a good reference on the reforms in the NHS in the 1990s. A useful survey of more recent NHS history is Oliver (2005). A brief discussion of Practice-Based Commissioning is in Curry and Thorlby (2007).

of the GP practices that operate throughout the U.K. under contracts with the NHS (that is, everyone must be on the "roster" of a GP practice). In addition to supplying diagnosis and treatment services for uncomplicated problems ("primary care"), the GP practices also have a "gate-keeping" function, in that a referral from the patient's GP is required if a patient is to receive the services of a specialist, or be hospitalized, with the costs being covered by the NHS. Since GPs also prescribe most of the out-patient drugs that are used in the U.K. (and paid for by the NHS), decisions made by GPs have a major influence on total costs in the system. Not only do GPs control the volume and cost of their own services, but through their referrals and prescriptions, their decisions also affect the aggregate cost of hospital and specialist services, and of pharmaceuticals.

The most important component of the system through which GPs are compensated is what is referred to as "capitation", meaning that each month the practice is paid a fixed amount for each patient that is on its roster, *regardless of the amount of services that the patient has received during the month.* Thus, the total revenue of a practice depends principally on the number of patients who have chosen to register with it, not on the volume of services that patients have received. Under a capitation system, therefore, a GP's incentive is to take on responsibility for as many patients as possible, but there is no incentive to supply a high volume of services to each patient.

A potential problem with a capitation system is that it indirectly creates an incentive on GPs to refer patients to specialists and hospitals. By doing so, a GP can shift the burden of caring for patients from his or her own practice to another provider. To overcome this problem, the capitation system can be modified so as to give GPs an incentive to limit their patients' use of specialist and hospital services, and pharmaceuticals, as well. For example, in addition to the capitation amount, a GP practice can receive a budget for the costs incurred by their patients for specialist and hospital services that they have received following GPs' referrals, and for the drugs they have used following their GPs' prescriptions. A financial incentive for GPs to limit these costs can then be created by allowing GPs to keep part of any surplus that remains in the budget, or by requiring them to pay part of any deficit out of the capitation amounts they have received. In the U.K., incentives of this kind have been created through the system of GP "fundholding" that was used in the 1980s, and it is also an element of the system of Practice-Based Commissioning that is currently being implemented.[4]

From the viewpoint of the citizenry, the NHS is a monopoly plan since the benefits offered through the NHS are the same for everyone. However, because citizens can choose to register on any GP's roster and are allowed to switch to another practice if they are dissatisfied with their current one, there is some degree of competition among GPs (although the competition relates only to the perceived quality of the GP practice's services, since no fees are charged, and since the capitation amounts paid to the doctors by the plan are the same for all GPs). Since patients can only be treated by specialists and/or in hospitals on the GPs' referral, patients' perception of the quality of care supplied by a given GP practice may also be influenced to some extent by the choice of specialists and hospitals that the practice offers its patients. Thus, in principle, and at least in major cities where there are several local GP practices, quality competition can be considered as taking place not just in the market for GP services, but also among the providers that are part of the various practices' referral network.

2.3. The Dutch model

At first glance, the Dutch (post-2006) model looks quite different, since in Holland there is not just one government-funded plan (such as the NHS), but many competing ones. Following the 2006 reforms, each Dutch citizen can choose to be covered by any one of the social insurance plans that offer coverage in the area where he/she

---

[4] Under Practice-Based Commissioning, groups of GP practices are also supposed to negotiate agreements with the hospitals to whom they refer their patients regarding the amounts that they will be paid for different services and other terms. This system is intended to replace the earlier model of a "purchaser-provider split" under which separate purchasing agencies were supposed to negotiate terms with the hospitals, as further discussed in the text below.

is a resident, or by a private insurance plan.[5] The premium revenue that each plan receives consists of two components: a risk-adjusted payment from a government fund (with the risk adjustment reflecting the estimated cost of care for each individual), plus an amount paid out of the insured individual's pocket (the "individual premium"). The latter can be different from plan to plan, but must be the same for each individual who is covered by the plan. Moreover, the rules require that each plan must accept all applications for coverage. Although plans are allowed to offer somewhat different menus of benefits, there are regulations that require each one to offer at least a specified minimum basket of benefits, if it is to be eligible for the risk-adjusted government subsidy.

Because there are many different plans with different individual premiums and somewhat different menus of benefits, the Dutch system cannot be considered equitable in the strict sense that all patients will receive precisely the same kind of treatment when they are ill (for example, if people with high income tend to choose more expensive plans with a somewhat broader set of benefits). However, it *is* equitable in the sense that everyone pays the same individual premium for a given plan, so that there is no discrimination according to factors such as family health history or previous illness, and no one can be denied coverage because of such factors.

With respect to the efficiency objective, the mix of demand-side and supply-side incentives that are used by different plans to promote cost-effective care is not specified, but depends instead on the contracts that the plans have with providers (primary-care doctors, specialists, and hospitals), and what out-of-pocket payments they require from patients. Since the plans compete with each other on the individual premiums that they charge and through consumers' perception of the quality of care that their providers supply, they do have an incentive to contract with providers and set consumer co-payments in such

---

[5]A good description of the principles underlying the Dutch model is, again, Flood (2000). For an updated account of the version that was implemented in 2006, see van de Ven and Schut (2008) or Enthoven and van de Ven (2007).

a way that the plan provides an appropriate mix of supply- and demand-side incentives to balance the cost control objective against the quality and quantity of care their members receive when they are ill.[6]

For example, if it is the case that the incentive structure under the NHS system with gate-keeping primary-care providers paid through a form of extended capitation (and zero out-of-pocket charges on patients) represents an efficient arrangement in this sense, one would expect that over time, many plans in the Dutch system would come to resemble the NHS model. Similarly, competition among plans would also give each one an incentive to rely on cost-effectiveness evaluations of new drugs or treatment methods when creating guidelines for their providers, along the same lines as those produced by NICE in the U.K.

It is possible, therefore, that over time, the plans in which most people in the Netherlands will be enrolled will come to resemble small-scale versions of the U.K. NHS. A major advantage of the Dutch system, however, is that it can, in principle, offer consumers in some places a choice between plans with different sets of incentives. Again, from the viewpoint of conventional microeconomic analysis, this should be considered an advantage if there are significant differences in consumer preferences. For example, consumers who are more risk-averse and have a high willingness to pay in order to avoid even a low risk of some kind of adverse outcome may choose a more expensive plan in which they are allowed access to a wide range of specialists and hospital care without referral from their primary-care provider; less risk-averse individuals may opt for lower-cost plans with more

---

[6]In principle, the plans can bargain effectively with providers since they are allowed to engage in "selective contracting" (that is, they are not obliged to offer the same contracts to all providers). The rules allowing selective contracting were passed only after considerable resistance from physician organizations, however, and insurers have only recently begun to exercise this option (Leu *et al.*, 2009). In the U.S., doctors' organizations have also tried to oppose the right of managed care plans to engage in selective contracting. In most U.S. states, however, managed care plans now have this right, and selective contracting has been an effective force to promote competition and lower costs; see Gaynor and Town (2012).

conservative referral requirements and more restrictions on their choice of providers.[7]

2.4. A digression: Why not use the U.S. or Japanese systems as a model?

As will be evident from the discussion in Chapter 3, the process of health system reform in China today is not closely following either the U.K. or the Dutch model. It is somewhat similar to the Dutch model in that there are government subsidies that help pay for certain groups' health insurance (the new CMS in rural areas, the urban residents' plan in urban areas), but it is also similar to the U.K. model in the establishment of a network of primary-care clinics where all residents will be eligible for subsidized care. Before turning to more detailed discussion of specific aspects of the Chinese reforms in later chapters and how they compare with the U.K. and Dutch approaches, we briefly consider two other countries that might also be expected to serve as partial reference points for China's future health care system, namely the U.S. and Japan.

The U.S., after all, is where the largest portion of advanced medical and pharmaceutical technology is being developed and applied in treating illness, and is generally regarded as having a very successful economy and society. Similarly, Japan has the most advanced society in Asia, whether measured by per capita GDP or by availability of high-level technology of all kinds. Moreover, its health care system appears to

---

[7]One important issue in the design of a model such as the Dutch one is whether the plans should be allowed to offer individual premium discounts to groups of individuals who enroll (for example, all employees of a given firm). The rule that insurers must charge every individual client the same individual premium may be justified as a means of avoiding problems of risk selection in the insurance markets. However, since it is difficult for individual people to acquire the expertise to compare different insurance plans, competition in insurance markets may be more vigorous if plans are allowed to offer group discounts, since this provides an incentive for employers to spend resources on comparing plans and negotiate premium discounts. In the current Dutch model, insurers are allowed to offer discounts of up to 10% of the individual premiums they charge when enrollment is through a group (for example, employees in a given firm); see Leu *et al.* (2009).

have been very successful, both in the sense of being efficiently managed and of having produced the longest life expectancy and lowest infant mortality rates of any country in the world.

2.5. *What is wrong with the U.S. model?*

While the U.S. health care system provides access to the most advanced medical technology available, the main reason it cannot be considered a good model for other countries is its very high cost. As Appendix Table A1 shows, the U.S. devotes a larger share of its total output to health than any other country, by a substantial margin. Since U.S. GDP per capita is also among the highest in the world, this means that the per capita cost of health care in the U.S. is very high indeed.

Part of the reason U.S. health care costs are so high is that many patients are treated using highly advanced technology and effective but expensive drugs. At the same time, however, data on male and female life expectancy and infant mortality from the U.S. do not compare favorably with those in other advanced countries.[8] That is, even though U.S. spends much more per capita on health care than any other country, its population's health status, if anything, appears to be below average for a high-income country. What explains this apparent low productivity of the U.S. health care system?

One contributing factor is likely to be that the costs per unit of certain major components of health care spending are high in the U.S., relative to other countries. For example, compared to doctors elsewhere, the net incomes of U.S. doctors are relatively high. Similarly, average costs per hospital day also are relatively high, in part because many hospitals in the U.S., even comparatively small ones, have acquired various kinds of advanced but expensive equipment. Thus, to some extent, high U.S. health care costs are explained by high costs per unit, rather than by a large amount of resource use.

---

[8]The U.S. data are considerably worse than those from Japan, and while they are better than the average for all of Europe, they are also worse than those in the high-income countries in western and northern Europe.

Another factor that has been cited to explain the relatively unfavorable U.S. population health status indicators is the uneven access to health care. Even though there are government insurance programs for certain population groups (the federal Medicare for persons over age 65, and state Medicaid plans for those with very low income), the U.S. system does not ensure universal coverage. While a majority of those not covered by government programs have private insurance, typically through their place of work, a substantial proportion of the population does not have insurance. As a result, there are large population groups in the U.S. who may have been unable to access needed care even when seriously ill because they cannot pay for it. The lack of insurance and hence deficient access to health care in these population groups is likely to be at least part of the reason why life expectancy is lower and infant mortality is higher in the U.S. than in other high-income countries that have universal insurance programs.

A third factor that is part of the explanation for high U.S. health care spending is administration costs, both in the insurance sector and for service providers. A portion of these costs are attributable to marketing costs of private insurance plans, but much of them are simply due to the fact that it is more difficult and costly to manage a system in which insurance is through many different plans. With a system of multiple insurers, not only are the costs of managing the plans themselves likely to be higher than they would be with a single plan, but it is also more complicated and expensive for hospitals and physician practices to deal with many plans, each one of which may have different rules and procedures for settling claims and reimbursing providers and patients.

While competition among insurers has been beneficial in helping to bring about some of the institutional changes that have taken place in the U.S. health care system over time, the high administrative costs and the uneven insurance coverage in the population are undeniable disadvantages. Attempts at reforming the system so that it would provide universal or near-universal coverage, and to reduce costs, have nevertheless resulted in only slow progress. Although the changes brought forward by the Obama administration have now been passed, it remains to be seen to what extent they will be implemented as originally planned. In any event, the controversy surrounding these initiatives was a clear illustration of the power of vested interests, including insurance companies and physicians' groups, to influence policy and resist major changes in the U.S. political environment. Although it seems probable that a model such as the Dutch one would be supported by a majority of people in the U.S. if it could be clearly explained to them, there seems little prospect that health care reform in the U.S. will bring about enough change to create that type of model in the foreseeable future.

2.6. *The Japanese system as a model?*

In contrast to the U.S. health care system which is much more expensive than those in other advanced countries, the Japanese one stands out by being *less* expensive. The most recently available data suggest that Japan devotes an even smaller share of its GDP to health care (less than 9%) than does the U.K. (and of course much less than the nearly 17% of GDP in the U.S.). Moreover, population health indicators such as life expectancy at birth and infant mortality in Japan are better than in any other country. Are there lessons to be learned by China from the apparently very efficient nature of the Japanese health care system?[9]

As in the U.K., the national, government-organized health insurance plan is universal, entitling every Japanese citizen to the same comprehensive set of benefits. Contrary to the U.K. system, people who utilize health services in Japan have to pay a significant share of the cost of their care out of their own pockets, but only up to a relatively low maximum amount per year. Costs beyond the maximum amount (including drug costs, which are included in the plan) are fully covered.

---

[9]The English-language literature on the Japanese health care system remains relatively limited, although the series on *Health Systems in Transition* published by the World Health Organization through the European Observatory on Health Systems and Policies now includes a volume on Japan (Tatara and Okamoto, 2009). The work of Ikegami and Campbell (1998) remains a helpful early reference.

There is no rostering or gate-keeping as in the U.K. system: the plan allows patients to go to any doctor or hospital, without referral.

Technically, financing of the insurance plan is through social insurance contributions to one of the many sickness funds that cover Japan's population. However, the contributions are mandatory, and citizens have no choice with respect to which fund to join. Which fund a person must contribute to depends on factors such as employment or (for retirees and the self-employed) where they live. Thus, these contributions are essentially equivalent to a tax, so in that sense the Japanese system is similar to the U.K. one (and not to the Dutch one, in which citizens can choose with which fund to register, and plans can offer somewhat different benefits).

Payment for both physician services and hospital services is through fee-for-service, but neither kind of provider has any freedom to decide what fees to charge. Payment for *every* kind of service is regulated in detail by the government. Unlike the case in the U.K., there is almost no provision of health care outside of the public system in Japan. Thus, one explanation why aggregate health care costs are relatively low in Japan is simply that fees for many services are fixed by government at low levels.

Another factor that may have helped keep costs low is that government has set the structure of fees so that provision of primary-care services is relatively profitable, but provision of various kinds of hospital services less so. As a result, most hospitals supply primary care in their out-patient departments, and there is keen competition between independent doctors and hospital out-patient departments to attract patients to whom they can supply primary care. Moreover, private doctors are said to be reluctant to refer patients to hospitals, as they fear that upon being discharged, the patients may choose to go to the hospitals' out-patient departments. The incentive that private doctors have to keep patients from going to hospitals may partly explain the relatively low hospitalization rates in Japan's population (even though it includes a large proportion of elderly people), and hence, indirectly, the relatively low aggregate health care costs.

While health care resources appear to be used efficiently in the Japanese system, it seems unlikely that reforms inspired by the Japanese model would be helpful at the present stage of development of China's system. First, it is not realistic at present to set a target under which every Chinese citizen, regardless of income, could expect to receive the same treatment for given illness conditions. Furthermore, designing a uniform fee schedule that would strictly regulate all physician and hospital services would be very complicated, and enforcing it would be difficult. Nevertheless, the Japanese experience does suggest certain principles that can be applied in other systems. One such principle is that incentives on primary-care providers to avoid referring their patients to specialists or hospitals may have a significant effect in saving aggregate health care costs. We will return to this idea in later chapters.

2.7. *Are health care systems converging?*

The principles underlying the two systems we have identified as potential models for China have been analyzed and discussed in the health economics community for a long time. The process of reorganizing the NHS so as to make more use of competition and decentralized management based on supply-side incentives was begun by the Thatcher government in the early 1980s, and the model of managed competition among insurance plans underlying the Dutch model was extensively analyzed by Enthoven in the 1970s.[10] Over time, similar ideas have influenced the health policy debate and the organization of health systems in other countries as well.

In particular, private managed care plans in the U.S. have increasingly used supply-side incentives based on principles similar to those in the U.K. model (rostering, capitation, drug budgets, and so on), and various forms of capitation to pay primary-care providers have been tried from time to time in countries like Canada and Sweden. A particularly important form of supply-side incentives in the hospital sector is episode-based payment based on Diagnosis-Related Groups. This method was originally developed by staff in the U.S. federal

---

[10]See Enthoven (1993).

Medicare plan, but has since spread all over the world.[11] Similarly, elements of the Enthoven model of competing insurers with risk-adjusted public subsidies have also been the basis for reforms of this plan (under the name of Medicare Advantage), and the reforms that have created near-universal insurance coverage in the U.S. state of Massachusetts have elements of this model as well.[12] It was also the basic model underlying the proposals for universal coverage advanced by the Clinton administration in the early 1990s. In Europe, it appears to have inspired the plans for reforming the German health financing system.

But while one may recognize bits and pieces of the principles underlying the U.K. and Dutch models in the health policy debate in many countries, the overwhelming impression in comparative analysis of health policy remains one of great diversity. Moreover, the descriptions of the prototype models above are somewhat idealized versions of the underlying ideas, and neither the U.K. nor the Netherlands have yet completed the process that would lead to fully developed Practice-Based Commissioning in the U.K., or extensive selective-contracting arrangements between providers and competing insurance plans envisaged for the system in Holland. Thus, even to those who believe that there is a degree of convergence of health care systems across countries toward one or the other of these models, it seems clear that it is occurring very slowly indeed.

Part of the reason the pace of health services reform in most countries has been very slow is the fact that health policy tends to be politically sensitive and controversial. This in turn reflects the fact that the health care sector everywhere is a major income source for large numbers of individuals, including highly educated professionals who tend to be influential in many political systems. Reforms that affect these

---

[11] See Schreyögg *et al.* (2006).

[12] Gruber (2009) discusses the Massachusetts experience. In their review of managed competition among insurance plans "within the context of a social health insurance scheme", van de Ven and Schut (2011) cite the following countries as having used this approach (in addition to the Netherlands): Belgium, the Czech Republic, Germany, Israel, Slovakia, and Switzerland.

groups' "vested interests" can therefore be difficult to implement, as we discuss in the next section. Although China's current political system is quite different from that of the developed Western countries from which most of the experience of health care reform is derived, vested interests are likely to be important in China as well. In the following section, we review some of the explanations that have been suggested for the power of vested interests in influencing economic policy in market-oriented economies, and consider the question to what extent these explanations apply in the Chinese context, with particular reference to the health care sector.

3. Why are Vested Interests So Powerful in Health Care?

3.1. *Government policy and vested interests: General considerations*

Analysis of vested interests in the context of Western economic and political systems tends to focus on actions by producers (or labor unions) for the purpose of influencing government policy that affects economic conditions in their industries. Often, these actions are intended to resist government policies that are perceived as increasing the intensity of competition among producers in an industry (or competition from new or foreign producers). A general principle that is often invoked to explain the perceived power of vested interests in many situations is that producers, because they are specialized, can be greatly affected by government decisions that affect an industry, whereas the interests of consumers, who purchase a great variety of goods and services, are more diffused. As a result, producers are more willing to devote resources to lobby for favorable government policy in each industry than consumers are.

More generally, the concept of vested interests need not just refer to private producers but can also be applied to people who may indirectly be affected by changes in an industry, for example, because the changes threaten their jobs. Interpreted this way, employees in both private and public sectors (including those in related government bureaucracies) may have a vested interest in not changing certain types of policy. The concept of "loss aversion" may also be relevant to the power of vested interests.[13] While policies that favor competition may be in the interests of not only consumers but also of new firms that are hoping to gain from entering an industry, the expected benefits to the latter groups are likely to be uncertain and speculative, whereas the losses of existing producers or employees resulting from a policy change can be predicted with more certainty. A generalization of the principle of loss aversion would suggest that these losses will tend to be given more weight than the speculative gains of potential innovators or entrants.

While vested interests are present in all industries, they are more likely to be politically influential in some industries than in others. In market-oriented economies, the general principle that consumers and society in general benefit from unrestricted competition among existing producers, and from new entrants or foreign producers, is, after all, widely accepted, and most such countries have competition and trade policies to ensure that this principle is respected. Vested interests are therefore more likely to be powerful in industries where a plausible case can be made that unregulated competition would not yield an outcome that would benefit consumers, so that some form of government regulation of private producers, or direct government intervention as a producer, is called for.

In regulated industries, vested interests may be effective in influencing the nature of the government's policies not just because they may be able to influence political decision-makers in various ways, but also because they can influence the bureaucrats that advise the politicians. According to the concept of "regulatory capture", the fact that regulatory bureaucrats need to have the same type of expertise as people in the industry, and in some cases are even former employees of industry firms, may create a tendency for the bureaucrats to develop not only an understanding of the industry's problems, but also some degree of sympathy for the positions taken by

---

[13] An early discussion of loss aversion is in Kahneman and Tversky (1979). Its empirical relevance is discussed in the influential paper by Kahneman, Knetsch, and Thaler (1990). A non-technical and highly readable exposition is in Kahneman (2011).

producers, even if these are to some extent in conflict with the public's interests.[14]

3.2. *Vested interests and economic policy in China*

Most analyses of the role of vested interests in economic policy-making have been conducted in the context of Western democratic systems in which the politicians in power are chosen in competitive multi-party elections. In such systems, vested interests can exert pressure on the politicians by influencing the voting patterns of some population groups (such as employees of particular firms, or members of particular labor unions), or via financial contributions to political campaigns. In a system such as China's with a single dominant political party, and with a smaller role for privately owned capital in the economy, the interaction between vested interests and those in charge of economic policy decisions will obviously take somewhat different forms. Indeed, it is possible to argue that economic policy in China will be less influenced by private vested interests than it is in the West, both because the large share of collective ownership reduces the impact of many economic policy decisions on private owners of capital, and because political decision-makers in a one-party system are less subject to pressure than in a system with many competing parties.

In recent decades, however, the gradual transformation of the Chinese economic system has greatly increased the degree of inequality in the distribution of real income, in large part because the new forms of economic organization have created opportunities for accumulation of private wealth that were not available earlier. Thus, there are now many cases in which economic policy decisions, and the way economic policies are enforced, can have a big impact on private economic interests. The incentives for private interests to influence these decisions, and the rules for enforcing them, are therefore much stronger than they were before, and when such incentives exist, they are likely to result in increased efforts to influence policymakers and officials, regardless of the nature of the political system.

---

[14]The concept is analyzed in the context of a theoretical model in Laffont and Tirole (1991). Stigler (1971) is an early influential discussion.

Moreover, even though electoral politics and private financing of political parties play a smaller role in the system through which China is governed than in the West, the Chinese system has other features which are likely to reinforce the potential influence of vested interests. One such feature is the high degree of decentralization of many aspects of economic policy, and the way central directives are implemented. While decentralization increases the ability of officials to respond to local conditions, it may also make it easier for vested interests to influence them without attracting a great deal of public attention, through personal contacts and relationships built on hospitality, gifts, and even bribes. The fact that local officials in China are still able to control the local media to a significant extent is also likely to contribute to this, although their ability to do so is gradually changing, both because of the increased importance of the Internet and because of central policies to strengthen the role of the traditional media.

3.3. *Vested interests in the health sector*

In the context of Western economic and political systems, the factors discussed earlier as explanations for the importance of vested interests on economic policy decisions make it plausible that the health sector is one in which interest groups can be quite influential.

To start with, health services are essentially non-tradeable, so that competition from foreign producers is not effective.[15] Moreover, the extent to which health policy in one country is influenced by experience in other countries is quite limited, as the understanding of the way other countries' systems of health care financing and health services production function generally is quite limited.[16]

More importantly, for reasons that have been extensively discussed in health economics, it is easy to make a plausible case to suggest that

---

[15] International trade in health services does exist to a limited extent, of course, when patients from Canada go to the U.S. for certain types of advanced care, or when high-income patients from other countries travel to places like Mumbai or Singapore because certain elective operations are offered there at a lower cost than in their home countries.

[16] Most people in both Canada and the U.S., for example, seem to be convinced that the health care system in their own country is superior to that in the other country.

unregulated competitive markets in health care would not function in a way that would benefit consumers. Although private insurance markets could, in principle, supply the risk-pooling arrangements that are needed in a well-functioning health financing system, there are well-known reasons why unregulated private health insurance markets might not produce outcomes that are equitable or efficient. For this reason, governments everywhere either heavily regulate private insurance markets (as in Holland or the U.S.) or supply risk-pooling through government plans (the U.K., Canada, most of the other countries of continental Europe, Japan).

The information asymmetry problem between patients and providers, together with the relative ineffectiveness in health care of methods that are used to ensure quality of products and services in other industries (such as warranties or legal remedies), has also led governments everywhere to heavily regulate entry into the medical profession and the nature of medical education. It has also delegated a major part of the responsibility to protect an imperfectly informed public to the medical profession itself, including the design of rules (such as those discouraging advertising by doctors in most countries) that govern the nature of competition among doctors. Thus, the nature of competition in both the markets for health insurance and health services is heavily regulated or non-existent everywhere, creating many opportunities for interest groups such as the medical profession, hospital employee groups, drug companies and private health insurers to influence the rules under which their industries operate.[17]

The dynamic of the interaction between the vested interest groups and the government, either as a regulator or as a financing agent, is also affected by the prevalence of third-party payment for health services. In other markets, the interest conflict to which policy must react tends to be between the producers (the owners of the industry's private firms,

---

[17]For a useful survey discussion of the way various interest groups interact in the health care reform process, see Tuohy and Glied (2011). An interesting comparative case study of the U.S., the U.K., and Canada, is Tuohy (1999). A detailed survey of the degree of competition in both the markets for health services (especially hospital services) and health insurance is Gaynor and Town (2012).

and sometimes its employee groups) on the one hand, and the buyers of the industries' products, on the other. But in health care, the definition of who is the buyer is not unambiguous. Are the "buyers" the patients who are ill and are seeking treatment and/or drugs, or are the buyers the set of insured individuals who pay private insurance premiums (or taxes) that finance most of the cost of health care everywhere?[18] In many cases when vested interests such as doctors, drug companies, or hospitals and their employees are resisting certain policies that are designed to reduce costs by changing incentive structures and competition, for example, they can argue that they are doing so in the interest not only of themselves, but also on behalf of the patients they will be treating. In open political systems in which decisions may be highly influenced by discussions in the media, coalitions of providers and patient groups are likely to be effective against the diffuse interests of the third parties (insurers or taxpayers) who pay most of the cost.[19]

3.4. *Health policy and regulatory capture*

The concept of regulatory capture is also likely to be relevant for health policy decisions, and the way they are implemented, in many countries. As an example, this seems especially likely in the context where health system reform has involved attempts to create an arm's-length relationship between health service providers (principally hospitals) and local financing agencies, in a situation where the hospitals were previously managed directly by the local governments that are now supposed to represent the taxpayers' interests against the providers. This logic seems to be relevant to the case of China at present. It may have been one reason why the attempt to create a "purchaser-provider" split at the local level in the early NHS reforms is widely regarded as not having been successful.

---

[18]In a theoretical model with a complete set of contingent markets, the answer would be "the latter". But in the real world with less complete insurance contracts, the answer is less obvious.

[19]Appeals for more resources to treat serious illness can often be justified by an appeal to the principle in the title of a famous paper by Thomas Schelling (1968): "The life you save may be your own".

Under the purchaser-provider split, the personnel in the local branches of the NHS bureaucracy that were previously responsible for managing local hospitals with funding from the U.K. government were divided into two departments. One group (the providers) continued to be responsible for managing the individual hospitals in the district, while the other group (the purchasers) was given the responsibility for allocating the district's hospital funding among the hospitals. In doing so, the purchasers were supposed to enter into explicit contracts with the hospitals regarding the types and volume of services they would supply to the district population, and on what terms the hospitals would be funded.

For example, rather than a hospital being given a global budget for the coming year, the contract might specify that part of the funding would be paid as a fixed amount for each patient treated for a specific condition. In negotiating these contracts, the purchasing department was supposed to act as a "prudent purchaser" of all required services on behalf of the district population, and to encourage local hospitals to compete with each other by offering to produce specific services on better terms than the others; a district purchaser was even allowed to contract for specific services with a hospital in another district if this resulted in the services being provided on better terms than local hospitals offered. Put differently, the experiment was intended to create the equivalent of an "internal market" in which individual hospitals would compete with each other for the right to supply (and be paid for) the services sought by the purchasing departments on behalf of the district's population.

While the model of funding hospitals through negotiations between hospitals and purchasers in internal markets may have worked well in some places, in many cases it appears to have had only limited success, in the sense that in practice, the "contracts" that were negotiated as the basis for funding the hospitals consisted of vaguely specified agreements under which the hospitals essentially agreed to continue providing services as needed, and funding continued to be in the form of an annual lump-sum. Effectively, therefore, the management system continued to operate pretty much as before, in spite of the attempt at differentiating between the purchaser and provider roles in the bureaucracy. The limited success of this form of a purchaser-provider split is part of the reason why the "purchasing function" in the U.K. is gradually being transferred to groups of primary-care providers, as discussed earlier.[20] We will return in Chapter 9 to the question of how an effective purchasing system can be created in China, if a model similar to the NHS is to serve as a template for its future system of financing and health services production.

3.5. *Vested interests in health care: Will China's experience be similar?*

The general conclusion suggested by the discussion above is that the health sector in most countries has characteristics that have tended to make vested interests relatively more influential in that sector than in most other ones.[21] As a result, convergence toward some version of an equitable and efficient system of health financing and health services production will tend to be very slow in countries where the current systems fall short on one or both of these criteria. As China embarks on its ambitious program of health system modernization, is it also going to be slowed down by entrenched interests? Can one use the experience of other countries to predict which interests are going to be most influential in China, and draw lessons about how they can be contained so as to speed up the process of creating a system that operates efficiently and equitably in the public interest?

In answering these questions, it must be recognized that any generalization about the health sector and health policy is risky, given the large differences between national systems.[22] The relative

---

[20]References to empirical studies of the effects of different forms of a purchaser-provider split in the U.K. may be found in Propper and Leckie (2011).

[21]Other possible examples may be defense industries (especially in the U.S., some European countries, and perhaps Russia) where, again, buyers are not individual consumers spending their own money directly, or agriculture in many countries (for different reasons).

[22]The question why national health care systems are so different in the first place falls beyond the scope of this chapter. Some explanations may go far back in history, for example, the strong influence of the guild systems in Europe that later gave rise to occupation-based social insurance schemes. However, some differences may simply be

influence of various interest groups may differ from country to country, depending both on the way the health sector is organized and on the way the political system functions. While doctors obviously play a major role in health policy in every country, the relative influence of primary-care providers and specialists can differ. In some countries, medical associations representing all doctors are strong, while in others it may be groups of senior physicians in teaching hospitals that have the most say, for example. In many countries, pharmaceutical companies (sometimes working together with physician interest groups) wield considerable power. In some systems, including China's, hospital managers (either individually at the local level, or as an organized group) can be very influential, whether they manage private hospitals or government-owned ones. In part, this is because hospitals are large employers so that large numbers of workers have an interest in the amount of resources the hospitals receive.

As suggested by the concept of regulatory capture, the way government bureaucrats in health ministries interact with providers may be an important determinant of the way interest groups influence policy, and in some countries one may be able to identify specific groups of people in the bureaucracy who should be classified as having a vested interest in their own right (for example, because they seek to increase their power by controlling a larger budget). This suggestion seems to be particularly relevant with respect to the case in China today, where most of the early resistance against health reform has come from bureaucrats in the state Ministry of Health who opposed many of the initiatives proposed by other ministries such as Finance and Labor and Social Security. While the Ministry of Health was not able to prevent the changes that took place in China's health care system during the 1980s

---

due to serendipity, together with the path dependence that results from the strong influence of national interest groups and the lack of competition among alternative models (compare the title of Tuohy, 1999). In an earlier era when medical technology was much simpler than today, the cost (in comparison with the economy as a whole) of failing to design an efficient system was also a great deal lower than it is now, so that countries could afford to preserve national idiosyncrasies, even if they were costly.

and 1990s, its officials have played a major role since the early 2000s as advocates of a return to a more centralized "command and control" approach in future reforms, as we noted in Chapter 1 and will discuss further in later chapters.

At the local level, the regulatory-capture concept has become increasingly relevant as hospitals and clinics have been given more freedom to generate revenue from patient charges and markups on prescription drugs. While most providers have continued to be owned by government, hospital managers and senior doctors are likely to benefit in various ways, from increased hospital revenue. If they are able to influence the local officials who are responsible for supervising them and implementing the rules under which they operate, the outcome is likely to be one in which costs to patients rise rapidly, as doctors tend to choose treatment approaches for which hospitals are allowed to charge high fees and to prescribe expensive drugs on which hospitals earn a high markup. As we will further discuss in Chapter 8, the tendency for local officials to sympathize with practices that enable hospitals to extract more revenue from patients is reinforced by the fact that it is the local government which carries the ultimate responsibility for ensuring that doctors and other hospital personnel are paid their salaries; indirectly, higher hospital revenues from patient charges and drug markups therefore reduce the pressure on local government budgets.

The dynamics of vested interests in the health care sector add to the urgency of resolving the ambiguities inherent in the central government's current health policy approaches, and settling on a clear direction for the future, whether it will focus on more direct government control over funding and production of health services, or on an enhanced role for market forces and competition. The longer drug companies, hospitals, doctors, and local governments are allowed to operate under the current hybrid system that allows them considerable scope for raising large amounts of revenue from patients in an environment with both relatively weak regulation and limited competition, the more entrenched will be their interest in the status quo, and the stronger their resistance to consistent future reforms.

3.6. *Conclusion: Which model for the long run?*

In a longer-term perspective, the problem that societies face in reconciling the power of vested interests in the health sector with the interests of the public and the objectives of equity and efficiency will only become more acute, as technological developments will increase the amount of resources that should be devoted to health care. As it is likely that public (rather than private) funding of health care will continue to dominate (this is true whether societies move toward a version of the U.K. model or the Dutch model), governments will gradually have to raise a growing share of national income as tax revenue, something that will intensify the competition among interest groups representing health care and other sectors (such as education), and also among different income classes as there will be a larger tax burden to share. It will also increase the urgency of resolving the fiscal issues that arise in countries that are federations, so that the responsibilities for raising tax revenue and funding different types of public expenditures are shared between central and local governments. This will be a particularly thorny issue in a country like Canada where health funding is a provincial responsibility, but where there are large transfers from the federal government to the provinces. It also exists in the U.S., and also in China, even though China is not legally classified as a federation.[23]

The power of vested interests will make it even harder to make the decisions necessary for health care reform, so the process of change will be slow and fitful, not only in China but in most other countries as well. Nevertheless, we believe that the inherent logic of the way the health care sector operates will produce a discernible trend toward either a version of the U.K. model (in those countries that continue along the path of a single universal government plan), or a version of the Dutch model. As medical and pharmaceutical technology advances and

---

[23]An intriguing question is whether certain kinds of vested interests can be more effective in influencing public policy in federal systems than in unitary ones. For example, are interest groups in Canada more able to resist health system reform because they can exploit competition between politicians at the federal and provincial levels in terms of being seen as protecting the health care system?

it becomes increasingly difficult to maintain a model where everyone receives the same health care when ill, there is likely to be increased tolerance of markets in which the wealthy purchase care privately, outside the public system, in countries that continue to offer a single universal public plan. Alternatively, more countries may switch from this model to a version of the Dutch model with public subsidies available to many competing private or public plans (as Germany may be doing over the next several years). We will return later, in Chapters 9 and 10, to the issue of which of these two models offers the best prospects for China in future years.

Appendix. Growing Health Care Costs: Wasteful or Economically Efficient?

Part of the reason health system reform is considered a priority in China today is that health care has become increasingly costly. As observed in Chapter 1, large expenditure on health care in cases of serious illness has become one of the most important sources of financial risk for families in China, and a major reason why many people in China continue to fall into poverty, even as per capita income was rising rapidly. The growth in insurance coverage through the social insurance plans described in the next chapter has reduced this problem to some extent. However, the growing cost of health care has also become a concern at the economy-wide level. As observed in Chapter 1, health care costs as a share of China's GDP rose from about 3.2% in 1980 to about 5.2% in 2010. These numbers imply that, on average, aggregate health care costs in China in real terms rose by more than 1.5 percentage points faster than real GDP every year. Since average real GDP growth over this period was some 10.1% per year, the average annual growth rate of health care costs in real terms would have been 11.6%, a high rate indeed. As China continues to pursue economic policies to raise the living standards of its citizens and catch up with the world's high-income countries, should it aim to reduce health care costs, or at least limit their rate of growth to the same rate as the rest of the economy, so as to prevent health care from claiming an ever-increasing share of the economy's total resources?

Health Policy Reform in China

Table A1.   Total national health care costs as a percentage of GDP.

	1960	1970	1980	1990	2000	2009
China			3.2	4	4.6	5
Canada	5.4	6.9	7	8.9	8.8	11.4
France	3.8	5.4	7	8.4	10.1	11.8
Japan	3	4.5	6.4	5.9	7.7	8.5*
Korea			3.7	4	4.5	6.9
Mexico				4.4	5.1	6.4
United Kingdom	3.9	4.5	5.6	5.9	7	9.8
United States	5.1	7.1	9	12.4	13.7	17.4

Source: OECD Health Data 2011 (http://stats.oecd.org/Index.aspx?DataSetCode=SHA).
*: 2008
Note: In U.K., in 2008 the figure was 8.8%.

The experience of today's high-income countries suggests that the goal of preventing health care costs from rising at a faster rate than GDP may be hard to reach. Data on health care's share of aggregate resource use in other countries show two clear patterns. First, there is a tendency for the share to be higher in countries with higher per capita income. For example, Table A1 shows much higher shares in the high-income countries of North America (Canada and the U.S.) and Europe (France, the U.K.), as well as in Japan, than the 5.2% that was the figure in China in 2010. Second, there has been a steady upward trend in the share over time, not only in China but in all the countries shown in the table.

Neither of these patterns necessarily implies that it will be in China's interest to allow the health care sector to absorb a larger share of total economic resources in the future than it does today. However, in trying to explain these patterns, the health economics literature has identified a number of underlying factors, some of which are likely to be present in China as well in future years. They include population aging, advancing medical technology, the notion that health care is a "luxury good", and a rising relative price of health services over time.

A.1. *Population aging*

Other things equal, the fact that older people tend to use more health services per capita than the young will obviously imply that a population with a larger fraction of people in older age groups tends to use more health services on average. However, demographic change takes place very slowly, so that the contribution of population aging to growth in health care spending each year tends to be quite modest. As an example, data from Canada imply that per capita health care costs of those over 65 on average is six times larger than for those below 65. In the period from 2011 to 2031, the share of Canada's population that is over 65 is projected to rise from 13% to as high as 25%. Although this will be the period in which population aging will be at its most rapid, these numbers together imply that aging by itself would only cause health care spending to increase by 1.56% per year, that is, by only a fraction of the observed growth rate in health care costs in recent years, and even a little below the historical growth rate of real GDP per capita. Thus, if population aging was the only reason why real per capita health care costs would rise over time, one would observe a stable or declining trend in the percentage of Canadian GDP devoted to health care, not a rising one.

In China, too, demographic trends imply that there will be a very rapid aging of the population, with the share of those over age 65 doubling from 8.2% in 2010 to 16.5% in 2030.[24] As in other countries, the prevalence of health problems in China is greater among the elderly than in the rest of the population, so population aging will translate into an increased per capita demand for health services. Moreover, since population aging in China mostly is the result of the very low fertility rates that prevailed after the adoption of the one-child policy in 1980, it will be accompanied by a reduced growth rate in the population of working age. Because this will tend to reduce the growth rate of GDP, other things equal, it will reinforce the trend toward health care accounting for a larger share of total economic activity. Nevertheless, as in the Canadian example, the demographic effects occur relatively

---

[24]The projections are based on the medium variant from the United Nations Department of Economic and Social Affairs, World Population Projections, the 2011 revision (available at esa.un.org/wpp). The projection shows a further increase, to beyond 25%, by 2050, until the share finally peaks at just over 30% in the latter half of the century.

slowly, so that by themselves, they should be manageable if the economy continues to perform well in general.

A.2. *Income and relative price effects*

The notion that health care costs as a percentage of GDP have been rising as a result of income and relative price effects is primarily based on empirical studies which have shown that in international cross-section and time series studies, the estimated elasticity of real per capita health spending with respect to real per capita income often is significantly above unity. This result is consistent with the idea that consumers' preferences typically are such that their income elasticity of demand for health care is above unity (that is, health care technically is a luxury good). In part, the result may also reflect the idea that, as per capita income grows in a country, there is a tendency for the price of health services to rise relative to other goods and services (for example, because health services are relatively labor-intensive, and real wages rise relative to the costs of other factors of production when per capita incomes rise). If it is further assumed that the price elasticity of demand for health services is less than unity, this would reinforce the tendency for per capita spending on health care to rise as per capita GDP rises.[25]

At the intuitive level, the idea that health care has the characteristics of a luxury good is difficult to accept if one thinks of services that are rendered to seriously ill people who, without them, would be likely to die or suffer a serious decline in their quality of life (for example, in the form of severe pain or major disability). However, one of the most important facts about health and health care is that there often is great uncertainty about what the outcome of an individual treatment episode will be, both because of the difficulty of obtaining an exact *ex ante* diagnosis for many kinds of health problems, and because there is randomness in the outcome of specific treatment choices for given illness conditions.

---

[25] For reviews of the evidence see Gerdtham and Jönsson (2000), Chernew and May (2011) and Chernew and Newhouse (2012).

Hence, while there certainly are some situations in which there would be a high probability of death or a serious deterioration in life quality if a particular treatment is not given, there also will be many cases in which there would be *some* probability of such an outcome, but where the risk of such an adverse outcome would be relatively low. Since the opportunity cost of providing a given quantity of health care is higher the lower is per capita income, people in poor countries may be less likely than those in rich ones to want to pay for diagnostic and curative health services which only have a low probability of improving health. This logic certainly is consistent with a pattern in which the share of health care spending in GDP rises (or at least does not fall) as per capita income rises.[26]

Another factor that may help explain the pattern under which health care's share of GDP tends to rise with per capita income is related to the influence of insurance. In many low-income countries, there are typically many people who have little or no health insurance coverage, as government plans often do not provide effective coverage, and because private insurance in poor countries tends to be purchased only by those with high income. In almost all high-income countries, in contrast, there are arrangements that result in universal (or near-universal) insurance coverage, reducing the barriers to access for the poor and leading to a higher health care spending share than in countries without universal insurance.

While the Chinese health care system until now only provides public insurance to part of the population, and relatively limited coverage to many, especially in rural areas, the expansion of the three social insurance plans described in Chapter 3 certainly provides a plausible factor that partially explains the rapid increase in health care's share in GDP over the last three decades. If, as seems likely, China continues to widen and deepen the coverage of the social insurance plans, aggregate spending may rise even further, unless this process is accompanied by

---

[26]The idea that a substantial portion of health care resources in high-income countries have only a low expected benefit in terms of health improvements is sometime referred to as "flat-of-the-curve medicine" (alluding to the relatively flat portion of a graph with health resources on the *x*-axis and some measure of population health on the *y*-axis).

other reforms that promote cost containment in various ways.[27] We will return to this issue later on.

The argument that the health care share rises with per capita income because the relative price of health services tends to increase with per capita income rests on three premises: that health care is relatively labor-intensive, so that its relative price will rise when real wages rise by more than the cost of other inputs such as capital; that real wages rise relative to the cost of capital when per capita income increases; and that the demand for health care is relatively inelastic with respect to price. There is considerable evidence that the second and third of these premises are true. While the demand for health care does respond to price changes to at least some extent, estimated price elasticities have been well below unity,[28] and it is well-established that the cost of labor relative to capital normally increases when per capita income rises. However, the evidence in favor of the suggestion that health care is relatively labor-intensive is less strong. Modern medical technology relies to a significant extent on advanced hospital facilities and expensive equipment for diagnosis and treatment. Moreover, most of the labor that goes into the production of health care is provided not by unskilled workers, but by highly trained professionals such as doctors, nurses, and pharmacists. Their earnings to a large extent reflect the return on the human capital that results from their long and costly training, not just on the labor time they provide. What will happen to the relative cost of health care in China over time will thus depend not just on the growth of real wages, but also on the efficiency with which health care professionals are trained in medical and other professional schools.

---

[27] The time path of health expenditures in Korea, where social health insurance became universal in 1989, is interesting in this regard. According to the OECD Health Database, health care costs as a percentage of GDP remained relatively constant around 4% in the first decade following this reform. Since then, however, the share has risen rapidly, reaching 7% by 2010.

[28] As discussed in Pauly (2011), the early estimates of the price elasticity implied by the famous Rand Health Insurance Study in the 1970s were as low as $-.1$ and $-.2$ for in-patient and out-patient care, respectively. Later studies have yielded somewhat higher values, ranging from $-.25$ to $-.5$ for in-patient care and $-.4$ to $-.8$ for out-patient care.

A.3. *Changing technology*

A positive relationship between per capita income and the share of health expenditures in GDP can partially explain why this share has risen in most countries, since per capita income has been rising in most countries. However, econometric evidence also is consistent with the hypothesis that advances in medical technology have contributed to rapidly rising costs. Since there is no obvious way in which technological progress can be measured, the approach in empirical studies typically is to treat it as a residual factor which causes health care costs to change over time, after controlling for other factors. When this approach is used and a time trend is introduced in equations that estimate the relation of health expenditures to other factors (such as income, relative prices, etc.), the coefficient on the time trend typically is positive and statistically significant, consistent with the idea that changing technology has tended to raise health care costs.[29]

In general, technological progress in a sector does not inevitably lead to higher expenditure on the sector's products. If the introduction of new production methods lowers the unit cost of a sector's products, and the price elasticity of demand for the products is less than one (in absolute value), consumers' spending on those products will fall, not rise. However, if technological progress takes the form of the introduction of new products that were not previously available in a sector, the result may be an increase in the total amount spent on the sector's output. In health care, much of the technological progress that has taken place appears to have been of the latter kind. It certainly is possible to think of some innovations that have reduced the cost of treating certain conditions that could be treated equally effectively with an older but more expensive method (for example, treating stomach ulcers with drugs rather than through an operation). However, technological change in health care has more often taken the form of introducing new drugs or treatment methods that made it possible to treat illness conditions that could not previously be treated, or to get

---

[29]Again, see Gerdtham and Jönsson (2000). A recent review of the evidence is Chernew and May (2011).

significantly better expected outcomes than with older methods, but at a higher cost. As a result, total expenditures have tended to increase.

In principle, one would expect that technological progress, by definition, would tend to make a society better off, even if it leads to more spending on the products of the sector where it has taken place. In an economy where resources are efficiently allocated, consumers will only spend more on a sector's products if the value they get from the extra output is larger than its opportunity cost.

One important strand in the health economics literature has suggested that in the case of health care, this logic may not always apply. Specifically, it observes that, since most health care costs are paid by third parties, the decisions by patients and their doctors whether or not to adopt various kinds of new technology may not be based on a comparison of its value with its full opportunity cost (because individual patients and doctors will not take into account the increased costs to the third party). As a result, new technologies may be adopted even though their full cost to society is higher than their value. Moreover, this problem may become worse over time because the firms that are engaged in the R&D that produces technological progress in health care focus too much on the development of new technologies that are attractive to patients and doctors because they yield additional health benefits, and not enough on inventions that reduce the cost of treatment methods that are already in use.[30]

To the extent that cost increases stemming from the inefficient introduction of costly technology are responsible for a large portion of the rapid growth in health care spending, they obviously represent a major policy problem, and society would be better off with slower growth in health care costs and a lower share of resources going to the health care sector. However, while the logic in the preceding paragraph suggests that this outcome is theoretically possible, there is not a great deal of independent evidence to substantiate that it is a significant problem in practice in most countries today. Part of the reason is that in

---

[30] For an exposition of this idea see, for example, the textbook by Folland, Goodman, and Stano (2007, Chapter 11). The first clear and rigorous exposition of the logic involved is Goddeeris (1984a,b).

response to rising costs, it has become more common for third parties to try to control rising costs by subjecting new technologies and drugs to some type of economic evaluation, so that the new technologies that are adopted do indeed have benefits that more than outweigh the costs to society as a whole (including the third-party payers). Many independent studies of specific types of new technology have supported this general conclusion, at least for the case of the U.S. and other developed countries.[31]

Nevertheless, while most developed countries may have found ways to make efficient use of advances in medical technology, there have been suggestions that overuse of advanced and expensive diagnostic and treatment methods has been a source of inefficiency and has contributed to the high cost of health care in many places in China. One reason why this may have happened is the way in which hospital fees have been regulated. As discussed in Chapter 5, while the central planning model in the health care sector has been modified so as to give hospitals more flexibility and autonomy in many respects, the fees for many established standard procedures have continued to be strictly controlled, often at levels that made it unprofitable for hospitals to use them in treating their patients. Since fees or markups for many newer treatment technologies or drugs were not regulated, hospitals have been able to set these fees and markups at levels high enough to make it attractive for them to treat patients using these drugs and technologies. To the extent that the hospital doctors' income has been tied to the hospitals' financial results, they have had an incentive to prescribe and supply these drugs and treatment methods to patients. The result may well have been an outcome in which, on average, the costs of dealing with patients' health problems have been much higher than they had to be.

A.4. Conclusion: Is the growth in health care spending sustainable?

If the rapid growth in health care expenditures in various countries has resulted mostly from the fact that consumers put a high value on better

---

[31] See, for example, Bunker, Frazier, and Mosteller (1994), and Cutler *et al.* (2006).

health and that technological progress has led to the development of more effective ways of reducing mortality and raising people's quality of life, then the increases in the amount of resources devoted to health care do not in themselves constitute a problem for society. Instead, a pattern under which society uses a growing share of its resources in health care constitutes an efficient response to citizens' preferences, and to new opportunities introduced by advances in technology. As observed earlier, in the debate over health policy, it is sometimes noted that a situation in which health care spending grows faster than GDP is not "sustainable", implying that deliberate government policies must be used in order to bring the increases in health care costs into line with the rate of GDP growth. The reasoning above suggests that this argument may be misleading: A pattern under which the share of health care spending in GDP continues to increase may in fact be efficient.[32]

This conclusion certainly may be applicable in China. Even though there is evidence that part of the reason for the rapid increase in health care costs has been due to excessive charges, overprescription of expensive drugs, and overuse of advanced technology, an equally important explanation surely must be that more and more people have been getting care for health problems that in the past would have gone untreated, or would have been treated using less effective methods. Thus, even if China is successful in eliminating much of the waste and inefficiency in its health care system, demand for effective health care may well continue to grow more rapidly than GDP as general living standards rise. To meet this demand, aggregate health care costs as a share of GDP will continue to increase.

However, even if keeping down health care costs should not be a primary focus of economic policy toward the health care sector, a growing ratio of health care spending to GDP does have important implications.

---

[32] In the long run, the issue of "sustainability" will probably receive less attention than the issue of how to better measure the contribution of the health sector's output to GDP. For two interesting conceptual discussions of this issue, see Usher (1973) and Nordhaus (2005). A recent survey is Triplett (2011).

As will be discussed in the next four chapters, there are large differences among countries in the approaches that are taken to managing resources in the health care sector, with some being less effective than others. As a larger and larger share of economic resources are used in that sector, the urgency of ensuring that a country is using an effective model for this purpose will become greater (perhaps suggesting an answer to the question implicitly raised earlier, namely why health reform has become an important part of the economic policy debate in many countries). A crucial element of such a model will be to have institutions that provide the proper information and incentives for health system managers, doctors, and patients, when making decisions as to what drugs and equipment will be used in the system, and what methods will be used in treating individual patients.

A central question in the debate over health policy, not only in China but elsewhere as well, has concerned the role that the government should play, both in paying for health care and in influencing the technology that is used in treating patients. With respect to financing, government now pays most of the cost in many countries. When health care constitutes a larger share of the overall economy, this implies that a growing share of total national income has to be collected by the government as tax (or social insurance) revenue. If it is recognized that collection of government revenue is costly in the sense that it has an excess burden, does this suggest that the optimal balance between government and private funding of health care should be changed?

With respect to influencing the use of different technologies, one obvious role for government is to encourage the use of economic evaluation of existing and new technology based on a consistent definition of cost-effectiveness analysis. One of the strengths of the U.K. model of health care organization has been its willingness to use this type of economic evaluation to govern the way patients have been treated in the NHS. Even in a system where a large share of health care costs are paid for privately, there is a strong case for an active government role in economic evaluation, since access to unbiased cost-effectiveness information makes it easier for patients, insurers, and health service providers to use health care resources more efficiently.

The question what role government should play in financing health care and influencing technology choices also raises a related one, namely to what extent it is appropriate for patients to have access to alternative ways of dealing with their health problems. To the extent that people have different values with respect to the way they would want to be treated when ill, conventional microeconomic analysis suggests that it is efficient to give them an opportunity to choose whichever approach they find most attractive, taking account of both the expected health outcomes and the cost of the alternatives. In an earlier era, when technology was such that health care spending only corresponded to a relatively small share of GDP, an approach in which every person would be treated the same way, regardless of their preferences, might be justifiable, given the advantages of such an approach in terms of simplicity and perceived equity. However, the implicit efficiency losses of this approach when there are significant differences in preferences may ultimately become so large as to justify a model in which there is more room for individual choices in health care. We will return to this theme in Chapters 9 and 10.

PART II

MAIN COMPONENTS
OF HEALTH REFORM

Chapter 3

STRENGTHENING CHINA'S SOCIAL INSURANCE SYSTEM*

1. Introduction: The Issues

As discussed in Chapter 1, China's health care system underwent major changes in the last two decades of the 20th century. While the changes were dramatic, they cannot be said to have resulted from a conscious effort by government to implement a consistent set of health policy reforms. They resulted instead from the general policy of reducing the role of the state in planning and managing the allocation of economic resources, and to strengthen that of voluntary transactions in free markets. But for the reasons discussed in Chapter 1, the health care sector has a set of special characteristics that impede the effectiveness of markets in allocating resources to and within it.

By the late 1990s, the tendency for health sector markets to fail had become increasingly obvious, and since that time the health policy community in China has been engaged in an ongoing debate about what policies should be employed to counteract this problem. The debate has been informed by the Western literature on health economics and the experience of health system reform in other countries to a considerable extent, and has involved experts and officials from many foreign countries and international organizations as well as from China. It has been confusing at times, with a bewildering variety of approaches

---

*Portions of this chapter have previously appeared as Blomqvist and Qian (2008).

being proposed and tested in pilot projects. In retrospect, this is perhaps not surprising, given the complexity and regional differences in current urban and rural health care systems, and the wide range of different approaches to health policy that have been tried in other countries. Moreover, as discussed in Chapter 2, although the kinds of vested interests that affect the health policy debate in China are somewhat different in kind from those in Western countries, they have a major influence in China as well.

It is perhaps also not surprising that the focus of the debate in the late 1990s was on the *financing* of health care. With fewer people being covered either by the Cooperative Medical Schemes in rural areas or by work-related insurance in the cities, and with hospitals and clinics raising treatment fees and drug prices, patients and their families were increasingly exposed to the risk of financial disaster or even of not being able to afford needed care, in case of serious illness. Under the circumstances, government measures to provide better risk pooling through third-party financing became the most important health policy priority.

With private insurance not being a realistic option, it was clear that government itself had to take a direct role in accomplishing this. But this role can take different forms. In the following sections, we focus on three questions that China's decision-makers had to consider in deciding how to strengthen the system of third-party financing. First, should the means for doing so be raised through general taxation or through a system of social insurance contributions? Second, should public funding be in the form of a single plan covering all citizens, or should there be different plans for different population groups? Related to this, should private insurance be allowed to play a role in the funding system, as a complement and supplement to public funding, or even as a substitute for it? Third, to what extent should the degree of risk-pooling be moderated by provisions to preserve incentives on patients to limit health care costs, through deductibles and co-payments, or by reserving a share of insurance funding to some type of medical savings accounts of the type that have long been used in the Singapore model of health financing?

1.1. *Government financing of health care: From general revenue or social insurance?*

As implied by the discussion in Chapter 2, the methods used to promote efficient and equitable forms of risk pooling in health care are quite different in different systems. In countries such as the U.K., Canada, or the Scandinavian countries where most health care costs are paid for out of general government revenue, risk pooling occurs implicitly as the costs are shared by all taxpayers. In many continental European countries (for example, Germany and France) and Japan that follow the social insurance approach, most health care costs are paid for out of special health insurance funds which receive their revenues principally from compulsory social insurance contributions from the citizens that are covered by the plans, though they sometimes also get some amount of subsidy from governments.

Although much of the literature on health financing has focused on the distinction between tax-financed plans and social insurance, the difference between these two approaches is not necessarily very significant in itself. In many countries that are conventionally classified in the social insurance category, contributions to the social insurance plan (or plans) are compulsory, for some or all population groups, and from the viewpoint of conventional economic analysis of the efficiency effects of different methods of raising government revenue, there is little substantive difference between a tax and a compulsory social insurance contribution. From a political-economy perspective, the difference may be somewhat important in that compulsory contributions to social health insurance plans have the characteristics of an "earmarked" tax, the revenue from which is associated with a specific government program. While such programs may be perceived somewhat differently by the public and politicians than those that are funded from general tax revenue, any such distinction obviously becomes less important in cases where social insurance revenue is supplemented by subsidies out of general revenue, as it is in Japan, for example, or if governments are able to draw on social insurance funds to finance other expenditures, as local governments in China are reported to have done in recent years.

But if the origin of the revenue out of which the government pays its share of the cost of health care is not of critical importance, another question is, as we will repeatedly stress in the chapters to come: whether the government performs its risk-pooling function indirectly, through contracts with providers that focus on the amounts of money that flow to them as total incomes or revenue, or through a system under which "money follows the patients" so that providers' revenue is determined by the product of the fees they charge for the services they provide to patients and the volume of these services.

While there is not a direct relation between the choice of these two approaches and the source of revenue to pay for the government's risk-pooling function, the countries that do so out of general revenue have historically been more likely to follow the former model. For example, the U.K., the Scandinavian countries, and Canada — all of whom have tax-financed plans — have traditionally funded their hospitals through negotiated annual budgets, while hospitals in the U.S., Germany, and Japan receive revenue from the respective social insurance plans in these countries in accordance with the volumes of specific services or the number of patient-days they have provided for the plans' members.

1.2. *Government-sponsored risk pooling: A single plan or multiple plans?*

Another question that probably is more important than whether a government-managed health insurance program is financed out of general tax revenue or compulsory social insurance contributions is whether the program is a single universal one that automatically covers every citizen, and whether coverage is available on "equal terms and conditions", in the phrase of the Canada Health Act that specifies the rules that all Canadian provinces have to abide by in designing their provincial health insurance programs. In countries like Canada, the U.K., and those in Scandinavia, all of whom have health care systems in which every citizen automatically belongs to the same government health insurance plan with the same set of benefits, and funding is through general tax revenue, both of these conditions are clearly fulfilled: Every citizen is entitled to the same benefits when they are ill, and the taxes that a citizen has to pay do not depend on his or her risk of illness.

In some countries with social insurance funding like the U.S., Holland, and Germany, on the other hand, the universality condition is not fulfilled: These countries do not have a single common plan to which every citizen belongs automatically. In the U.S., government plans only cover those over age 65 and those with income below specified limits, while citizens in Holland and Germany can choose from a menu of different subsidized plans, private or public, with different (but regulated) benefit structures, and premiums that differ according to plans (but not according to factors such as individuals' risk of illness). At the same time, the social health insurance plans in countries like France and Japan *are* universal (in the sense that all citizens are entitled to the same benefits when ill), and while the compulsory contribution rates may differ across population groups, they do not depend on factors related to individuals' risk of illness.

The classification of different methods of government-sponsored risk-pooling is further complicated by the fact that insurance plans can differ not only with respect to what population groups are covered, but also in terms of what kinds of costs are included in their coverage, and what role private insurance is allowed to play alongside government funding. In a number of countries where government insurance is relatively incomplete, attempts are made to encourage additional risk pooling through private insurance, subject to various forms of regulation and subsidy. The most important example in this category is of course the U.S., where private employment-related insurance covers most of the population; but private insurance accounts for a substantial share of aggregate health care financing in many other countries as well, even those where there is a universal public plan that covers all citizens.[1]

The extent of coverage in the government plan may affect what role private insurance is likely to play alongside it. As an example, in each

---

[1]A comprehensive discussion of different roles that private insurance plays in OECD countries is Colombo and Tapay (2004).

Canadian province, there is only a single government plan that covers every citizen against the cost of physician services and of in-patient care in hospitals, but not for the cost of out-patient drugs. As a result, private health insurance plays a significant role in the Canadian system by offering plans that cover the cost of out-patient drugs and other items, such as dental care, that also are not included in the provincial plans.

In the terminology that has been proposed by the OECD, by covering certain kinds of costs that are not included in the government plan, private insurance in Canada plays the role of a *complement* to the government plan. In France, or in the regular Medicare plan for U.S. retirees, the government plans have deductibles and co-payment features that require patients to pay a substantial share of the cost of certain kinds of covered services out of their own pockets. In both cases, there are many individuals who both belong to the public plan and have private *supplementary* insurance that reimburses the patients for their out-of-pocket costs under the public plan. In China, private health insurance currently offers plans that complement and supplement the government plans in certain markets, and as we will discuss in Chapters 9 and 10, a case can be made for allowing it to play an even greater role in future years.[2]

1.3. *Medical savings accounts and the Singapore model*

The question whether government should strengthen its role in pooling health care costs through direct payments to providers, as in the tax-financed U.K. model, or through an insurance plan that reimburses patients for part of their health care costs, as in the U.S. Medicare plan or the Dutch or Japanese social insurance systems, has been the most controversial one in the Chinese debate about health financing over

---

[2] OECD uses the term *substitute* private insurance to include cases where certain population groups are covered by private plans either because they are not eligible for coverage through the public plan (as in the U.S.), or because government pays a subsidy toward the premium of a private plan of the citizen's choice, as in Switzerland, Holland, or Israel. We discuss the possibility of using this approach in China in future years later, in Chapter 10.

the last several years. Somewhat surprisingly, however, the design of the rural and urban social insurance plans that have evolved over the last decade has drawn heavily on an important feature of the system in another neighboring Asian country, namely Singapore's Medisave accounts.[3]

In the Singapore system, employers must deduct a certain percentage of every employee's earnings as contributions to a Central Provident Fund and to a Medisave account. While these compulsory contributions are similar to those that individuals in many other countries must make to social health insurance and retirement income schemes, the term "insurance" is somewhat of a misnomer in the Singapore context since no risk-pooling is involved: The total amounts that individuals are able to draw from the CPF when they retire, or from their Medisave accounts for eligible health care costs when they become ill, are limited to the accumulated balances they themselves have contributed in the past (including interest at a statutory rate). Plans with this characteristic might therefore more properly be referred to as *forced savings plans*, rather than as social insurance. In a social insurance plan, the value of the benefits that a person receives (for example, the total retirement income over his or her lifetime, or the total amount of reimbursement for medical expenditures) is not linked directly to his or her past contributions.

Many analysts have been very critical of Singapore's system, partly because the general conclusion from conventional microeconomic analysis is that, by themselves, forced savings plans are likely to be ineffective or inefficient, or both.[4] However, the conventional analysis typically proceeds from two fundamental assumptions. First, it postulates that individuals are willing and able to make savings and insurance decisions today that are based on reasonably accurate anticipation of their future resources and needs, and on rational reactions to various risks, including the probability of serious illness and need for costly medical care. Second, it assumes that there are well-functioning markets where

---

[3]For a review of Singapore's system of health care financing, see Lim (2004).
[4]On the Singapore case, see Hsiao (1995). A more general discussion of proposals to introduce the model in other countries is in Hurley and Guindon (2008).

individuals can borrow and lend, and obtain insurance on reasonable terms.

Needless to say, these assumptions may be unrealistic, and retirement income support programs with significant elements of forced savings enjoy high levels of popular support throughout the world. However, compulsory medical savings accounts take the concept of forced savings a step further, in that they require people of working age to save *for a specific purpose* (to pay for medical services). The rationale for such a scheme is much less clear, especially if there is a social insurance scheme that pools the risk of illness in the population, and Singapore is, to our knowledge, unique in having a system of compulsory medical savings accounts combined with a limited government role in ensuring that there is effective pooling of the financial risk associated with the need for expensive health care.

2. Reforming Urban Health Care: The Basic Health Insurance Scheme

As China moved to re-establish a strong system of risk-pooling in the health care sector in the late 1990s, it was perhaps not surprising that the focus initially was on a version of the social insurance approach under which "money follows the patient". A return to a system based on direct government funding of health care providers out of general government revenue would have been hard to reconcile with the broad strategy of more reliance on market-based transactions in the economy in general. A social insurance approach, on the other hand, could be designed in such a way as to maintain the principle that providers should derive most of their revenue from charging for the services they supply, while at the same time reducing the burden on individual patients through insurance-based risk pooling.

Another reason for choosing a social insurance approach was administrative. While the direct government funding of health care providers that had been the basis for the risk-pooling system in the pre-reform era had been channeled through the Ministry of Health, the shift to the social insurance model was accompanied by a major reassignment of administrative responsibility for health care financing to the Ministry of Labor and Social Security. Because MLSS had not previously been involved in the health care sector to a significant degree, its officials, along with those in the Ministry of Finance which also has been heavily involved in the reforms since the 1990s, could be expected to be more willing to support market-based approaches than those in the Ministry of Health who had worked closely with providers in the past and might be more sympathetic to those who wanted a return to a system with a larger role for direct government funding and management.

2.1. *The first step: Urban employees*

Introduction of the new system began with a well-defined population: workers in the formal urban sector. Following lengthy pilot projects in the cities of Zhenjiang and Jiujiang from 1994, the State Council in December 1998 announced a "landmark decree" concerning the establishment of the Basic Health Insurance System for Urban Staff and Workers. The system (henceforth referred to as BHI) was based on the following simple principles.[5] First, risk-pooling and plan management was through a Social Insurance Bureau in each large Chinese city. The basic version of the plan covered only current and retired employees (but not their dependants) of participating employers, who can be either the government, SOEs, or private firms. The intention was that the BHI plan would gradually replace the Government Insurance Scheme and the Labor Insurance Scheme that previously covered government employees and employees in SOEs and be compulsory, but in practice, many employers in these categories were slow to sign up, and even today, the goal of enrolling all eligible workers in a BHI plan has only been partially met.

Funding of the plan is through payroll deductions which, at a minimum, have to be at the level of 8% of the worker's salary (6% from the employer and 2% from the employee). In accordance with the principle of incorporating a medical savings account element in the

---

[5]The following account draws on Liu (2002). Another useful reference is Wong *et al.* (2007). Various acronyms have been used to refer to this plan in the English-language literature, including "UEBMI" (for example, Ho (2010)).

plan, this amount is then split between an "individual account" which belongs to the worker, and which can be used to pay for both out-patient and in-patient care, and a "social pooling account". In the early versions of the plan, the split was 3.8% to the individual account, 4.2% to the social pooling account. In case the individual has an illness episode requiring in-patient care, he or she can get reimbursement from the social pooling account for expenses in excess of a deductible (in the basic plan, equivalent to 10% of the worker's wage), subject to a locally determined co-insurance rate, and subject also to an upper limit equivalent to 6 times the average annual wage in the city.

There were two additional important provisions. First, coverage included only drugs and procedures on an explicit list of Essential Drugs and Essential Services; drugs and services not on the list were not covered. (The relevant legislation provided for some, but not unlimited, discretion for local authorities to decide what items would be included on the list.) Second, reimbursement could only be made for services received from hospitals and clinics that had been approved by the city's Social Insurance Bureau.

2.2. *The BHI in international perspective*

In comparing the BHI plan with social insurance plans in other countries that use that approach, such as Japan or the countries in continental Europe, the most significant difference of course is that the BHI is not a universal plan, as it only covers a subset of the population. However, the universal plans that exist in Japan and these European countries today also developed from earlier non-universal plans, and the BHI can be seen as a first step toward a future universal plan in China as well.

Since the most important function of any insurance scheme, government or private, is to accomplish risk pooling so that consumers are protected against illness-related financial risk and are able to access necessary care when they need it even if they have limited resources of their own, one of the most important criteria to be used in evaluating an insurance plan is to what extent they actually accomplish these objectives. But in considering the design of an insurance plan, one must keep in mind that a trade-off is likely to exist between the degree to which a plan protects against risk and removes financial barriers against needed care, on the one hand, and how costly it will be, on the other hand.

In particular, a plan that gives consumers complete protection against the financial burden of health care costs by paying 100% of what they are charged for the health services and drugs they use may be very costly. A population of fully insured consumers who pay nothing out of their own pockets for health services or drugs is likely to incur much higher costs for these items, on average, than in a population in which consumers have to pay a significant share of the costs out of pocket. Thus, a higher degree of insurance protection will translate into higher insurance premiums or government expenditures for subsidies to health insurance, giving rise to a trade-off between the degree of insurance and costs. The nature of this trade-off, and the question of how the objective of better insurance protection should be balanced against its cost, constitutes one of the most important areas of theoretical and empirical research in the field of health economics.[6]

Although there are examples of government insurance plans that come close to covering all the costs consumers incur for physician and hospital services, and prescription drugs, in most plans there are attempts to limit the plans' costs by requiring consumers to pay a portion of the costs out of their own pockets. As in the basic model of the BHI plan, this is normally done by defining a deductible under which the consumer must pay 100% of the relevant costs up to a specified limit (which may be defined in terms of annual expenditure, or per illness episode), and a co-payment provision under which the consumer pays a share (say, 20%) of costs beyond the deductible.

In health economics, deductibles and co-payment provisions are often referred to as *demand-side incentives*, since they shift some of the costs to the patients who seek out and receive health services and drugs. High deductibles and co-payment percentages imply a reduced degree of insurance since they imply that consumers may have to pay a relatively

---

[6]A clear and concise survey of the literature on this issue is Pauly (2011).

large share of their health care costs out of pocket. However, in order to limit individuals' and families' exposure to illness-related financial risk, the rules on deductibles and consumer cost-sharing are often supplemented by some type of "stop-loss" provision which specifies an upper limit on the amounts that they have to pay out of their own pockets per year or illness episode.

In comparison with other social insurance plans, even those with substantial patient co-payments such as those in Japan or France, the design of the original version of the Chinese BHI implied only a relatively limited degree of insurance. Even if the locally determined co-payment percentages were not especially high, a deductible set at 10% of the worker's annual wage is fairly high. More importantly, social insurance plans in other countries typically cover not only hospital in-patient expenditures, but also physician and hospital services that have been provided on an out-patient basis, while coverage under the risk-pooling provisions of the BHI was limited to the cost of in-patient services. (Although individuals could be reimbursed for some out-patient costs from their individual accounts, this did not reduce financial risk since the balances in individual accounts were limited to each person's own past contributions.) Moreover, the upper limits on the benefits payable under the BHI plan implied a residual risk for those few individuals with very large costs. While such limits exist in many private health insurance plans, social insurance plans typically specify upper limits on each patient's out-of-pocket payments instead.

Finally, in addition to the demand-side cost sharing in the form of a deductible, co-insurance, and an upper limit, the extent to which the BHI has reduced risk has also been limited to a significant extent by the fact that in order for patients to be able to claim reimbursement, the services and drugs that they have paid for must appear on the list of Essential Drugs and Essential Services referred to above. The fact that hospital patients may be asked to undergo procedures or use drugs that are not on the list (in part because the hospitals have an incentive to recommend such procedures or drugs, since their prices are not controlled) effectively reduces the extent to which the insurance protects them against financial hardship. To deal with this problem would require either making the list more inclusive (which would raise costs), and/or changing the incentives on providers (hospitals) so that they no longer have an incentive to recommend such procedures or drugs except in urgent cases.

2.3. BHI and purchasing

The demand-side incentives and limitations on coverage discussed above obviously are important parameters in evaluating the initial model of the BHI and the modified versions that have been developed in China's urban areas since the late 1990s. Another set of features of social insurance plans that may be at least as important in influencing the health care sector are the rules they contain with respect to patients' choices of what providers to use, and the terms according to which the providers are paid for their services.

In the past, private and public insurance plans in most countries gave patients an essentially unrestricted choice of providers, and paid their share of the fees that patients had been charged by any licensed doctor or accredited hospital. More recently, the trend everywhere has been toward various forms of *selective contracting*. With selective contracting, patients in a given insurance plan are covered only for the cost of health services that are supplied by doctors or hospitals that have accepted the terms of the plan's contract regarding such things as what fees they can charge, how they are going to be paid, and sometimes with certain restrictions on how the patients can be treated.

Although the guidelines for the BHI did not go into details, they did specify that coverage would be limited to services of providers that the local Social Insurance Bureau had approved, on the understanding that this would give the SIBs the ability to negotiate with providers regarding fee levels and other terms. Many observers anticipated that the SIBs would use their market power to promote methods of payment that implied incentives on providers to be productive in the sense of taking responsibility for many patients and keeping down the cost of the care the patients received. Payment methods with such "supply-side incentives", such as capitation in primary care and prospective payment for hospital services based on Diagnosis-Related Groups, have become increasingly common not only in the U.S. managed care plans, but in other countries as well. While payment methods with supply-side incentives were not used everywhere, some cities began experimenting with them even in the early years of the BHI.[7]

While the BHI was a carefully constructed and internally consistent blueprint for urban health insurance reform, it left a number of questions unanswered, in part because it was intended to allow for a substantial degree of local variation in the final plan design. In the time that has passed since its introduction, a clearer picture has emerged regarding how it will evolve in various dimensions.

2.4. *The BHI plans since 2000: Differentiation and growth*

Since its beginning in the early 2000s, the BHI has evolved rapidly. The number of individuals it covers exceeded 260 million in 2012 (Figure 1). While the number of enrollees has been increasing rapidly, it still falls far short of 100% of eligible employees in some cities. According to statistics from 2010, BHI covered 234 million people in total at the end of that year.[8] The total number of urban employees at the end of 2010 was around 322 million, while retirees numbered about 60 million. Thus, BHI enrollment was still only about 60% of the number eligible by 2011.[9] Nevertheless, the system appears to be firmly established, and one can expect that most employees and retired workers will ultimately be enrolled; the new guidelines issued in 2012 confirm that this is the intention (see below).

---

[7]Yip and Eggleston (2004) is an interesting account of an example where reimbursement methods of this type were tried. Blomqvist (2011) reviews the arguments in favor of the view that these methods are more likely than fee-for-service to promote cost-effective treatment decisions in any health care system. Gu (2010) has remained a strong supporter of the principle that the Social Insurance Bureaus should attempt to control costs by acting as large "purchasers" of health care on behalf of their plan members, and exercise their market power to negotiate favorable terms of service provision from hospitals and clinics.

[8]Chinese Government website (http://www.gov.cn/jrzg/2011-09/04/content_1939943.htm), accessed on July 31, 2013.

[9]Note, however, that some urban residents are still covered by GIS/LIS, and some have private commercial health insurance.

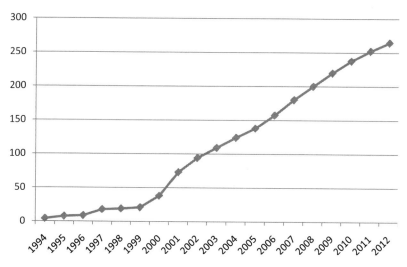

Fig. 1. Number of enrollees under BHI (million).

Source: *China Labor and Social Security Yearbook*, various years.

As aggregate enrollment has increased, another notable feature has been the high degree of differentiation in the way the BHI has been implemented and managed. As an example, while the initial guidelines recommended an employer contribution of 6% of each employee's wages, the actual rates have often been higher, though in some cities they have been lower than 6%. In Shanghai, employers contribute 10% of the worker's wages, while the lowest employer contribution rate is 3%, and the national average was about 7.4% in the mid-2000s.[10] Some cities with good fiscal capacity offer more generous benefits, and complementary social insurance beyond the basic BHI can be offered to improve coverage. Currently in Shanghai, the deductible for in-patient treatment is set at 1,500 RMB and a "threshold" is set at 280,000 RMB. Below this threshold, the reimbursement rate is 80% or even higher. Above it, there is a complementary social insurance plan that also

---

[10]http://www.npc.gov.cn/npc/zt/2008-12/23/content_1463573.htm, accessed on July 31, 2013.

pays 80% of eligible costs.[11] In Xi'an, the deductible is set between 200–950 RMB, depending on the hospital's grade. Beyond the ceiling specified in the BHI, there is a complementary social insurance plan with a co-insurance rate of about 10%–20% (that is, the plan's coverage is 80%–90%). The complementary plan specifies a second ceiling set at 400,000 RMB; above that ceiling, patients have to pay 100%.[12]

As previously noted, there has also been a great deal of variation across cities with respect to the way Social Insurance Bureaus have used their ability to negotiate with providers regarding payment methods. In most cities, hospitals that treat insured workers are still paid via the traditional fee-for-service method, but methods such as capitation and global budgets have been used to pay hospitals in Zhenjiang city since 2001. Guidelines issued in early 2012 specify that there will be payment method reform in 300 county-level hospitals nationwide starting later in 2012, in which the traditional fee-for-service payment system will be replaced by various alternative payment methods to control hospital costs.[13]

In some cities, local governments have contracted with private insurance companies to either offer complementary coverage for workers insured under BHI, or participate in the administration of the local BHI plan. For example, the local government in Zhanjiang, Guangdong province, uses 15% of the social insurance funds to purchase reinsurance from private insurance companies under which the extent of coverage under the BHI plan is augmented by decreasing the co-insurance rate and increasing the benefit ceiling. In Fanyu city, Guangdong province, private insurance companies have been contracted to manage various social insurance funds under arrangements that give them incentives to use health insurance funds more

---

[11] http://www.shyb.gov.cn/ybzc/zcfg/01/201103/t20110325_1128736.shtml & http://www.shanghai.gov.cn/shanghai/node2314/node2316/node2331/node2504/userobject6ai269.html, accessed on July 31, 2013.

[12] http://www.chira.org.cn/xinwenzhongxin/chengzhenjiminjibenyiliaobaoxian/new335752.html, accessed on July 31, 2013.

[13] Xinhua News Agency, March 11, 2012 (http://news.xinhuanet.com/yzyd/legal/20120311/c_122818239.htm), accessed on July 31, 2013.

efficiently.[14] The role that private insurance will play alongside the BHI plan may well expand in the future. In September 2012, the central government officially encouraged local governments that had surpluses in their social health insurance funds to work with private insurers to offer supplementary private insurance to extend the basic coverage. We will come back to the important question of what the future role of private insurance is going to be later in the discussion.

3. Risk Pooling in Rural Areas: The New Cooperative Medical Scheme

Some four years after the decree establishing the BHI, a major joint announcement of the State Council and the Central Party Committee set the direction for future reform of health care financing in rural areas.[15] As in the case of the BHI, the centerpiece of the new strategy was a mechanism to encourage a higher degree of risk pooling in the financing of health care, following the reduction in the extent of direct collective funding of the production of health services. This was to be accomplished through a revival of the earlier Cooperative Medical Schemes which had paid for part of rural residents' health care costs before the 1980s, but which had collapsed with the dissolution of the agricultural communes at that time.

Although the New Cooperative Medical Scheme model (henceforth NCMS) is usually interpreted as another element of the social insurance approach to health financing, one of its important characteristics is that, in line with the goal of limiting the tax burden on rural residents, membership in the scheme is not compulsory. In principle, each resident is allowed to choose to not join in the local NCMS plan, in which case he or she does not have to pay the individual premium that is required for coverage.[16] However, in order to encourage enrollment,

---

[14]http://health.people.com.cn/GB/17408848.html, accessed on July 31, 2013.

[15]The announcement was made following an international conference on the topic of rural health care: the China National Rural Health Conference, held in October 2002 (see Liu and Rao, 2006).

[16]Interestingly, Wikipedia defines social insurance so as to include programs in which participation is voluntary or subsidized to a sufficiently high degree so that almost

the individual premium was initially set at a very low level (10 RMB per person per year), with subsidies from both the central and local levels of government for each enrollee contributing a large share, initially two-thirds, of the plans' revenue. While local governments were allowed to specify higher individual premiums and pay larger subsidies to the plan, most initially chose the minimum amounts specified by the central government.

With annual revenues of only 30 RMB per enrollee, the benefits that plans could offer in the early stages could not be very generous. They were limited not only by rules specifying deductibles, co-insurance requirements, and upper annual limits on plan payments, but also by restrictions on what types of services and drugs were eligible for coverage, and in some cases also by lists that limited coverage only to patients who suffered from particular kinds of serious illness.[17] Not surprisingly, the number of people who enrolled in NCMS plans was relatively small in the first few years. However, the size of the local and central government subsidies increased rapidly, and benefit packages became more generous. As can be seen from Figure 2, by 2013, the minimum subsidies had grown from 20 RMB to 280 RMB per enrollee (shared equally between the two levels of government), and while the minimum individual premium required for coverage had also grown (to 60 RMB per year), the increased subsidies had made possible substantially enhanced benefit packages, and enrollment has grown rapidly. By 2012, the number of rural residents enrolled in the plan already numbered some 812 million, accounting for some 95% of China's rural population.[18]

---

everyone participates. In the U.S., the Medicare plan that covers all U.S. citizens over age 65 is technically voluntary, but participation is almost universal since the premium cost is heavily subsidized.

[17] For a detailed discussion see Ma, Zhang, and Chen (2012).

[18] See http://finance.chinanews.com/jk/2012/09-17/4188276.shtml (accessed on August 6, 2013). Part of the reason for the rapid increase in enrollment may have been that local governments had a strong incentive to encourage people to join, as we further discuss in Chapter 8. There have even been reports that governments in some places actually have paid the individual premiums on behalf of residents in order to encourage larger enrollment.

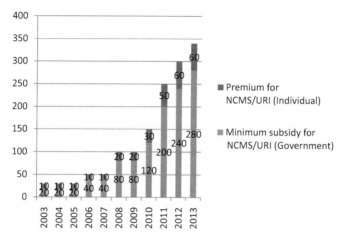

Fig. 2. (Minimum) Government subsidy per enrollee under NCMS/URI from 2003 to 2013* (RMB).

*The data for Urban Residence Insurance (URI) is from year 2007.

Source: Ministry of Health, Ministry of Labor and Social Security, various years.

As in the case of the BHI, local governments are given considerable leeway with respect to how they design and manage the local NCMS schemes. As already noted, a local government can choose to pay more than the minimum subsidy; if it does, the state subsidy is increased so as to match the local one. As a result, there is considerable variability in total plan revenues per enrollee. For example, most NCMS plans in Hubei and Shandong provinces in 2012 collected total revenue per enrollee of no more than 300 RMB per year, corresponding to the minimum specified by the state guidelines, while in rural areas around Shanghai, total annual plan revenue per enrollee was 980 RMB, around two-thirds of which consisted of government subsidies.

There has also been considerable variability in the composition of the benefit package. In some cases, what is covered under the NCMS plans is limited to the same services and drugs as those covered in the BHI plans (this has been the case, for example, in Guangdong province[19]), and some of them also divide their funds

---

[19]See the website http://www.gdwst.gov.cn/a/200718wj/200903186546.html, accessed on July 31, 2013.

into the equivalent of individual accounts and a county-wide social pooling account. Coverage typically includes not only part of the cost of in-patient hospital care but also out-patient services at the village level and above. However, because the resources of the plans are limited, the degree of coverage is typically reduced by deductibles and substantial co-insurance rates (sometimes well in excess of 50%), as well as by relatively low ceilings that limit what the plan will pay out per year or illness episode. On balance, therefore, most of them offer considerably less complete insurance protection than the BHI plans.

3.1. *Integration of financing and health services production in rural areas*

Although there are some similarities between the NCMS plans and the BHI plans in various cities, there are important differences in the way they are managed. In particular, management of urban BHI plans is by Social Insurance Bureaus (SIBs) which are under the jurisdiction of the Ministry of Labor and Social Security at the state level. The NCMS plans in rural areas, in contrast, are managed by the local Health Bureaus which come under the jurisdiction of the local and state Ministries of Health. This difference is potentially important because it influences the relationship between the social insurance plans and the hospitals and clinics that provide health services: the latter are mostly state-owned and report to the Ministry of Health.

In urban areas, it is therefore possible, in principle, to create an arm's-length relationship between the SIB and the providers, since they do not fall under the same ministry. As purchasers of health services on behalf of the insured workers, the SIBs can more easily use their market power to put pressure on providers to produce services on favorable terms and in a cost-effective way. In rural areas, where the NCMS plans and service providers are regulated and supervised by the same Health Bureau officials, such an arm's-length relationship is more difficult to create, and there is a greater risk that the NCMS plans will be seen primarily as vehicles that can be used to increase the resources of local governments and incomes of providers, with less attention to the interests of the insured population. We will return to this issue in Chapter 8.

The different approaches to managing the urban and rural social insurance plans also reflect differences in the conditions under which health services are supplied in rural and urban areas. In densely populated cities, it is possible to supply most health services in relatively large clinics and hospitals, and patients can have some degree of effective choice among several competing hospitals and clinics within a reasonable distance. In rural areas, in contrast, the question of functional differentiation among clinics and hospitals is more important than in an urban setting. Specifically, while economies of scale might cause one to favor concentration of most health care resources in a relatively small number of large hospitals in urban areas, such a pattern is less likely to be efficient in the countryside since it will entail long and costly trips (or delays in treatment) for patients who need hospitalization.

The pattern of hospital services production during the pre-1980 period reflected this, in the sense that a large number of small township hospitals with relatively basic facilities co-existed with a small number of large county hospitals with more advanced equipment. The extent of utilization of these different hospital types was governed by a clearly defined system of referrals under which treatment in a township hospital was only allowed on referral from the village doctor, while treatment in a county hospital required a referral from the township. This system appears to have functioned quite well in the sense that patients were treated in the least costly facility appropriate to the seriousness of their condition.

However, following the shift to less collective financing, there was also a major change in the way the rural health services production system functioned. In particular, the role of smaller township hospitals declined substantially, and while they typically continued to operate, statistics suggest that they have not been heavily utilized until recently. In part, this has been the result of a vicious circle under which the increasing profitability of supplying high-level services with advanced equipment caused many of the good doctors who previously worked in township hospitals to seek employment in better-equipped central county hospitals. As patients have observed this, they have become distrustful of the quality of care offered in smaller township hospitals and clinics, and have frequently chosen to go directly to the central county hospitals. This has made it even less profitable for good doctors to stay in the township hospitals, accelerating the process. Many rural health care providers also switched to private practice, and a large portion of rural health care at the village level in the 1990s and 2000s was provided by private practitioners (doctors or other health professionals) who were paid on the basis of fee-for-service and augmented their income with the markups they earned from selling pharmaceuticals.

3.2. *Varieties of NCMS models*

With the revival of the rural community medical schemes, many of the local county health bureaucrats that are responsible for the NCMS plans have begun to experiment with new forms of organizing the production of health services in their counties, and with alternative methods for paying the providers.[20] There are as yet few signs that China's rural health care system will converge on a single model of financing and organization, but valuable lessons are being learned both from the experiences with different approaches taken by local governments in various parts of China as they respond to the central government's encouragement and financial incentives, and through a number of pilot projects, completed or ongoing, that are being conducted with support from international agencies such as the World Bank, the WHO, the U.K. Department for International Development, and others. (Appendix Tables A1 and A2 give examples of the kinds of features that have been tried in various models.)

To improve the system's cost-effectiveness, some of the pilot projects include various features intended to improve the way treatment decisions are made. Several of them have organized bulk purchasing of drugs and include attempts to get primary-care providers to follow standardized treatment protocols and prescription patterns. They may

---

[20]See Cheng (2013) for some recent rural pilot projects on payment reform.

also devote resources to personnel training, especially at the village and township levels.

   Another feature of some of the pilot projects is that they are trying to reinstate the system requiring a referral from a village- or township-level provider before an individual will receive care at the township or county level (or higher). In at least one case, the pilot project has featured payment of village-based primary-care providers on the basis of salary and a bonus (rather than fee-for-service), under an arrangement with the NCMS plan, and the plan also negotiates terms for care delivered to its members in township and county hospitals. That is, the plan in this project functions somewhat like an HMO or a managed care plan which not only helps pay for its members' health care but also gets involved in negotiating with providers at different levels regarding the terms on which the care is delivered.[21]

   While responsibility for managing the local NCMS plans rests with county governments, the early pilot projects were often undertaken and managed at the township level. (Traditionally, many of the earlier CMS plans were also organized and managed at the township level.) Because of the importance of local knowledge and a close working relationship between plan managers and village-based providers, decentralized management with substantial financial and organizational responsibility at the township level may seem a promising approach to creating a system that can contain costs in a way that is efficient and focus on the health problems that are most significant in the respective localities.[22] Township-level management may also improve the likelihood that a multi-level referral system will work well. In a project being organized in collaboration with a team from Harvard University, substantial management responsibilities have even been given to elected committees at the village level, who supervise the primary care and public-health

---

[21] For further description, see Hsiao (2004).

[22] Models where publicly funded systems of health insurance and service delivery have delegated substantial administrative responsibilities to low-level administrative units include the experiments with fundholding GPs (and its successor, "practice-based commissioning") in the U.K., and with primary-care centered management in certain counties in Sweden in the 1990s (Blomqvist, 2001, 2002).

services delivered in the village, and appoint representatives to the board that manages the plan at the township level.[23] The board's responsibilities, in turn, include contracting for services from health centers and higher-level hospitals.[24] In the long run, therefore, it is possible that there will be considerable decentralization of responsibility for managing important components of the rural health care system, especially primary care, to the township and village levels, even if county governments will continue to be responsible for setting the main parameters for the basic risk-pooling function of their local NCMS plans.

3.3. *Implementing rural health reform: A role for the private sector?*

As evidence accumulates from pilot projects and from other countries regarding what is a good model for rural health care reform, the question arises how a blueprint for reform in China would be implemented. We expect that such a blueprint would involve use of tools such as treatment protocols, drug formularies, and a referral system. It will also make use of methods such as bulk purchasing of drugs, and payment mechanisms and pricing of health services that are different from conventional fee-for-service. An important issue will be whether the system that ultimately emerges will be entirely managed by government employees, or whether there will be a role for the private sector.

The organization and management of a rural health care system with these kinds of features will be a complex task, and will require development of a large body of skilled managers, especially if the system is to be managed in a decentralized fashion, for example, at the

---

[23] Again, see Hsiao (2004).

[24] For an eloquent and convincing discussion of the effectiveness of local management in the context of using common property resources in rural areas, see Ostrom (1990). Although the underlying economic problems are somewhat different, a cooperative rural insurance system also involves certain issues that require collective action and some degree of monitoring (such as support for community members who are at high risk of illness, and monitoring of both local service providers and plan members' use of the system).

township level. Although it may be possible for township and county governments to acquire the relevant expertise by training existing staff or by hiring new staff with the required skills, it is also possible that some or all of the management functions could be provided by the private sector under contracts with local boards or governments. Privately contracted managers could then be assisted by specialized firms providing services such as updating of treatment protocols and drug formularies, as well as supplying drugs under bulk purchasing arrangements. They could also develop model contracts between NCMS plan managers and service providers, both those supplying primary care at the village level and for hospital care at the tertiary level.

Experimentation with a model of private management has been conducted in five counties in Fujian province. In these experiments, it has been observed that enrollees may see private management as an advantage to the extent that they want to reduce the influence of outside officials in the system, a point that is also relevant to models under which plans are managed by locally elected committees.[25]

4. Filling the Gaps: The Urban Resident Basic Medical Insurance

While the urban BHI plans constituted an important step in the development of a Chinese social health insurance system, the fact that it was offered only to persons employed in the formal urban sector limited its scope. As the NCMS plans grew to cover a majority of the rural population, large numbers of urban residents remained without coverage. By 2007, the population covered by BHI only accounted for some 30% of the urban population.

However, local governments in some cities had already begun to offer voluntary plans to those not eligible for the BHI plan (for example, students, the self-employed or those not in the labor force, and many retirees). For example, in the city of Xiamen, persons who were self-employed or temporarily unemployed were allowed to join the

---

[25]The Fujian experiments are discussed in Lin (2007), while Hsiao (2004) comments on the advantage of management by elected local committees.

BHI on a voluntary basis by paying a premium linked to the average annual wage in the city. In addition, the city government subsidized an even more basic voluntary plan (with higher co-insurance rates than the BHI plan) for particular categories of individuals (the elderly, the disabled, people who receive low-income support). Similar plans existed in other cities as well, in Jiangsu province and elsewhere.[26] In Jilin province, there was a "residents' plan", described as having a benefit level somewhere between that of the BHI and rural NCMS plans (in terms of co-insurance rates, deductibles, and benefit ceilings). For example, the ceilings for different versions of the plan ranged from 35,000 to 45,000 Yuan, with annual premiums of 120–200 Yuan. In press interviews, officials estimated that even when benefits did not hit the ceiling, they typically covered no more than 60% or less of individuals' actual expenditures because many drugs and services they had to pay for were not on the plan's approved lists.

In 2007, the central government added its formal support to these local efforts by offering to extend the principle of matching grants already in use to support the rural NCMS system, to local plans for urban residents not eligible for coverage through a BHI plan. The minimum subsidy offered under these plans was 120 RMB annually from the central and local governments, with a premium payable by the insured set at a minimum level corresponding to around 2% of the average disposable income in each city. Plans of this type, often referred to in English as Urban Resident Basic Medical Insurance (URBMI), are now being offered in all large cities, and enrollment has been rising rapidly in recent years.

Like the NCMS plans, the URBMI plans remain voluntary, with coverage being conditional on payment of an individual premium, though enrollees often join the plans in groups (for example, students in a particular institution). The plans are managed by the same Social Insurance Bureaus that are responsible for the local BHI plans.

As with the other social insurance plans, there are large differences, in terms of cost and coverage, among URBMI plans in different cities.

---

[26]See http://news.xinhuanet.com/misc/2007-03/05/content_5802384.htm (accessed on June 13, 2013), and Ren *et al.* (2007).

For example, in Shanghai, the premium for a person 70 years old or above is 1,500 RMB per enrollee and there is a government subsidy of 1,260 RMB per enrollee.[27] The reimbursement rate varies from 50% to 80% depending on the grade of the hospital where the patient is treated. In Lanzhou city, Gansu province, by way of contrast, the premium is 160 RMB per enrollee and the government subsidy is 80 RMB per enrollee.[28] The reimbursement rate ranges from 50% to 65%, and the ceiling for reimbursement is 18,000 RMB.

4.1. Risk pooling in China's health care system: Toward universal coverage

By the end of the first decade of the 21st century, China could point to great progress in terms of the degree of risk pooling in its health care system. In terms of the questions raised in the introduction, it had accomplished this by opting for a social insurance approach, rather than implicit risk pooling through direct financing of health care out of tax revenue, and by initiating three different government-sponsored plans rather than a single one for all residents. Enrollment in the BHI had climbed rapidly, from less than 50 million workers in 2000 to some 250 million by 2011 (Figure 3). Data on coverage of the rural population through the NCMS plans were even more impressive, with the number of insured quadrupling from less than 200 million in 2005 to more than 800 million in 2011, and URBMI membership statistics showed around 200 million enrollees by 2011. In total, the three schemes covered more than 95% of China's population, so the goal of universal coverage by 2015 announced by the central government in 2012 seemed within easy reach.

While these data are impressive in terms of the percentage of the population covered, however, it must again be recognized that the degree to which the plans help pay for the health care costs of the insured is relatively low on average, and varies a great deal across plans.

---

[27] http://www.zgylbx.com/pNMalvXRKUaInew17408_1/ (accessed on July 31, 2013).
[28] http://www.lanzhou.gov.cn:8080/root84/srmzfbgt/201105/t20110520_40845.html (accessed on July 31, 2013).

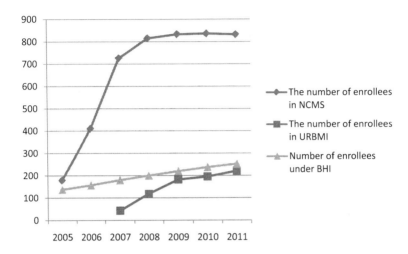

Fig. 3. Number of enrollees under the three social insurance plans (million).

Sources: China Health Statistical Yearbook, various years, from the website of the Ministry of Health; and *China Labor and Social Security Yearbook,* various years.

In particular, the degree of coverage is generally lower in the NCMS plans than in the urban ones, and in the URBMI relative to the BHI, but as already discussed there is also a great deal of variation across cities and provinces within each plan.

The differences arise partly because of variation in the size of the deductibles, cost-sharing percentages, and limitations on the maximum benefits that can be paid to a patient in a given year. Equally important are differences in the rules regarding what services and drugs are covered, and the extent to which hospitals and clinics charge patients for services and drugs that are not on the eligible lists. In part, the degree of risk pooling is smaller than one might expect from the given amounts of plan revenue because part of the contributions that are made by or on behalf of enrolled members go into individual accounts that are not part of the pool, following the principle that applies in the Singapore model.[29]

---

[29]Although we have not seen any explicit suggestion that the decision to incorporate the medical savings account concept in China's health insurance plans was motivated by the Singapore example, it most likely was. It is clear that China's leadership has

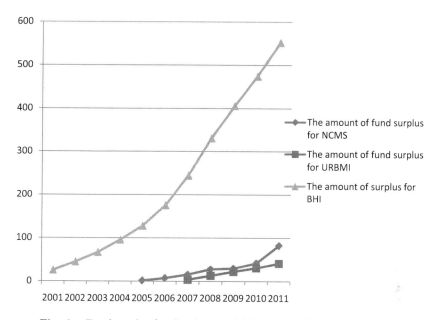

Fig. 4. Fund surplus for the three social insurance plans (RMB billion).

Sources: Ministry of Health, *China Health Statistical Yearbook*, various years; *China Labor and Social Security Yearbook*, various years; *Insurance and China's Health Reform*, Economic Science Press, Beijing.

One consequence of the restrictive limits and rules for reimbursement has been that, on average, the revenues of the social insurance plans — in the form of individual premiums, contributions from employers and employees, and (in the cases of the NCMS and URBMI plans) government subsidies — have been considerably greater than the amounts paid out as reimbursements. As Figure 4 shows, the result has been accumulated surpluses in all three plans that have been growing steadily since they were started. In the BHI it increased by more than four times between 2004 and 2010, from 100 billion to over 470 billion RMB; this surplus was equivalent to over 140% of the total amount of reimbursements in 2010. For the NCMS and URBMI plans, the

---

paid close attention to the Singapore model in general over the years; see, e.g., Vogel (2011). Dong (2008) provides a detailed and critical discussion of the early experience of Shanghai with medical savings accounts.

growth rates for the surplus were even faster. For the NCMS there was an increase from less than 10 billion RMB in 2006 to over 70 billion RMB in 2011, roughly 44% of the total amount of reimbursement in that year, while for URBMI the accumulated surplus grew from less than 5 billion RMB in 2007 to over 30 billion RMB in 2010, 115% of the total amount of reimbursement in 2010. Social insurance plans in other countries also build up and maintain reserves over time, but they typically average around 10% of annual reimbursements, compared to well over 100% in the Chinese plans, which was equivalent to more than 27% of the aggregate total of all health expenditure in 2010.

In spite of the limitations of the plans' coverage, however, the data nevertheless do show that the expansion in the number of people enrolled has had a significant effect in helping shift the overall burden of health care costs from individual patients to third parties (governments and insurance plans). As Figure 5 shows, the share of total costs that patients have paid out-of-pocket has fallen from a high of 60% in 2001 to around 35% in 2011. Over the same period, the share paid for by the social insurance system rose from around 5% to 25%. The remainder, 35% in 2001 and 40% in 2011, includes government payments for public health services and direct subsidies to providers which increased from 11% to 17% over this period, as well as the cost of health services supplied directly to employees in clinics and hospitals owned and managed by their employers. It also includes costs reimbursed by private insurance plans, though this component has remained relatively small: in 2011, it accounted for only about 3% of total health expenditures, although the share had been somewhat larger in previous years.

5. The 2009 State Council Guidelines: New Directions for Health Reform?

Expansion of the social insurance system can be said to have been the main thrust of health policy reform in China during the first decade of the 21st century. While the need for improved risk-pooling and protection of patients against the high cost of health

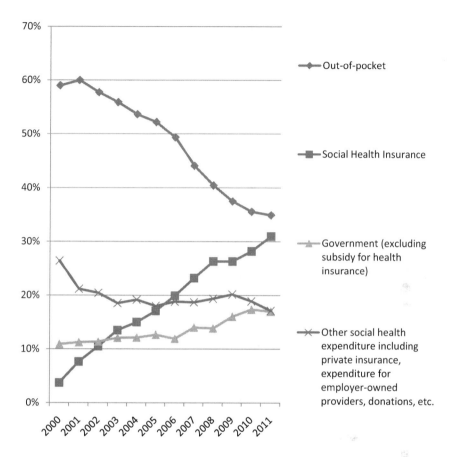

Fig. 5. Composition of health expenditure in China.

Source: Ministry of Health, *China Health Statistical Yearbook*, various years.

care was widely recognized, however, not everyone was in agreement with the government's focus on strengthening the social insurance financing mechanism as the main method of alleviating these problems.

Among those critical of the focus on the social insurance approach were Ministry of Health officials who continued to favor a stronger role for government in direct financing and management of hospitals and clinics, as under the pre-reform model. In part, this may simply have been because MOH officials wanted to reverse the lessening of their power and influence over the health care system: With the focus on social insurance, other ministries such as Finance, and particularly the Ministry of Labor and Social Security which oversees the urban social insurance plans, were playing a more central role in the development of health policy.

But critics of the focus on social health insurance also included many conservatives within the party who believed that China had moved too rapidly in reducing the role of central planning throughout the economy. To the conservatives, high costs and deteriorating access to health care were clear examples of problems that would arise if the strategy of relying on markets and competition was used in sensitive sectors where the previous system of centralized management had worked reasonably well, and where there were well-known reasons why markets might not work.

In a report circulated in 2005, a group of experts working at the Development Research Center of the State Council expressed strong doubts regarding the effectiveness of current reform approaches, and its concluding chapter includes a recommendation that the state (central government) should fund and operate a network of township health centers and urban community hospital clinics that will provide basic medical care at low charges for a range of "common and frequently occurring diseases".[30] These proposals were taken seriously by the leadership: In Premier Wen Jiabao's speech to the Fifth Session of the

---

[30] Although an early English-language version of the report circulated as a supplement to Volume 7, No. 1, March 2005, of the DRC's *China Development Review*, this version no longer appears on its website, although a later version is listed there as a supplement to Volume 9. A Chinese-language version of the report can be found in Ge *et al.* (2007), and on the DRC's website. Another interesting critique of the current model for urban health insurance reform in China is in Dong (2006), in which the author argues that the attempt to emulate the successful Singaporean approach to cost containment in health care did not work well because of the different socio-economic characteristics of the two countries. It may be worth noting as well that one reason the government-sponsored plans can take a relatively limited role in paying for health care in Singapore is that employer benefits and private insurance pay for a substantial portion of the health care costs in that country, as much as 40% in the early 2000s (Dong, 2006, p. 211). These funding sources only play a minor role in the Chinese system today.

Tenth National People's Congress of March 5, 2007, he referred to large allocations from the central government budget for the purpose of ultimately setting up a government health clinic in every town and township, as well as funding to support the establishment of new urban community facilities to deliver primary care in cities in China's western and central regions.[31]

The relative merits of the social insurance approach and one that would restore a greater role for direct government funding and management of health services continued to be debated over the next few years. In an approach that was somewhat unusual in the debate over China's social and economic policy, the central government commissioned several university-based think tanks, international organizations, and even an international consulting firm, to prepare reports with recommendations for what approaches should be taken in future health policy. Among these reports, some supported a strategy of continued reliance on the social insurance approach, while others favored the direct funding approach with a stronger central management role.

The eagerly awaited guidelines for the future of health reform in China that were released by the State Council in April 2009 did not settle the contest between these two approaches. Instead, it outlined a strategy that combines elements of both, and that tries to keep alternative options open.[32]

In the guidelines, five tasks are outlined for the first phase of health reform between 2009 and 2012. First, a target is set for social health insurance to achieve universal coverage by 2012. Second, a system will be established to define a set of essential medicines that are supposed to be the most cost-effective ones for different conditions, and that will be sold without price markup in publicly owned primary-care clinics. Third, a network of primary-care clinics paid for and managed by the government will be created. This will be accomplished by upgrading the infrastructure of 2,000 county hospitals, over 30,000 township health

---

[31]See http://www.js.xinhuanet.com/xin_wen_zhong_xin/2007-04/11/content_9751797.htm (accessed on June 14, 2013).

[32]For an early review of the guidelines, see Yip and Hsiao (2009).

centers and over 14,000 urban community health centers throughout China; training general practitioners for these primary-care clinics will be put on top of the agenda.

Fourth, government will increase spending on public health services, in particular for lower income regions. Fifth, there will be changes in the methods used in funding and governance of public hospitals. Revenue from the sale of drugs will be decoupled from public hospitals' revenue, and government will increase the amount of subsidies allocated to public hospitals.

In an implicit recognition of the continuing debate between the two fundamental approaches, the guidelines state that one principle that will apply to the implementation of these five major tasks during the first phase is that government will play the leading role in the reform process, while market mechanisms will be complementary. But consistent with China's gradual and pragmatic approach to many aspects of social and economic policy, the guidelines also note that local pilot programs will be conducted to explore methods of implementing these objectives, and that the results of these programs will be pivotal in setting directions for future health reform.

Further indications of the central government's plans for future health reform were given in March 2012, as part of the State Council's blueprint with targets under the 12th 5-year plan, and in a subsequent document with more details on social security reform specifically.[33] In these guidelines, measures to further strengthen the social insurance programs are described, including a reaffirmation of the target of universal coverage, increased minimum subsidies under the NCMS and URBMI plans of 360 RMB per enrollee, and a minimum reimbursement rate of 75%. There is reference to the goal of attaining portability of the social insurance plans across regions (that is, ensuring that individuals can be covered by membership in a plan in their home region even when they have health care costs in another region

---

[33]http://www.gov.cn/zwgk/2012-03/21/content_2096671.htm (accessed on July 19, 2012); http://www.gov.cn/zwgk/2012-06/27/content_2171218.htm (accessed on July 19, 2012).

where they may have travelled for work). The guidelines also make explicit mention of plans to further develop the role of the social insurance plans as purchasers of care, with more use of new payment methods such as capitation, pay-for-performance, global budgets and Diagnosis-Related Groups that may help contain expenditure and induce more cost-effective methods of care and patterns of drug prescription.

At the same time, the guidelines also outline plans for a continuation of the initiatives under which government will be more directly involved in funding and management of health services. The number of pharmaceuticals included on the list of essential medicines will increase, and the local governments' responsibility for financing the operation of the expanding network of primary-care clinics is noted; there are also plans for training 150,000 new general practitioners specifically for these clinics. Thus, there still is no clear indication as to whether China's future health care financing system will evolve into one that is dominated by the social insurance approach, with more autonomy for health services providers and more competition among private and public providers, or whether government will retain or even expand its role in directly financing and managing the institutions that produce health care services and supply patients with drugs. We will return to this question in later chapters.

5.1. *The way forward*

Even if China continues to be successful in maintaining a high rate of economic growth so that she will gradually catch up with today's rich countries in terms of the per capita income of her citizens, there is little doubt that the resources spent on health care will continue to grow even faster than the economy as a whole, resulting in further increases in the ratio of health care costs to GDP. This would almost certainly be true if medical technology in the future were to be similar to what it is today. The U.S. today already spends nearly 18% of GDP on health care, about three times the corresponding figure in China today. Moreover, medical technology will continue to progress, and if past patterns continue to hold, this will result in even more pressure to raise spending on health care. For these reasons alone, policy toward the health care sector is likely to be at least as important a part of the debate over economic and social policy in future years as it is today.

In addition, the central role of health policy will be reinforced by the increasing preoccupation with effective means of alleviating the high degree of economic inequality that has been produced by China's rapid economic growth during the last three decades. In historical perspective, the objective of ensuring greater equality of access to health care has been an important component of social and economic policy in all of today's rich countries, and almost all of them now have systems that accomplish this objective through universal, or near-universal, insurance protection that covers most of citizens' health care costs. While China has made great progress toward wider insurance coverage, as discussed in this chapter, the health financing system remains a work in progress. Major questions remain unanswered, in particular, to what extent the different health insurance models that now cover different segments of China's population will be integrated into one that offers similar coverage to all residents. Moreover, it is still not clear whether the government's future role in health care will focus on health financing (through further development of social insurance), with increasing decentralization and privatization of health services production; as discussed above, there are many who support the model under which the government maintains or further expands its role as both owner and manager of the hospitals and clinics where health care is produced. The change in China's top leadership in 2012 has added to the uncertainty, since it is still too early to predict whether the new leaders will continue moving toward further liberalization and decentralization in general, or conversely, try to slow the process down and maintain or strengthen the state's control in various ways.

Appendix. Alternative Models of Local NCMS Pilot Projects

Table A1. Management and features of four rural health insurance projects.

	RMHC*	Health VIII**	CASS in Shanxi province***	New rural CMS in Yunnan province****
Who manages the funds?	Fund Board elected from village level	County government?	Cooperatives at township-village level	Township government
Who monitors the fund management?	Indirectly monitored by enrollees	County government?	Cooperatives at township-village level	County/Township government
Is the plan voluntary?	Voluntary	Voluntary	Voluntary	Voluntary, but with "mobilization" from local governments
Level of risk pooling	Township	County?	Township	County
Out-patient co-payment rates	60% (village), 65% (township and above)	30% at village level, 35% at township level, and 40% at county level	N/A	Not much difference between township/village-level providers, 60%–70% in practice
In-patient co-payment rate	70% (township), 70% (county and above)	30% at village level, 35% at township level, and 40% at county level	N/A	76% on average

(Continued)

Table A1. (*Continued*)

	RMHC*	Health VIII**	CASS in Shanxi province***	New rural CMS in Yunnan province****
Deductible	No Deductible	N/A	N/A	Various deductibles from 0 to 300 RMB, or deducted from individual medical account
Ceiling on coverage	300 RMB (out-patient), 350 RMB (in-patient for township provider), 1,850 RMB (in-patient for county and above providers)	N/A	N/A	1,500–2,500 RMB

Table A2.   Supply-side interventions in three rural health insurance projects.

	RMHC*	Health VIII**	CMS in Yunnan province****
Drugs	Bulk purchasing of drugs/Information sharing on drug management	Standardized procedures of treatment/ Essential drug list	Bulk purchasing of drugs/ Information sharing on drug procurement/ Regulation of quantity of drugs per visit
Doctors	Use competition to selectively contract with village doctors; Pay village doctor by salary plus bonus	Training of doctors; Standardized procedures for diagnosis and treatment	N/A
Referral system	From low- to high-level provider	In both directions: from low- to high-level provider and from high- to low-level provider	From low- to higher-level provider
Hospital	Fund Board of the plan contracts out services to health centers and hospitals	Facility improvement/ Information system	N/A

Sources:
*Rural Mutual Health Care, by Harvard research team; Hsiao (2004), Yip *et al.* (2008).
** World Bank Health VIII project; Wagstaff (2007), China Development Brief (2003).
*** Chinese Academy of Social Sciences, Department for International Development, UK and Amity Foundation, HK in Shanxi province; Cai (2007).
**** CMS project survey in Yunnan province, China; Chapters 6 and 7 in Gu *et al.* (2006).

Chapter 4

PROVIDING PRIMARY CARE

1. Introduction

Following the discussion of the financing side of China's health reforms in Chapter 3, in this and the next two chapters we turn to the reform initiatives that related to the production of health services. In this chapter, we consider the role and organization of primary care. As we have seen, the plans for creating a government-managed network of clinics for the provision of "basic medical care" was a central, though controversial, component of the reform plans announced in 2009. The hospital and pharmaceutical sectors are discussed in the following chapters; again, the 2009 announcement outlined plans for new initiatives in those areas as well.

The chapter is organized as follows. In the next section, we briefly discuss the relationship between primary care and the rest of the health care system, including the important role it has with respect to the resources devoted to services that are classified under the rubric of "public health". We then consider the way China's primary-care system changed between the 1980s and the early 2000s, and how the changes that took place then were the most important reason for the deteriorating performance of the system as a whole during that period. As a prelude to the discussion of the plans to once again strengthen the role of primary care in China, we then describe and analyze the way primary care is organized in some other countries, with particular emphasis on the U.K. model. We then review the progress that is being made in establishing the planned network of basic care clinics, and some of the models that are being tried for bringing about closer integration between these clinics and the rest of the system. In the final section, we consider alternative ways in which primary care in China may be organized in future years, and to what extent there may be a role for competition between government clinics and privately practicing providers in it. We also comment briefly on the importance of making the regulatory decisions, and decisions about provider training, that will influence the mix of personnel that will supply primary care in the future, at what cost and quality.

2. Definition of Primary Care

In discussing the structure and performance of the health care sector, it is customary to make a distinction between the provision of primary, secondary, and tertiary care. Although the exact classifications may vary, secondary and tertiary care is normally defined as that which is supplied by doctors who are experts in treating particular diseases only ("specialists"), as well as care provided in hospitals, especially to in-patients who have been admitted to the hospital and will spend one or more nights there. Primary care, in contrast, is typically provided on an out-patient basis (that is, patients return home after being seen), and often by doctors who are not classified as specialists but instead are "general practitioners".[1] In most systems, a patient's first contact with the health care system when they have a health problem is with a primary-care provider. While primary care provided to out-patients typically accounts for a smaller share of total health care costs than treatment of in-patients in hospitals in most health care systems, it nevertheless accounts for, by far, the largest share of the total number of treatment episodes. This just reflects the fact that most of the health problems that occur during a year to people in a given population are

---

[1] In some countries, including China and Japan, a substantial proportion of patients go directly to a hospital when they are ill. In such cases, many hospital patients are treated as out-patients and are sent home after being seen, implying that the hospitals' out-patient departments really should be classified as a part of the primary-care system.

In some countries, the distinction between specialists and general practitioners has become somewhat obsolete, with most doctors who supply primary care being classified as specialists in the field of "family medicine".

relatively minor ones that either are self-limiting or can be resolved after treatment by a general practitioner or even a nurse or pharmacist, often after the prescription of a drug.

Even though primary care usually accounts for a smaller share of aggregate health care costs than the hospital sector, or even a smaller share than pharmaceuticals, the performance of the primary-care system is, indirectly, of critical importance in influencing the functioning of the health care system as a whole, both with respect to its success in dealing with the population's health problems and with respect to aggregate costs. In part, this reflects the fact that, as consumers of health care, patients typically do not have the information they need in order to make choices with respect to what health services or drugs they need, but instead have to rely on someone with medical expertise to make these choices on their behalf.

The quality of the decisions that are made when the patient first contacts a primary-care provider, including decisions with respect to the diagnosis of the patient's problem, is often critical in ensuring that the patient will be treated appropriately, and in determining how costly it will be to deal with the problem. In particular, primary-care providers in a well-functioning system should have both the expertise and the equipment to make the right decision with respect to what drugs the patient should be using, and whether they should treat the patient themselves or send him or her on for further diagnostic tests or treatment in a specialist clinic or hospital. Bad decisions at this stage can result either in adverse outcomes that could have been avoided — if the wrong drug is prescribed, or if patients needing advanced treatment are not sent on to more advanced providers — or in high costs to the system, if many patients who could have been treated at low cost in a primary-care facility are sent on to hospitals and specialists, or if expensive drugs are chosen when cheaper ones are available.[2]

---

[2]There is an extensive literature on the special role of primary care in countries' health care systems. For example, Glied and Smith (2011) has three chapters that deal with various aspects of primary care.

2.1. *Link between primary care and public health*

Another reason why the primary-care sector can be of critical
importance in a health care system is related to its role with respect to
those determinants of a population's health that are often collectively
referred to as "public health". Although the public health concept is
not always clearly defined, in the terminology of economic analysis
it can be described as relating to health problems and environmental
factors that affect not just the health of a single individual, but have
spillover effects on other members of the community as well. The most
important examples of health problems in this category are infectious
diseases and certain environmental factors such as sanitation.[3]

In high-income countries, most health problems do not involve
public health issues. The incidence of most types of contagious disease is
limited, in part as a result of near-universal immunization of the children
against many forms of contagious disease, and specialized public-
health departments in cities and rural communities are responsible
for enforcing effective rules regarding environmental factors such as
sanitation and food handling. In such countries, the number of deaths
that occur as a result of communicable disease is relatively limited,
and most of the health problems for which individuals seek care are
the result of non-communicable disease that only affects the individual
himself or herself.[4] In low-income countries, and even in rural and poor
areas of middle-income countries, however, communicable disease and
environmental factors that affect health continue to cause significant
health problems. When resources are deployed to improve population
health in such places, it frequently makes sense to supply regular health
care and many kinds of public health services together.

---

[3]Wagstaff *et al.* (2009) distinguish between public health services such as sanitation
and vector control that are provided to the community as a whole, and those that are
supplied to individuals (such as vaccinations, or treatment of infectious disease) but
are of benefit not just to the individual receiving them but to others in the community
as well.

[4]Of the 54 chapters in the survey volumes in health economics in Glied and
Smith (2011) and Pauly, McGuire, and Barros (2012), only two contain significant
discussions of public health issues.

As an obvious example, primary-care providers in rural or poor urban areas who supply regular maternal and child health services can also be given responsibility for vaccination campaigns, and even for promoting sanitary waste disposal. It is well-established that much of China's success in improving its population's health status in the era of central planning before the 1980s was due to the success of the authorities in reaching high standards of public health through immunization campaigns and improved environmental standards, and the personnel in charge of the public health functions at that time were often the providers of regular primary care as well. As China continues to develop, the public-health function of the health care system will become more specialized, and account for a smaller share of total health care costs, as has happened in today's developed economies. At present, however, strengthening the public health function remains an important task in many places, and it continues to make sense to integrate the development of the primary-care system with planning the public health function. As we discuss further below, this may have implications for the way primary-care providers should be financed.

3. Primary Care in China's Health Care System: The Years of Decline

The weakening of the Chinese health care system that took place in the 1980s and 1990s appears to have disproportionately affected the primary health care system.

As noted earlier, during the central planning era, most Chinese residents in both rural and urban areas did have access to basic primary care supplied by rural health workers employed by the agricultural communes in rural areas, or by nurses and doctors employed by their work units in urban areas. Generally, those who supplied primary care were salaried employees, with responsibilities for many local public health functions as well as for provision of basic curative care and prescribing and supplying subsidized drugs.

As the agricultural communes were replaced by the family responsibility system, commune health workers lost their jobs, and while many of them tried to continue as private practitioners, what they could earn by charging patients for acute care, or by supplying drugs, was often not enough to replace the salary they had received under the earlier system. As a consequence, more rural residents became dependent on hospitals for both primary and higher-level care, and some public health functions were weakened as well.[5]

Similarly, as urban employers came under increased financial pressure when their subsidies from the state were reduced, some of them responded by laying off the nurses and doctors that supplied basic health care to their current and past employees. Again, the result was that more urban residents turned to hospitals for care. In both cases, the result was in part a tendency for people to delay care until they were seriously ill, resulting in more adverse health outcomes, and also tending to raise aggregate health care costs, both because it costs more to supply basic care in a hospital setting, and because delays in treatment raise costs because they result in patients becoming more severely ill.

While state subsidies to hospitals were restrained as well, hospitals were better able than primary-care providers to compensate for the lagging growth in subsidies by increasing the revenue they earned from patients. Partly this was because in comparison with primary-care providers, a large share of the patients that hospitals treat are seriously ill and are willing to pay for costly treatment or drugs; also, primary-care providers devote a relatively large share of their activities to public health functions, for which individual patients are less willing to pay than for acute-care services. Moreover, hospitals are owned by county or municipal governments who have more resources than smaller local rural communities, and who were responsible for continuing to employ hospital personnel even after the reforms began in the 1980s.

Another contributing factor to the decline of the primary-care sector in the 1980s and 1990s appears to have been a high degree of public distrust of the quality of care patients could expect from providers outside of major hospitals. This problem may of course have existed even before the reform, but may not have been as obvious

---

[5]Wagstaff *et al.* (2009, Chapter 2) describe these trends and even show data that indicate how the weakening of the system led to a deterioration in some measures of population health.

then because under the old system, patients were compelled to go through their primary-care providers in the first instance, as referrals were required in order for a patient to receive treatment in a hospital. To some extent, however, it may also reflect increased public suspicion regarding the nature of the care given by non-hospital providers who depend on the fees or drug revenue they can earn from their patients, rather than on a salary. People may realize that in this situation, non-hospital providers have an incentive to supply more expensive types of services or drugs than strictly justified by the patients' health problem. (A common observation is that non-hospital providers have a tendency to supply medications that are injected even when drugs taken by mouth would be equally effective, because they can charge more for an injection than they would earn from the markup on an oral drug.) They may also fear that providers with these incentives may fail to refer patients to a hospital even in cases where this would be warranted, since they earn no revenue from referrals.

The result of these trends has been the development of a health care system dominated by the relatively large county and urban hospitals to which patients have gone not just when they have known themselves to be seriously ill, but for relatively routine primary care as well. At the same time, data on the utilization of smaller facilities, especially in rural areas, display very low levels, especially in the early years of the 21st century, as shown in Figures 1 and 2.

By the early 2000s, there was some evidence that the downward trend in utilization of lower-level facilities had been reversed. In part, the increase in visits to township and community health centers is likely to have resulted from measures by the social insurance plans in rural and urban areas to encourage patients to visit less advanced facilities before going to major hospitals. Another reason may have been that many new doctors have been entering the system in recent years, and as some of them have not been able to find jobs in major hospitals, they have gone to lower-level facilities. This in turn may have raised patients' confidence regarding the quality of care they can expect to receive in such facilities.

There is also anecdotal evidence regarding a growing role for non-hospital primary care outside of the organized health care system, in a

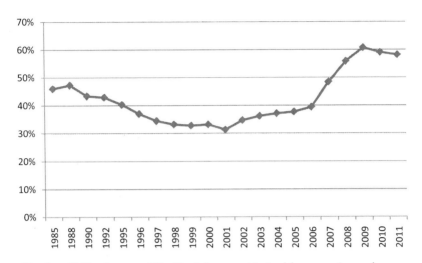

Fig. 1. Utilization rate (%) of beds in township health centers in rural areas.
Source: *China Health Statistical Yearbook*, various years.

Fig. 2. Number of visits to township health centers (100 million).
Source: *China Health Statistical Yearbook*, various years.

"gray market" for out-patient physician services in Beijing and other major cities. In these markets, newly trained young doctors who have not been able to find positions in major hospitals supply primary-care services to patients such as migrant workers who may not be able to obtain, or cannot afford, hospital treatment.[6] While the clinics in which this care is delivered are technically illegal, newspaper accounts suggest that the rules against them are not strictly enforced.

3.1. *Reversing the decline: The 2005 proposals*

By 2005, there was clear recognition in China that measures to strengthen the primary-care system had to be a high priority for future health policy. The analysis in the important report by the Development Research Center of the State Council referred to in Chapter 3 identified the problems in this sector as the main reason for the disappointing developments in the health care system as a whole. The preliminary English-language version of the report[7] consists of eight essays and reviews the organization of the system in the era of central planning before the late 1970s and how it had been affected by the new departures toward economic management in the subsequent quarter-century. It is very critical of the policy approaches that led to the changes, specifically the idea that hospitals and health clinics should be expected to raise a larger share of their total revenue from charges for medical services and drugs, along the same lines as firms in other sectors. Consistent with the observations above, the report singles out two subsectors for particular attention: public health and primary care. These subsectors were particularly affected by the abolition of the agricultural communes (in rural areas), and by the incentives that state-owned urban firms had to cut spending by no longer paying for employees' basic health services in their own clinics.

Considerable attention was paid to the organization of the health care systems in other countries in the report. There are frequent

---

[6]See, for example, a report in *China Daily*, downloadable from www.chinadaily.com.cn/life/2009-12/07/content_9128192.htm (accessed on June 13, 2013).
[7]See Chapter 3, footnote 30.

references to other countries' experiences, and the introduction lists the World Health Organization and the U.K. Department For International Development (DFID) as sponsors of the report and acknowledges the assistance of foreign experts. In the discussion of models of governance and management for the institutions that supply health care, the choice between direct government provision, one the one hand, and government purchases of services from privately owned and managed facilities, is considered.

Although the report remains generally critical of the role of private ownership and the profit motive in health care, it makes occasional reference to the possibility that private ownership and competition may lead to improved efficiency, and suggests that there may be a role for private institutions, for-profit and non-profit, alongside government-owned ones in the provision of "non-basic" (secondary and tertiary) services. However, for primary care, it argues strongly for a model under which it is supplied by providers who are paid and managed by the government, in a network of government-owned clinics.

Several arguments are advanced in support of this choice. One is the idea that such clinics should have a major role in strengthening the public health function, and that it is difficult to ensure that it receives priority if primary care is supplied by private agents. Another is simply that government employees in publicly owned providers can be more effectively supervised and monitored so as to prevent the harmful practices (supplier-induced demand, use of fake drugs) that private practitioners had sometimes engaged in. The DRC report also paid attention to the question of what level of government should be responsible for the management of the clinics and their personnel. While it suggests that the central government should bear most of the responsibility for financing, it recognized the advantage of management by local government, specifically, at the county level.

As we noted in Chapter 3, these recommendations were ultimately heeded in the guidelines for health reform that were issued by the Hu–Wen government in 2009. One of its cornerstones was a plan to construct a China-wide network of clinics that would be responsible for public health and basic medical care. We will return to the progress that has been made so far in implementing this plan. First, however, we will briefly review the way primary care is organized in other countries, and consider to what extent there are lessons to be drawn from their experiences in making decisions about the way these clinics should be managed and integrated into the rest of the health care system as it continues to evolve.

4. Primary Care in Other Countries: What Lessons for China?

The way primary care is supplied and paid for differs widely across countries. While medical doctors are the key actors in the primary-care system in every country, the kind of training required to become a doctor differs substantially from country to country. Moreover, there are large differences in the extent to which certain types of primary care is delivered by personnel who are not qualified doctors (for example, nurse practitioners), and in what kind of training these providers receive. In many countries, most doctors supply their services as self-employed professionals in "solo practice", while others do so in group practices in which several doctors work together as partners or part owners who share certain facilities; in other countries, most primary-care doctors are employees of firms or clinics. While all these are important aspects of a country's primary-care system, economic analysis of physician services markets has traditionally focused on another aspect: how the primary-care provider is paid.

4.1. *Payment mechanisms and incentives in primary care*

In history, medicine has been practiced both by physicians with permanent attachment to an employer from whom they received a regular salary (for example, court physicians in ancient China), and by doctors practicing independently whose income was derived from the fees they charged individual patients for their services. With respect to the provision of primary care, both of these methods of compensation are found in today's developed societies. The fee-for-service model remains the most common one, and is used in, among other countries, France, Germany, the U.S. and Canada, and Japan. The salary model has been used in some countries, such as Sweden, where primary care is often delivered by salaried doctors in public clinics; as discussed earlier, it has also been the predominant model in the Chinese health care system.

However, an increasingly common method of paying for primary care is capitation, along the lines of the U.K. model that was briefly discussed in Chapter 2. A capitation system is similar to the salary model in that the doctor's income does not depend on the volume of services he or she has produced during a given time period. Instead, it depends on the number of patients with whom the doctor has contracted to provide primary-care services as needed. From the viewpoint of the patient, a disadvantage with capitation schemes is that it ties the patient to a single primary-care provider for the duration of the capitation contract (generally, public or private insurance programs that pay primary-care doctors through capitation do not cover the cost if a patient goes to another provider), but this disadvantage may be offset by the tendency for the capitation model to result in lower costs of health care than fee-for-service based models.[8]

The U.K. is probably the best-known case in which primary care is supplied by doctors under capitation contracts, but the capitation model is also extensively used in the Netherlands, and also in many of the managed care plans that are offered in the private market for health insurance in the U.S. In practice, no country uses a pure capitation system. For example, only about half of the income of the General Practitioners who deliver primary care in the U.K. comes from capitation: The rest of their income comes partly from a fixed salary from the NHS, and partly from the fees they can charge for certain specific services (including certain forms of illness prevention).

4.2. *Paying for physician services: Competition vs. regulation*

Historically, the fees that independently practicing physicians charged for their services under the fee-for-service model were allowed to

---

[8]The different incentive structures in primary care have been extensively studied in the Western health economics literature. Recent surveys can be found in, e.g., McGuire (2011) and Scott and Jan (2011).

be determined in the same way as fees and prices in other markets: by agreements between willing buyers (patients) and sellers. In some countries, they still are (for example, in the U.S., or in the U.K. when patients choose to go to privately practicing providers outside the NHS plan). However, as the technology involved in medicine became more and more complicated, it was more and more widely recognized that patients, as the buyers of health care, usually are not in a position to bargain effectively with doctors over fees. Patients typically do not have the specialized knowledge to decide whether the drugs and services that doctors recommend are the appropriate ones, or whether the fees being offered are reasonable. Moreover, they also often are in no position to search in the market for the services of competing sellers, for example, when they need treatment urgently.

Several responses to patients' lack of bargaining power have emerged in the marketplace for medical services. In countries with universal health insurance plans (Germany, France, Canada, Japan), all doctors must abide by fee schedules that are negotiated between the government, representing the public insurance plan, and physician representatives. Since the government insurance plans in these countries completely dominate the demand side of the market, this model is essentially equivalent to a form of central price regulation.

In the U.S., the weak bargaining position of individual patients has been one of the forces driving the development of insurance plans with "selective contracting" and "patient steering" (these plans are also often referred to as "managed care" plans). When a patient is covered by such a plan, he or she is restricted to seeking care only from doctors that appear on the plan's list of approved (or "preferred") providers. The names on these lists consist of doctors with whom the plan has negotiated in advance regarding the fees they will charge, and other terms according to which they will provide their services. Thus, in markets where selective contracting is common, the fees charged by providers continue to be determined by negotiations between willing sellers and buyers in the marketplace, but the buyers are not individual patients. Instead, they are insurance plans that negotiate the fees and other conditions in advance, on behalf of the patients that will subsequently use the sellers' services. When managed care plans pay primary-care providers through capitation, the amount that doctors are paid per patient is also determined through competition among doctors to be included in the plans' lists of preferred providers, and among plans to attract good doctors.

In China, the doctors and other personnel that have supplied primary care in clinics and workplaces in the past have typically been employees paid by salary at rates that have been set by the government. More recently, with private practice having become more common, many have also been paid via fee-for-service, even though most hospital doctors still are paid mainly by salary. If these patterns continue, the experiences in other countries with payment methods such as capitation, or payment rates negotiated via selective contracting, are irrelevant. However, we will argue later that a case can be made for using the capitation principle as an element in the funding of primary-care clinics, and perhaps also of privately practicing doctors who compete with them. Moreover, the principle of selective contracting may be relevant for urban Social Insurance Bureaus when negotiating with government hospitals and clinics (and perhaps with competing private providers) regarding the terms according to which they will supply services to patients covered by the social insurance plans. We will return to this issue in a later section, and also in Chapters 9 and 10.

The method according to which doctors are paid for their own services is one way in which primary-care systems differ among countries. Another important difference is with respect to the primary-care doctors' role in determining the drugs that their patients use, and their use of the services of specialist doctors and the services of hospitals.

4.3. *Primary care and pharmaceuticals*

Prescribing the drugs that their patients use is one of the central functions of primary-care doctors in all health care systems. However, one important difference among countries is with respect to how the drugs are supplied. In the U.S. and Canada, while drugs are prescribed by doctors, drugs used by out-patients are not supplied by these doctors, but by independent pharmacists. In some other countries, notably in Japan, however, doctors are allowed to not only prescribe the drugs, but also supply them to patients. In such cases, part of the doctors' income consists of the markups they are allowed to charge for the drugs they prescribe. Depending on how these markups are set, this may give the doctors an incentive to prescribe relatively large amounts of drugs, and to choose drugs with high markups in preference to others in certain cases. This issue, of course, is one that has been highly relevant in the case of China, where markups on the drugs doctors supply have long made up a substantial share of the revenues earned by hospitals and clinics from patients.

As will be further discussed in Chapter 6, various measures have been used in different countries to restrain the costs of the drugs prescribed by primary-care doctors. These have included separating the authority to prescribe drugs from the right to supply them, so as to remove the incentive from doctors to prescribe drugs with high markups, or regulating the size of the allowable markups. In addition, managed care plans in the U.S. and the NHS in the U.K. have imposed restrictions on what drugs plan doctors have been allowed to prescribe, and/or used financial incentives on doctors in capitation plans to reduce the cost of the drugs they have prescribed for the patients that have registered with their practices.[9]

4.4. *Primary care and referrals*

Primary-care doctors in all health care systems also have major influence on the extent to which patients use the services of specialist doctors and many kinds of hospital services. One of their most important functions is to establish the initial diagnosis of patients presenting with health problems, and advise them on whether they should obtain further tests, or seek treatment from specialists or in hospital. The advice they provide in these respects can be major determinants not only of population health, but also of total health care costs. By following conservative strategies, for example, by not recommending further tests or specialist

---

[9]Danzon (2011) and Morton and Kyle (2012) briefly comment on the role of prescribing physicians in influencing drug costs.

and hospital treatment in doubtful or marginal cases, they can restrain costs, even if this increases the workload in their own practices. If they follow this strategy judiciously, there need not be significant negative effects on health outcomes.

While referrals to specialist and hospital providers is a major function of primary-care providers in all systems, referrals from primary care are not formally required everywhere. For example, all patients in Canada and many in the U.S. are covered by government or private plans that allow them to seek care from specialists or in hospitals on their own initiative, even though in practice most patients choose among specialists or hospitals on the advice of their primary-care provider. However, in the U.K. NHS, and in many managed care plans in the U.S., patients are only covered for specialist or non-emergency hospital care if they have been referred by their regular primary-care provider. In the U.K., this is expressed by saying that the GPs whose referral is required for such services have a "gate-keeping" function: Patients are only covered for such services if their GPs have recommended them.

In the previous section, we discussed some of the advantages with capitation as a way of paying doctors in primary care. However, in systems where primary-care doctors have a gate-keeping role and are paid via capitation, a problem arises: Such doctors have an indirect financial incentive to refer many patients to higher-level providers, other things equal. Under a capitation scheme, a doctor's income is higher the more patients there are on his roster, and the fewer the services he has to supply to each patient, the larger the number of patients he can manage. Referring patients to higher-level providers is one way for him to reduce the need for providing his own services to the patients, and hence make it possible to accept a larger number of patients on his roster.

Insurers or government funding agencies in systems where primary-care doctors are paid via capitation have attempted to counteract this tendency by introducing offsetting financial incentives. In some U.S. managed care plans, insurers keep records on the cost of services that insured clients have been using on referral from their designated primary-care providers, and the latter are eligible to receive bonus payments if these costs are below budgeted amounts that have been established in advance. (Similar approaches may be used to give capitated doctors an incentive to limit the costs of the drugs they prescribe for their patients.) In the U.K., a system referred to as "fundholding" was used in the 1990s. Under this system, the GPs who supply primary care in the U.K. system were given notional budgets for the prescription drugs and the costs of certain elective services that their patients might use following the GPs' prescriptions or referrals, and if the actual costs were less than the budgeted amounts, the GPs were allowed to use part of the surplus for enhancing their practice facilities. While the fundholding approach is no longer used, a system referred to as Practice-Based Commissioning that is being implemented contains incentives similar to those in the fundholding scheme.[10]

The balance between the resources used in primary and higher levels of care may also be affected by incentives that influence the referral decisions of primary-care providers in systems where they are paid via fee-for-service. For example, one explanation that has sometimes been given for the relatively low cost of specialist and hospital care in the Japanese health care system is that the regulated fees paid for primary-care services are relatively high. This has led many doctors to establish independent primary-care practices, and many hospitals to establish out-patient departments to supply primary care. The competition between the independent doctors and the hospitals' out-patient departments has been cited as one reason why the doctors are reluctant to refer their patients to a hospital in cases when they are able to treat them in their own clinics. Independent doctors fear that patients who have been referred to a hospital may subsequently choose to receive their primary-care services from the hospital's out-patient department, thereby reducing the doctors' potential revenue.

---

[10]The literature on the economic aspects of physicians' referral role is surprisingly small. Mention is made of fundholding and similar arrangements in U.S. managed care plans (under the name of "withholds") in Baker (2011) and Barros and Olivella (2011). A theoretical analysis is in Blomqvist and Léger (2005).

4.5. *Licensing, regulation, and manpower substitution*

The choice of payment mechanisms in primary care, and the restrictions and incentives that affect referral behavior, are important determinants of the balance between the resources allocated to primary care, on the one hand, and specialist and hospital care, on the other hand. Another important aspect of this issue is what type of training should be required of primary-care providers, and what rules and regulations should govern the scope of their practice.

In some systems, a large amount of primary care is supplied by nurse practitioners whose training is less long and comprehensive than that of medical doctors, and who therefore have to rely more extensively on referrals to higher-level providers for diagnosing and treating more complex problems. In other systems, most of the primary care is supplied by family doctors who are classified as "specialists in family medicine", and who have undergone training and internships that may be as long and rigorous as that of other specialized doctors. Because of their advanced training, these doctors can diagnose and treat a wider range of diseases than, for example, nurse practitioners, and hence can refer fewer patients to specialists and hospitals. While this means that fewer resources are needed for the provision of these more advanced levels of care, the longer and more extensive training means that it is more costly to train each primary-care provider. Deciding where the best balance lies is a difficult task, and different countries have made different choices. It will be an important issue for China as programs are designed to train the personnel that will work in the strengthened primary-care system in future years, an issue to which we will return below.

4.6. *Payment methods and the organization of primary care: Private or public?*

Much of the discussion about primary-care reform in China has centered on the question of whether it should be supplied through public or private providers. This is perhaps not surprising: Many of the critics of government health policy in the 1990s and early 2000s were arguing that the problems in the sector to a large extent stemmed from an uncritical application of the shift toward privatization and reliance on competitive markets that had been successful in other sectors. To the critics, therefore, a return to a greater role for direct government provision seemed a natural response.

The question whether primary care should be supplied through private or public providers is not the same as the issue of how they should be paid. In principle, doctors may be paid through any of the methods of fee-for-service, capitation, or salary in either the private or public sector. In practice, however, the two issues are related. In most systems in which primary-care doctors are paid through fee-for-service, they are classified as private providers. Conversely, salaried primary-care doctors are typical of systems in which providers are public.

As previously noted, fee-for-service remains the most commonly used approach to paying doctors, and in all the countries noted above where it predominates, primary-care provision is in privately owned facilities. In countries such as the U.S., Germany, France, Canada, and Japan, primary care has typically been supplied by private practitioners ("general practitioners") in offices that they themselves owned, and in which they were the only doctor ("solo practice"), and the only employees were nurses and perhaps a receptionist or administrative assistant. While arrangements under which several doctors practice together ("group practices") in facilities which they own jointly, or in clinics that are owned by independent investors, are becoming more common, the solo practice model still predominates. It is noteworthy that private fee-for-service practice continues to flourish not only in systems where practitioners are privately paid (by their patients or private insurers), but also in systems where payment is from government-sponsored social insurance plans (Canada, France, Japan, for example).

Among high-income countries, provision of primary care through clinics in which the doctors are salaried employees is relatively uncommon, though the model is used in the Nordic countries. It is also used in many middle-income and low-income countries (India, Indonesia), and it was also the predominant model in the countries of the former Soviet Union and Eastern Europe. In all these cases, the clinics in which doctors are paid by salary are owned by the government, which also pays the salaries of the nurses and administrative personnel who assist them. The model in which salaried doctors provide primary care in privately owned clinics is uncommon, but it has been used in some of the Health Maintenance Organizations that made up a large share of the U.S. health care system during the early phases of the evolution of the system of managed-care insurance that now dominates the market for private health insurance in that country.

As noted above, the U.K. National Health Service is the system that is most clearly identified with the use of capitation in primary care. Because most health care in the U.K. is paid for by the government which also owns most of the system's hospitals, it is sometimes believed that the General Practitioners who supply primary care in it are government employees. Technically, however, this is not correct. While U.K. GPs receive almost all their income from public funds (including not only the capitation component but also a fixed salary and a "practice allowance"), they are in fact private practitioners who are entitled to retain any net profits their practices are able to earn after their expenditures have been covered.

However, the market in which GPs supply their primary care is heavily regulated, including the restriction that they cannot charge their patients any fees, and the government controls where practices can be set up. Moreover, the GP practice contract regulates in considerable detail exactly what services each one must supply to enrolled patients. With these regulations and contractual provisions placing relatively tight constraints on how the GPs can practice, it may not make a great deal of difference whether the facilities where they work are privately owned or owned by the government; what is more important are the incentive effects inherent in the capitation model of compensation, and the incentives to control the costs of drugs and higher-level care their patients receive.

This may be the most important lesson from China's point of view for the design of the future primary-care system: Even if it is accepted that the bulk of it will be produced in clinics owned by the government, this still leaves a range of options open with respect to issues such as how the clinics and their employees will be paid, what restrictions and incentives they should face with respect to drug prescriptions and referrals, and so on. In answering these questions, China's policymakers can make extensive use of the lessons that have been learned from other countries, even within the framework of a system dominated by government-owned clinics.

5. China's Network of Basic Care Clinics: Progress So Far

There has been substantial progress in implementing the plans announced in 2009 to strengthen China's primary-care system. The plans were ambitious in foreseeing a vast network of facilities, calling for 5,000 township health centers and 29,000 township health clinics in rural areas, and 3,700 community health centers and 11,000 community health clinics in urban areas.[11] Some of these are being newly established, while many others that existed before are being refurbished and their staff and facilities are being strengthened. In an announcement in late 2009 from the State Council, it was stated that the salaries of employees in these institutions should be "performance related" (绩效工资 in Chinese)[12]; this can perhaps be taken as partial recognition of the fact that in many cases, employees had continued to collect salaries from the local governments even as the decreased rate of utilization of the facilities had left them with little work to perform.

The system is also being strengthened through re-establishing a better-defined set of rules for funding the operating costs of these facilities. As subsidies to them gradually came to cover a decreasing share of their operating costs in the 1990s and early 2000s, they were forced to cover more of their costs through charges to patients, and via markups on the drugs they supplied. Beginning in 2009, all of the clinics and centers that are owned by the government will receive subsidies to allow them to decouple their salaries and other expenditures from the revenue they raise from patient charges and drug markups. In particular, each publicly owned facility will be obliged to supply all drugs from an established list at a zero markup, and the prices of

---

[11] See http://www.moh.gov.cn/publicfiles/business/htmlfiles/mohzcfgs/s7846/200907/41882.htm and http://news.xinhuanet.com/2010-06/10/c_12207179.htm (accessed on May 29, 2012). There are about 40,000 townships in China.

[12] See http://news.xinhuanet.com/politics/2009-09/02/content_11985468.htm (accessed on May 29, 2012).

the basic services they supply will be strictly regulated.[13] Funding for the providers' subsidies are either directly from the local governments' budgets, or from the social health insurance funds, which are used not only to pay the fees charged for services delivered to insured clients, but also sometimes to pay collectively for public health services; the latter practice illustrates the fact that the funds collected by local governments under the social health insurance plans that they manage are not always managed separately from the governments' general budgets, as further discussed in Chapter 8.

Another element in the campaign to strengthen China's primary-care sector has been attempts at creating closer integration between the primary-care facilities and the hospitals that have come to dominate the health care system. Although formal compulsory referral systems are not typically used, patients are encouraged to first go to a primary-care facility for diagnosis before deciding whether they need to go to a hospital for treatment. The social insurance plans may also contain financial incentives for patients to do so by offering more favorable reimbursement rates for services supplied in a primary-care facility. Furthermore, government officials have also tried to strengthen the reputation of the primary-care facilities by getting qualified hospital doctors to spend part of their time providing services to patients in these facilities, rather than in the hospitals where they are based.

Finally, there has been discussion of a strategy under which there would be a significant role for privately practicing providers to supply primary-care services alongside the government facilities. One element of this strategy would be to make private providers eligible for the same subsidy as government clinics in return for charging zero markups on basic drugs. It is not clear whether this means that local governments are actively encouraging private providers (through licensing and in other ways) to directly compete with their own facilities, or whether they are trying to complement the operation of the government clinics by allowing private provision of certain specialized services that the former do not provide. It is, in any case, interesting that there

---

[13]See http://www.gov.cn/zwgk/2010-04/19/content_1586732.htm (accessed on May 29, 2012). We will return to the rules regarding pharmaceuticals in Chapter 6.

is active discussion of an approach in which potential competition between private and public providers may be used as an instrument for encouraging better quality health care, and which draws attention to the need for a "level playing field" (such as similar degrees of subsidization) if it is to be effective.

5.1. *Integration of primary and higher-level care: Pilot projects*

As discussed above, a great deal of attention has been paid in other countries to encouraging an efficient division of labor between primary and higher levels of care, through restrictions and incentives that reinforce the role of primary-care providers as gate-keepers to higher levels of care. The problem of making the different levels of care work well together has also been addressed in local pilot projects in China.

In an April 2010 Ministry of Health document, guidelines were suggested for attaining more efficient use of publicly owned hospitals and health care clinics in rural areas by more integrated management.[14] A natural first step was to bring about closer integration between township health centers and local village clinics, and evidence from pilot projects suggests that this approach has been useful in improving service quality (Wagstaff *et al.*, 2009, p. 143).

In rural areas surrounding Foshan city in Guangdong province, this approach has been taken a step further, in that county hospitals and village and township clinics and health centers are funded and managed jointly, something which can facilitate creation of a referral system and better joint use of all facilities together.[15] In Zhenjiang city, Jiangsu province, a different model of integration has been implemented. Two hospital groups were formed in November 2009. All public hospitals and community health centers are allocated to one of these two groups, with representatives from the local government sitting on the board. According to official sources, such an arrangement of hospital groups

---

[14]See http://www.gov.cn/zwgk/2010-04/07/content_1575036.htm (accessed on May 29, 2012).
[15]See http://medicine.people.com.cn/GB/132552/188880/189037/11640591.html (accessed on May 29, 2012).

serves two purposes. First, it encourages competition between these two hospital groups. Second, similar to the case in Foshan city, it speeds up referral decisions between primary care and tertiary care units within a hospital group in a hierarchical manner.[16] Another example comes from Shanghai, where the municipal government released a health reform proposal in May 2011. The main feature of the proposal is the establishment of a "health conglomerate" in each district, consisting of a general hospital, several smaller hospitals, and a number of community health centers. Patients have to go to a community health center to obtain a referral before they can visit a higher-level hospital. Currently, two such pilot health conglomerates have been established in 2011 in two districts of Shanghai, and this institutional arrangement is expected to expand to the entire city over the next three to four years.[17]

6. Primary Care in the Future

The performance of the primary-care system, and how it interacts with the hospitals and other institutions, will be critical determinants in influencing the aggregate costs and quality of the health care system as a whole in future years. The pilot projects that are being undertaken to test different models for integrating them will therefore be followed with great interest, to see which ones can best serve as templates for reform elsewhere.

The methods that will ultimately be chosen by local governments to manage and integrate the system will be of great significance in predicting the answer to the big question that was introduced in the first two chapters: Will the "government camp" or the "market camp" prevail in health policy? That is, will China's health care system gradually return to a model in which its resources are directly managed by government departments with responsibility for the local system as a whole, or will the trend be toward more decentralization and autonomy for providers and more widespread use of incentives and competition to promote efficiency?

---

[16]Du and Zhang (2009, p. 141).

[17]*Economic Observer*, May 4, 2011, http://www.eeo.com.cn/Politics/by_region/ 2011/05/04/200472.shtml (accessed on May 29, 2012).

While the 2009 guidelines suggested that there could be a role for both approaches, the nature of the local experiments described above seems to suggest a tendency toward more focus on models of strong government oversight and control than on incentives and competition. We think a good case can be made for additional pilot projects that draw on lessons from the experience in other countries and experiment with more decentralized government approaches that rely on performance-based funding, rather than on official oversight, to manage the system.

6.1. *Incentives and competition in primary care*

As in other industries, the performance of the primary-care sector may be strongly influenced by the incentives to which the managers and providers who work in primary-care clinics are subjected. In industries that are highly competitive, there is a tendency for the incentive structure on decision-makers in individual firms to promote efficiency, since inefficient firms will not be able to survive. To some extent, this logic may be applicable in health care as well, but only if government chooses to regulate health care in such a way as to bring about competition among autonomous providers. Moreover, even if the clinics that supply primary care are owned by government, incentives can be used to promote efficient performance by clinic employees.

If resources in primary care are allocated through fixed budgets to each clinic, and employees are compensated through fixed salaries — the prevailing model in China today — there are no direct financial incentives on the providers to perform efficiently. This approach may nevertheless lead to acceptable performance if employees and managers are motivated by a strong sense of professional and social responsibility, and because there is implicit recognition that in the long run, budget allocations will not continue to be made to clinics that do not perform well, and that salaried employees will ultimately be terminated if they are not productive. However, allocation of primary-care resources through fixed budgets and employee compensation through fixed salaries are less common than approaches that rely at least partially on methods with stronger financial incentives for performance, such as fee-for-service or capitation.

As discussed in Chapter 2, under the fee-for-service method, providers' income is derived from payments by patients, or their insurers, for itemized individual services; thus, a provider's revenue from each treatment episode is higher the more services that have been provided. Fee-for-service, therefore, encourages producers to be productive in the sense of supplying a large volume of services, in contrast to salaries or fixed budget allocations that have no direct link to the volume of services. It is the predominant method for allocating resources to primary care in most advanced countries (for example, the U.S. and Canada, Japan, and France and Germany). While it is primarily used in systems where primary care is mostly supplied by independently practicing GPs or family doctors, it can also be used as the basis for determining the amount of revenue and resources received by hospitals and primary-care clinics. As is happening in many places in China today, the incentives inherent in paying hospitals and clinics this way can be transmitted to the doctors who work in them, by paying them bonuses that depend on the institution's revenue, or even on the revenue generated by patients treated by specific departments or doctors.

But as also noted earlier, in the health care market, the incentive structure inherent in the fee-for-service method of compensation is flawed to some extent, partly because patients do not have the information necessary to decide which health services are of most benefit to them, and therefore have to rely on the advice of their doctors when deciding what health services to utilize. If doctors can earn more revenue by treating individual patients more intensively, or with more advanced methods or drugs than really needed, they may end up supplying more services and more expensive drugs to the patients they treat, rather than dealing with patients' health problems as efficiently, and at as low cost, as possible. That is, even though a fee-for-service system rewards doctors for supplying a large volume of services, it does not imply an incentive for them to allocate these services to the people who need them the most in order to stay healthy. One indirect consequence of this may be to make it difficult to attract doctors to under-serviced areas: In a system based on fee-for-service, providers may be able to earn more revenue in more prosperous areas, even if there is a relatively large number of doctors per capita in these areas.

Capitation, the other principal method used to pay for primary care in countries like the U.K., implies a different incentive structure. It rewards providers who take responsibility for supplying primary-care services as needed, to as large a number of people as possible. Put differently, it gives providers an incentive to keep as many people as possible healthy, not to provide a large volume of services to each one. A potential disadvantage with capitation, of course, is the risk that it will lead to a relatively low quality of care. With many patients, providers may not have much time or energy for each one. However, a commitment to professional responsibility, as well as a desire to protect the clinic's reputation and avoid complaints, partially serve to offset this possibility, and the experience of the U.K. and Holland, as well as many U.S. managed care plans, suggest that the capitation method may work well in practice.

The capitation model in these countries is typically used as the basis of compensation of individual doctors, but it can also be used as a method to allocate resources among competing clinics. For example, in urban areas where patients may be able to choose from among several competing clinics, patients could be given a choice with which clinic to register, and funding for the clinics could be based, in whole or in part, on the number of patients who had chosen to register with them. In rural areas, competition of this type may not be possible, since there might only be one clinic within patients' reasonable travel distance. However, capitation could also be used to compensate individual doctors in clinics with several physicians, thereby inducing an element of competition and incentive to take care of many patients and provide high-quality care at the level of the individual doctor, as well as at the clinic level. We will return to these issues later in Chapters 9 and 10.

With respect to attaining an efficient division of labor between primary care and care in higher-level institutions (hospitals and specialist clinics), the capitation model has the potential disadvantage that it implies an incentive on primary-care providers to reduce their own costs and resource needs by referring patients to higher-level institutions more frequently than is medically justified. However, as discussed previously, techniques for overcoming that problem have been developed in the U.K. (for example, the fundholding approach) and in U.S. managed care plans. With appropriate modifications, these methods could become part of China's future primary-care system as well, as could the idea of drug budgets, to create incentives on clinics and individual doctors to control the cost of the medications they supply to their patients. Indeed, drug budgets could serve as a supplement to the enforcement of the restrictions requiring primary-care providers to limit their prescriptions to drugs from an approved list, and to supply these drugs to patients at zero markup, along the lines of the recently introduced measures to restrain drug costs.

6.2. *Should private practitioners be publicly subsidized?*

Earlier it was argued that allowing doctors or nurse practitioners to supply primary-care services through private practice could serve as a useful safety valve that would allow newly trained health professionals to supply services, at least temporarily, even if they could not quickly find jobs in government-owned clinics. Allowing primary-care doctors to practice privately could also be beneficial in creating competition for government clinics, strengthening their incentives to offer care of high quality.

A number of issues arise in designing a system in which independent private practitioners would be allowed to compete with government clinics. One question is whether individual doctors who are employed in government clinics should also be allowed to work part-time in private practice; as will be discussed later, this is the model that is used in the U.K. for some hospital-based specialist doctors, and there are other countries where this has been allowed as well. In rural areas, allowing doctors to work part-time in private practice may make it easier to attract qualified practitioners to government facilities in small communities. However, it can also be problematic in the sense that doctors who are allowed this form of "dual practice" may be tempted to use various strategies to raise their income by encouraging patients to be treated privately rather than through the government clinic, for example, by reducing the number of effective hours worked in the government clinic, or by holding out the prospect of more careful diagnosis and treatment for patients who see the doctor privately.

In such cases, the result of allowing private practice will not be quality-enhancing competition, but just increased cost.

The effectiveness of competition between government clinics and full-time private practitioners also depends on whether or not it takes place on a "level playing field". One way of accomplishing this is to ensure that public subsidies similar to those available to government clinics are also available to private practices. To make this possible within a given total subsidy budget implies sharing this budget between government and private clinics, in some fashion. A natural way of doing this would be if most of the public subsidy to government clinics came in the form of a capitation payment to the clinic with which the patient had signed up. This could be accomplished in a system where each patient would be required to register with a clinic in order to be eligible for subsidized care and drugs, as discussed earlier. In a system where private providers are able to compete with the government clinics as well, however, the patient would not just have a choice between different government clinics, but would also have the option of choosing a private clinic instead.

The effectiveness of competition between government clinics and private practitioners would also depend on the range of services that government clinics supply. For example, in many places, government clinics would most likely be responsible for a variety of public health services, and may also be equipped with certain basic diagnostic and laboratory facilities. The question would then arise with respect to the extent to which patients who had chosen to register with a private practice would have access to these public health services and diagnostic and laboratory services. If the rule was that patients registered with private practitioners would not have access to any of the services offered in government clinics, private practices would have to offer the same range of public health services and facilities as government clinics, in order to compete effectively. Alternatively, contractual arrangements could be made under which private practices only receive a partial subsidy (that is, a lower capitation amount than government clinics), but patients registered with a private practice would continue to have access to some of the services (public health services, diagnostic and laboratory facilities) of the government clinics.

6.3. *The supply of primary-care providers*

Finally, it is clear that no matter what institutional arrangements and incentives are used to manage the primary-care system, none of them will make it work efficiently unless it is staffed by properly trained and motivated doctors and nurses.

One of the reasons for the decline of primary care in China's health care system in the post-1980 period appears to have been a loss of public confidence in the quality of care that was offered by providers outside hospitals, especially in rural areas. As funding for primary care was decreased, qualified and experienced doctors had more incentive to practice in hospitals rather than in health centers or primary-care clinics, and some of the providers who continued to practice outside hospitals (often those with relatively little training) struggled to survive by supplying services and drugs that yielded more revenue from patients, as they received less government funding. As older practitioners have retired and not been replaced, the number of experienced primary-care providers outside hospitals is now relatively limited. An important priority for future health policy therefore will be to find a way of ensuring that there will be enough qualified personnel to staff the increasing number of primary-care centers and clinics in both urban and rural areas.

In the short run, the approach of recruiting some of the doctors who are supposed to work in the basic care clinics from among doctors currently working in hospitals certainly makes sense; it may be the most effective way of convincing members of the public that there is a strong commitment to offering care of high quality in these clinics. In the longer run, however, most of the personnel that will be working in primary-care clinics will be new graduates from medical schools in China. This, therefore, raises the issue: What types of training programs for primary-care providers should medical schools be encouraged to focus on?

As noted earlier, there is great variety across countries with respect to the training required of those who supply primary care. Specifically, while some countries have restrictive rules under which the public insurance programs will only pay for primary-care services supplied by licensed doctors, others allow a large share of primary care to be provided by persons with less extensive training, for example, nurse practitioners. Staffing the primary-care system mostly with nurse practitioners is less expensive to society in the sense that it is less costly to train a nurse practitioner than it is to train a medical doctor. However, to the extent that a less highly trained provider has a higher probability of misdiagnosing a patient's condition, or to choose less than optimal treatment methods, substitution of nurse practitioners for medical doctors can result in a lower average quality of care. Moreover, if nurse practitioners have a higher probability than medical doctors of referring patients to higher-level care, there may be an offsetting cost increase.

In systems where nurse practitioners have a major role in providing primary care, the above issues are typically addressed through a system in which these practitioners work closely with medical doctors to whom they refer patients in cases where there is uncertainty about either the diagnosis of the patient's condition, or the proper drug or treatment methods. While such a system does not completely address the issue of the quality of care provided, it clearly can help, and there is a substantial literature to suggest that nurse practitioners or other auxiliary health workers may be a cost-effective substitute when there is a shortage of medical doctors to work in the primary-care sector.[18] However, whether this conclusion is the appropriate one in the context of China's future health care system also depends on the relative cost of training primary-care doctors and nurse practitioners, and this relative cost, in turn, depends on the standards that are set for the training programs.

While international models from advanced countries may yield useful insights when it comes to designing the programs that Chinese health practitioners will be going through, the desirability of attaining high standards modelled on these countries must be weighed against the high cost of doing so. The Cuban approach has been to reduce the cost of training medical doctors by requiring fewer years of training

---

[18]Scott and Jan (2011) discuss this issue and provide references. Nicholson and Propper (2012) is a very comprehensive survey of issues relating to government policy with respect to the training and regulation of health sector manpower.

than in advanced countries, and it is often held up as a successful model for middle-income countries. Another possible model would be one based on a combination of a relatively small number of highly trained primary-care specialists working together with a large number of nurse practitioners or some other type of "physician extenders". Whether this would be preferable to a strategy modelled on the Cuban approach is an issue that is worth further discussion and research.[19]

7. Conclusions

Earlier, we observed that the debate over health policy in China has to some extent come to serve as a forum in which the differing views regarding economic management in general are more openly displayed than in other areas. This tendency appears to have been particularly evident in the discussion about primary care.

Some will see the 2009 decision to strengthen China's primary-care system through a network of government-owned clinics as a setback for those who favor further liberalization of economic management, with a continuing trend toward a greater role for markets, incentives, and competition. As we have made clear in this chapter, however, we do not necessarily share this view.

Even if the primary-care clinics are owned by the government, their managers can be subject to incentives similar to those in private firms. For this approach to work effectively, it must be clear that they have a high degree of autonomy with respect to the decisions they make, especially those relating to employment and the way their doctors and other staff are paid, and they must be subject to hard budget constraints. Furthermore, competition between government clinics and privately practicing providers can be allowed to play a role, with the financing system being designed so as to ensure that the competition takes place on a "level playing field". While the 2009 decision was an important one, it did not settle the broader debate between the two competing views about China's future health care system. We will return to this issue in Chapters 9 and 10.

---

[19]An interesting account of the Cuban model of training doctors is in WHO (2010).

Appendix. Statistics for Primary-Care Service Providers in China in 2011

	No. of providers	No. of visits (millions)	No. of registered doctors	No. of nurses	No. of beds	Fee per visit (out-patients)	Fee per visit (in-patients)	Total expenditure (billion RMB)	Salary expenditure (billion RMB)
Overall primary-care clinics	918,003	3,805	959,965	492,554	1,233,721	n/a	n/a	252	87
Community health centers and stations	32,860	546	158,554	119,834	187,132	81.5	2,315.1	66	21
Township health centers	37,295	866	408,587	203,339	1,026,251	47.5	1,051.3	128	44
Village clinics	662,894	1,792	1,060,548	30,502	n/a	n/a	n/a	29	11

Source: China Health Statistical Yearbook, 2012.

Chapter 5

THE HOSPITAL SECTOR
AND HOSPITAL REFORM

1. Introduction

Although primary care plays a central role in the health care system of every country, statistics on health care expenditure typically show that the largest portion of the national health care budget goes to hospitals — that is, to what is usually referred to as secondary and tertiary levels of care. For example, data from around 2010 show that in the U.S., over 30% of total health care costs were for hospital care, while the cost for physician services (which includes almost all primary care) was about 20% and the cost of prescription drugs around 10% of the total. In Canada, the picture was similar, with data showing 29% of the total for hospital costs, although the share for physician services was lower at around 14% while pharmaceuticals accounted for 16% of the total.[1]

As the data in Table 1 show, the hospital sector accounts for an even larger share of total health care spending in Chinese statistics. The total revenue paid to government-owned hospitals had reached as high as 45% of total national health expenditure in 2010. In interpreting and comparing these data, however, one must keep in mind certain institutional differences between China's health care system and those in North America. First, the doctors who treat patients in North American hospitals are typically paid separately for their services, meaning that the data on the cost of hospital care in the U.S. and

---

[1]For U.S., see Martin *et al.* (2012); for Canada, see Canadian Institute for Health Information (2011, p. 17).

Table 1. Different components of revenue of government-run hospitals as a share of total national health expenditure.

	2005	2006	2007	2008	2009	2010	2011
Total hospital revenue (%)	42.73%	40.94%	42.36%	41.90%	42.51%	45.24%	44.85%
Revenue from providing services (%)	20.30%	19.81%	20.55%	20.05%	20.20%	21.74%	21.90%
Revenue from selling drugs (%)	18.38%	16.91%	17.48%	17.64%	17.88%	18.87%	18.13%
Revenue from fiscal grants (%)	n/a	n/a	3.42%	3.39%	3.61%	3.86%	4.05%

Source: *China Health Statistical Yearbook*, various years.

Canada do not include the cost of their services. In China (and in many European countries as well), the salaries paid to the doctors who work in hospitals are included in the data on hospital costs. Second and more importantly, while the cost of drugs supplied to hospitalized patients is included in hospital costs in both the North American and Chinese data, in North America it makes up only a very small share of these costs. In China, in contrast, the revenue that hospitals generate by selling drugs to their patients makes up a big portion of the total gross revenue shown in Table 1 — over 40% in 2010 and 2011. When these factors are taken into account, the differences between the systems in terms of the relative share of hospital costs become much smaller.[2]

Another difference between the current pattern of Chinese health care costs and that in most developed countries stems from the fact that in recent years, hospitals in China have supplied a relatively large share of out-patient primary-care services, as fewer people have visited rural-area health centers or depended on primary care in urban health clinics or at their place of employment. Because the primary-care sector in

---

[2]As we will further discuss in Chapter 6, however, a big difference between the pattern of health care costs in China and that in the rest of the world is the much higher cost of pharmaceuticals (bought not only in hospitals but in clinics and independent pharmacies) in China. Recent estimates put the share of pharmaceutical costs at above 40%, much higher than the shares in North America or other high-income countries.

China is now being refurbished and expanded, the number of hospital visits may gradually be reduced, at least as a share of the total number of treatment episodes. As a result, the pattern in China will become more like that in developed countries in this respect as well, with a relatively smaller number of patients and treatment episodes in hospitals, but a rising cost per treatment episode as hospitals acquire more advanced equipment and employ specialists with more extensive training, and concentrate more on treating patients with relatively severe illnesses.

In the rest of this chapter, we discuss issues relating to the reform of China's hospital sector within the context of health services reform more generally. As a background, we briefly discuss the historical evolution of hospitals in other countries, and how their functioning and roles in all health care systems have changed in response to the development of medical technology. As in the chapter on primary care, we then turn to an analysis of the way hospitals are financed. In that section, we consider the division between public and private financing, and review the international experience with different methods of payment as third-party payers have tried to introduce incentives designed to control hospital costs and promote efficiency in the hospital sector. We then turn to a discussion of the evolution of China's hospital system over the last several decades, and the guidelines for hospital reform that were outlined in the 2009 blueprint for China's future health policy. We describe some of the pilot projects that currently are underway, and conclude the chapter with a discussion of possible lessons for future policy toward hospitals in China based on the experience in other countries.

2. Hospitals in Historical Perspective

The hospital sector in a modern society encompasses a range of institutions that provide many different types of services. At a time when medical technology was not very advanced, there was less differentiation. Most hospitals were simply institutions where people were housed when they were too sick to continue living at home, or had no relatives and friends to care for them. Most hospitalized patients stayed there until they died.

Today, there is more variety. In some countries, there are specialized long-term care hospitals and nursing homes that provide simple care for old and/or chronically ill patients who do not suffer from acute illness but who cannot function independently in the community. Others, often referred to as *acute-care* hospitals, focus more on providing the advanced kinds of care that modern technology now offers to people with many types of serious acute health problems. While many of the patients treated in acute-care hospitals today are very seriously ill, most of them are expected to recover, and in comparison with nursing homes and long-term care hospitals, the length of their stay on average is much shorter.[3]

Of the total costs that are attributable to the hospital sector, a large share consists of wages and salaries. Many of the people who work in hospitals are professionals with extensive education and training, not only doctors and nurses but also various kinds of technicians and pharmacists. Professional employees account for a large share of total costs partly because they are paid more than unskilled workers, but large numbers of relatively unskilled employees in positions as nursing assistants, orderlies, cleaning staff, and so on, also add to the total.

But modern acute-care hospitals also can be very capital-intensive facilities, with large amounts invested in the equipment that is needed to deliver various forms of technologically advanced care, such as in intensive care units, operating theaters, and facilities where radiation treatment is given to cancer patients. Most hospitals also have expensive equipment such as X-ray machines or scanners for more advanced imaging technology, as well as laboratories and pharmacies.[4]

---

[3] One definition of "acute illness" is that it requires treatment within a short time (say, 48 hours) after it has been diagnosed, in order to avoid serious adverse outcomes such as death or long-term disability. Some patients with chronic illnesses may require acute care if their illness enters an acute phase.

[4] The education and training that providers of various professional services must undergo is often interpreted as a form of capital ("human capital"), and part of the salaries and other income they receive for their services can then be interpreted as a return on the past investments in their training. Once this is taken into account, it is no longer clear whether the health care sector is in fact relatively labor-intensive, as is often thought to be the case.

Even within the acute-care hospital sector there is great variety. Major hospitals in large cities can have facilities to treat a wide range of serious illness using state-of-the-art equipment, while those in smaller cities or county hospitals in rural areas may lack some of the most advanced equipment and facilities. In the U.S. and elsewhere, a distinction is sometimes made between hospitals that make up most of the secondary care sector[5] and the most advanced ones that provide tertiary care. While it is not always clear precisely where the line between the two categories should be drawn, a tertiary-care hospital is either an acute-care hospital with a full range of facilities for treating all types of acute illness, or a hospital that is highly specialized in the treatment of a particular type of illness, sometimes using advanced technology that is not available elsewhere. Another similar distinction is often made between teaching hospitals that are affiliated with major medical schools and others; teaching hospitals clearly belong in the tertiary sector, as do some of the specialized hospitals in large cities that focus exclusively on treating patients with certain specific kinds of illnesses, using state-of-the-art methods.

In Chinese statistics, Ministry of Health guidelines list three categories of hospitals: primary, secondary, and tertiary. The categories are not distinguished primarily through what range of services are supplied, but in terms of the number of beds and personnel that each one has. Primary hospitals are township or community hospitals with 20–99 beds, and at least 0.7 health workers per bed (with a minimum of 3 doctors and 5 nurses), while secondary and tertiary hospitals have 100–499 beds and over 500 beds, respectively, with a minimum of 0.88 and 1.03 health workers per bed. Primary hospitals are responsible for providing preventive and basic health care and rehabilitation services, while higher-level hospitals are required to produce more comprehensive and specialized care, as well as some

---

[5]The term "secondary care" sometimes is also defined to include care by specialist physicians who practice in their own offices or in clinics that only treat patients with the particular type of illness that they specialize in treating. In China, this type of practice is still rare.

Table 2. Number of institutions and beds by level of hospital, 2012.

	Number of institutions in 2012	Number of beds in 2012
Tertiary hospital	1,624	1,469,737
Secondary hospital	6,566	1,827,240
Primary hospital	5,962	312,866

Source: Statistical Communiqués on health and family planning in 2012, Ministry of Health.

education and training and (for tertiary hospitals) scientific research as well; see Table 2 for an overview.

Although exact comparisons are not possible, it seems likely that much of the basic care that is provided in institutions that are classified as primary hospitals in China consists of care that is similar to primary care that is produced in clinics or individual physician practices in Europe and North America, and hence would not be classified as part of the hospital sector in statistics from these regions.

2.1. *Hospital financing and ownership: Charities, patients, and investors*

Historically, hospitals in today's industrialized countries were charitable institutions, and most were built and operated by religious orders that did not expect payment from the patients they cared for. Later, as responsibility for supporting the poor was taken over by secular society, hospitals were also built and operated by local governments. As the function of hospitals gradually changed from simply housing the sick and destitute to providing a place where doctors could restore patients to health with the aid of advancing medical technology, the responsibility for paying the hospitals' operating costs was gradually shifted to the patients who were treated there, or to the doctors who used the hospitals' facilities but who in their turn charged the patients for their services.

As developments in medicine made it possible to treat more and more diseases, the demand for hospital capacity increased. In part, the increasing demand was met by expanding the capacity of the existing hospitals owned by religious institutions or local governments, who covered their rising operating costs through charges to patients or their insurers, but who typically chose to operate as non-profit entities that only charged enough to cover their operating costs. In some countries, however (for example, the U.S. and Japan), new hospital capacity was also created by private investors who expected a return on the capital they had invested. To accomplish this, the hospitals had to charge patients and their insurers enough to cover not just their operating costs, but to leave room for a profit margin as well.

With aging populations, investment in hospital capacity is a large component of total investment expenditures in most countries today, and the cost of allocating a large share of society's capital to hospitals represents a significant share of the opportunity cost of providing health care. This is true whether hospitals are owned and operated by governments or by private owners, and whether or not they are operated as non-profit entities. Whenever society invests in a hospital, the resources needed to build and equip it could have been used for some other type of investment that would have yielded a stream of future benefits.

From the viewpoint of society as a whole, it is the streams of foregone future benefits from alternative investments that represent the true cost of expanding hospital capacity, and this cost is the same regardless of who pays for it, and whether or not it is subsequently operated as a for-profit entity. Conventional measures of health care spending and costs do not always fully recognize this. For example, they may not include depreciation charges on existing hospital capacity as part of aggregate health care costs, or include a component of capital cost in economic evaluations of proposals for new treatment facilities.

It is sometimes argued that government investment in hospitals should not be required to yield a rate of return as high as that on other investments because, in addition to the value of the services they provide to patients they actually treat, they also yield collective benefits to all members of the community who feel more secure knowing that a local hospital is available should they need its services. (In the language of economic theory, this amounts to suggesting that a hospital partly has the characteristics of a local public good.) While this argument has some merit, it should also be recognized that if individuals cannot be treated in a local hospital, they can typically get treatment for most diseases by travelling to a hospital elsewhere. For this reason, it is important that savings in travel costs should be included as part of the return to investing in a local hospital (especially in remote communities in thinly populated areas), but provided these benefits have been properly taken into account, there is no reason to require a lower return on investment in health facilities than in other projects or facilities.

3. Methods for Funding Hospitals

As in the case of primary care, a range of different methods have been used across the world to pay the providers of hospital care for their services. This is not surprising, given the differences across countries not only in terms of who owns the hospitals (governments, charitable institutions, private investors), but also with respect to who pays for hospital care (patients, private or government insurance plans, or governments directly). In the next subsections, we describe the most important methods.

3.1. *Charging patients or their insurance plans: Itemized billing*

In some countries, notably Japan and the U.S., almost all of the revenue that hospitals receive comes from charges payable by patients or their insurance plans after each admission and treatment episode. Under this method of funding, the basis of payment is typically a bill in which hospitals' billing departments show exactly what services (and drugs) each patient has received while being treated, and add up the charges that the hospital makes for each unit of service. This method is sometimes referred to as "itemized billing"; it is similar to the method of fee-for-service in the provision of primary care and specialist physician services.

In high-income countries that rely on itemized billing as the principal method for funding hospitals, the proportion of the total cost that is paid by patients out-of-pocket is typically fairly small as most of the cost is covered by the patients' insurance plans. These plans may be private or public, or both. In some places, the bill is payable by the patient, who then obtains reimbursement after filing a claim with the insurance plan. In other cases, all or part of the bill is sent directly to the insurance plan, and any co-payment required from the patient may be collected either by the hospital or by the insurance plan.

A key question in systems that rely wholly or in part on itemized billing is how the charges for the individual services, or the markups on the drugs the hospitals supply, are determined. In some places, hospitals are allowed to decide their own charges, without restrictions. The expectation in such cases is that competition among hospitals will be sufficiently effective to protect patients (or their insurance plans) from charges that exceed the hospitals' costs by an excessive margin, especially in situations where many hospitals in the market are operated by government or by non-profit entities, so that their managers are not expected to make a profit.[6]

As the costs of hospital care have been increasing, however, governments have intervened in various ways to restrict and control hospital charges. For example, while hospital funding in Japan continues to be on the basis of fee-for-service, central government regulation now determines what hospitals, private or public, can charge for every kind of service for which they bill patients' insurance plans. Even in the U.S., the charges that hospitals make for treating patients over age 65 who are covered by the federal Medicare plan are controlled by a system known as Diagnosis-Related Groups, further discussed below. Nevertheless, among countries where hospitals continue to be funded through itemized billing to a large extent, the U.S. remains one of the systems in which there is least government regulation of hospital fees. In part, this is because competition in U.S. hospital markets has become more intense as a result of an increasing role of private insurance plans as purchasers of hospital services on behalf of their clients, as also further discussed below.

---

[6]Recent surveys of the effectiveness of competition in the markets for hospital care in various countries are Propper and Leckie (2011) and Gaynor and Town (2012).

3.2. *Itemized billing and fee-for-service: Hospitals as doctors' workshops*

Most of the doctors who treat patients in Western hospitals are specialists who deal only with particular types of illness conditions (except perhaps for doctors who supply primary-care services in hospitals' outpatient or emergency departments). Many of the specialists who supply secondary or higher-level care do so in hospitals because their patients need to spend part of their convalescence in hospital as in-patients, or because the hospitals have the kind of advanced equipment that they need to treat the patients. However, certain kinds of specialist services can also be provided in clinics outside hospitals. In high-income countries, specialties such as ophthalmology (dealing with diseases of the eye) often are practiced by private doctors in their own clinics. Many other specialists also supply some of their diagnostic and continuing-care services in clinics of their own, although they perform some of the procedures that require advanced equipment, or a period of in-patient convalescence, in hospitals. Some specialists, finally, perform all their services within the hospital.

In specialties where some or all of the treatment is performed in a hospital, the beds, equipment, and ancillary services provided by the hospital can be regarded as one of the inputs that is used in conjunction with the services of the specialist doctors in the treatment process. For this reason, hospitals have sometimes been referred to as doctors' "workshops", by analogy with the way production takes place in, for example, the repair and maintenance of motor vehicles, where skilled mechanics use the facilities and equipment of repair shops to do their work.[7]

In activities of this type, the services of the professional and the workshop may be supplied as a package consisting of the services of both the professional (the doctor) and the workshop (the hospital), by a single producing firm which owns the workshop facilities and employs the skilled professional. This is the way hospital services are produced

---

[7] The expression became popular following the publication of the book titled *Doctors and Their Workshops* by Pauly (1980).

in most countries, for example, the U.K., Japan, or Germany, where most specialists are employed by the hospitals in which they work, and the hospital pays them out of the revenue they collect from patients and insurers.

However, an alternative model is when the skilled professionals (the specialist doctors) sell their services individually to patients, while the facilities of the workshop (the hospital) are provided by a separate firm which may be paid either by the professionals (the doctors, who pay for the services of the hospital out of the revenue they collect from the patients), or by the buyers (patients or their insurers) separately. As noted above, this model is the one that has traditionally been used in the U.S. and Canada, where most specialist doctors are not employed by hospitals, though they treat their patients there. In the U.S. and Canada, most specialists are paid independently by patients or their insurers via fee-for-service, while the hospitals in which they work are paid separately via itemized billing (the U.S.) or through global budgets (Canada; see below).

In China today, most specialist services are supplied by doctors who are hospital employees, but we will return later to the issue of whether there may be a role for independently practicing specialists in China's health care system in the future. To some extent, the two models can be combined, as they are in the U.K. where specialist doctors are employed by the hospitals in which they work, but they are allowed to practice privately on a part-time basis. In some cases, they are allowed to treat their private patients in the hospitals where they are employed. When this happens, the patient is typically not billed separately for the hospital services (as they are in the U.S.), but the revenue that the doctors can earn by treating private patients in the hospital can be taken into account when negotiating the doctor's salary from the hospital. This form of "dual practice" may be a useful model in certain places in China.

3.3. *Financing hospitals through global budgets*

While itemized billing has been the most common way of paying for hospital services in places where most hospital revenue comes from patients or private insurers, other methods have been more common in countries where health care financing is dominated by direct funding from government, or from government-organized social insurance plans. In the U.K. and Canada, where acute-care hospitals are funded directly by governments and patients pay nothing out of their own pockets, the method used is that of a "global budget". Under global-budget financing, each hospital submits a budget at the beginning of the fiscal year in which it provides estimates of the resources it needs to pay the salaries of its employees and other costs. This budget is then the starting point for negotiations between the hospital and the local government funding agency, which result in a revised figure that becomes the hospital's adjusted global budget for the following year.[8]

From the viewpoint of the government officials who are in charge of financing the hospitals, an advantage of funding through global budgets is that, in principle, it allows a high degree of control over aggregate costs. However, from the viewpoint of the system as a whole, a disadvantage is that there is no direct and transparent link between the budget that each hospital gets and the services it produces, as further discussed below. While funding agencies may collect and compare data on various aspects of their operations from the hospitals and adjust funding in accordance with various productivity measures over time, in practice, adjustments are incremental, meaning that budgets only change slowly, even in cases where there are big differences in the efficiency with which different hospitals use their resources. Moreover, since circumstances change from year to year, hospital managers must have some flexibility and be allowed to spend beyond their budgets at least temporarily. But in some cases, letting them do so has resulted in protracted deficits that in the end have been covered by government, meaning that in reality, the funding agencies have not been able to

---

[8]The term "global" is used as an indication that hospital managers have a high degree of discretion in terms of how they distribute their total budget across different expenditure items, as long as they stay within the given total budget. In earlier models, it was common for managers to get separate budgets for different types of expenditure, with little or no authority to use surpluses for one budget item to cover deficits for other ones.

exercise effective control over aggregate spending. That is, hospital managers have not always been subject to "hard budget constraints".[9]

Funding of hospitals through direct government subsidies can of course be combined with other methods. While hospitals in China in recent years have covered most of their costs through charging patients or markups on the drugs they have sold, most of the government-owned ones have continued to receive at least some direct subsidies from local governments. The extent of these government subsidies has varied from place to place, so that the aggregate statistics in Table 1, for example, are averages that may differ a great deal from the corresponding figures in different provinces or individual cities or counties. Similarly, the rules that determine the subsidies may be different as well, so that while hospital managers in some places may face hard budget constraints, others do not.

3.4. *Prospective methods: Capitation and case-based funding*

Itemized billing by hospitals and through fee-for-service by doctors are methods of paying providers that share an important characteristic: The amount that a patient or his/her insurance plan is required to pay is determined *after* treatment has been completed, so that the quantity of each different service that has been performed is known. For this reason, these methods are referred to in the literature as "retrospective". This distinguishes them from certain other payment methods that are described as "prospective", meaning that the amount of payment is determined, at least in principle, *before* treatment has actually taken place. Under prospective payment methods, therefore, providers are not paid for the services they have actually performed in treating their patients. Instead, they are paid in return for an implicit promise to provide whatever services the patients need. Since the quantities of different services that will be needed and performed when individual patients are treated for different health problems cannot be exactly predicted, prospective payment methods are sometimes said to "put

---

[9]As an example, a recent newspaper headline from the U.K. states: "Ailing NHS hospital trusts receive multi-million pound bailout" (*The Guardian*, July 5, 2012).

providers at risk". A provider who is unlucky and treats patients that are difficult cases and require a large volume of services is paid the same as one whose cases are straightforward and easy to treat.

Payment of primary-care providers through capitation, discussed in the previous chapter, is an example of a prospective funding method. Under capitation in primary care, the providers agree to supply whatever primary-care services their patients need during the contract period, in return for an agreed payment for each patient on their list. In principle, capitation can be used in funding hospitals as well. That is, a hospital can agree to supply a specified set of services to anyone from a given patient population who needs them, in return for a fixed payment per person in the population.[10] However, in financing hospitals, another form of prospective funding has gradually become more common, originally in the U.S. but later throughout many other countries elsewhere: case-based funding.

The basic principle underlying various forms of case-based funding is a list of well-defined health problems and their associated treatment approaches. For example, it will include various kinds of surgery: heart operations, knee and hip replacements, eye surgery, etc. For each item on the list, a payment to the hospital is specified, and the hospital receives this amount for each patient who is admitted for this type of treatment. In principle, the amount that the hospital will receive for each such patient, therefore, is determined in advance, before it is known how long the patient stayed in the hospital, or what services were actually performed while the patient was there.

The most well-known form of prospective case-based funding is probably the system of Diagnosis-Related Groups (DRGs). While the DRG approach was initially developed for use in the U.S. Medicare

---

[10] In the U.S. health care system, many patients are insured through membership in a Health Maintenance Organization (HMO). Under HMO plans, the HMO undertakes to provide patients with all primary care and hospital services they need during the contract period, in return for a fixed premium. Health insurance through membership in an HMO can be regarded as a comprehensive capitation contract that covers all needed health care, with the premium taking the place of the capitation payment. Shanghai has started a pilot project by reimbursing primary hospitals on the basis of capitation for enrollees under NCMS. See *Xinmin News*, August 26, 2012.

plan, it has subsequently come into use in many other plans, including not only private-sector managed care plans in the U.S., but also to some extent in countries with universal government-organized plans. For example, versions of the DRG system have been used for systematic cost comparisons among hospitals in some Canadian provinces, or as the basis for negotiations between local funding agencies and individual hospitals in the U.K. NHS, even though financing through global budgets continues to be the predominant method in both those countries.

The list of diagnoses used in the U.S. Medicare's DRG plan is an extensive one. When it was first introduced, it contained some 470 different disease conditions, differentiated not only by disease types but also by factors such as co-morbidities, degrees of severity, and so on. In principle, the amount of revenue that the hospital will receive for treating a patient with a given condition is then supposed to be fixed once the patient has been placed in one of the DRG categories, and will not vary depending on the types and quantities of specific services the patient receives while in hospital. In practice, there may be some exceptions (such as "outlier" payments for patients who end up needing exceptionally large amounts of services), but the fundamental idea that for most patients, hospitals should not be rewarded for producing a large volume of services, has generally been respected.[11]

4. The Markets for Hospital Services, Incentives, and Competition

As is evident from the above discussion, very different methods are used for financing and managing hospitals in different countries. They may be private or owned by government, and if privately owned, operated as either non-profit or for-profit firms; their operating costs can be covered by direct subsidies from government, by publicly organized social insurance programs and/or private insurance plans, and by patients directly, in combinations that differ widely from country to country. Questions regarding the relative role of private

---

[11] An analysis of the effects of outlier payments under DRG-type systems is in Felder (2009).

and government hospitals, or with respect to what sources will be used to finance their operations, are important elements in the formulation of a long-term health policy strategy in China.

However, the efficiency of the hospital sector is not directly determined by whether hospitals are privately owned or owned by government, or what the source of their funding is. Instead, as in any organization, their performance depends largely on the quality of the decisions made by those in charge of the hospital's activities, principally its managers, but also the doctors who treat its patients. These decisions, in turn, are influenced by the incentives to which managers and doctors are subjected.

In this section, we discuss how the incentives on hospital decision-makers differ across the different funding mechanisms described in the previous section. But while the choice of funding method is the main determinant of the *direction* in which their decisions are steered, of equal importance for the sector is the *strength* of the incentives to which they are subjected. To what extent are hospital managers and doctors rewarded for using resources efficiently and for reducing the costs to society of providing health care?

The answer may partly depend on whether the hospitals are owned by government or by private investors, and whether they are operated as for-profit or non-profit entities. It may also depend on the degree of competition in the local market for hospital services. If there is little competition, individual hospitals do not have to be concerned about losing patients to competitors and are less motivated to control the costs of producing services. Indirectly, the intensity of competition may also depend not only on whether there are both government-owned and private hospitals in the system, but also on the extent to which their revenue comes from government or patients and private insurers, and, again, on which of the different funding methods is the predominant one.

4.1. *Global budgets and incentives*

The methods of payment that are generally regarded as having the weakest incentives for efficient performance are global budgets for hospitals, with fixed salaries for their doctors — methods that have been used at various times in countries like the U.K., Sweden, and Canada, and that were predominant in the Chinese system during the era of central planning.

Under the global budget model, each hospital is simply allocated a fixed sum from which it must cover its operating costs in the coming year, and each doctor's salary is fixed at the beginning of each year. The reason these methods are considered as having weak incentive effects is that the amounts that hospitals and doctors will receive do not explicitly depend on measures of their activity (services produced, or patients treated). Implicitly, there is obviously an expectation that a hospital will only continue to be funded if its performance meets at least some minimum standards of productivity, and salaried employees are subject to sanctions or dismissal if they shirk their duties. However, the links between reward and performance are not immediate, and threats of drastic consequences such as closing the hospital or dismissing an employee are likely to be somewhat ineffective except in very blatant cases.[12]

When hospital funding is through global budgets and fixed salaries, competition among providers is also likely to be weak. Once a hospital's budget for the year has been fixed, its managers are not rewarded for attracting additional patients during the year, for example, by trying to raise the quality of the services they provide. Neither are they rewarded for trying to reduce costs so as to produce a surplus; doing so may simply result in the payer reducing the size of the budget in future years.

4.2. Itemized billing and cost per case

When hospital funding is through revenues earned by itemized billing of patients or their insurance plans for the services they have received, as in Japan or the U.S., the incentive on providers is to provide a large volume of services since this raises their income. But while an incentive

---

[12]Christianson and Conrad (2011) review and compare the incentive effects of fixed budgets and salaries and other payment methods.

to produce a large amount of output generally is consistent with the objective of encouraging good performance in other industries, in the context of health care it may not be so.

The reason is that in health care, the amount of services supplied to an individual patient sometimes is larger than the amount that would be efficient from an economic point of view. This may happen partly because when patients are insured, they may pay much less than the full cost of the services they receive, so their incentive to limit the cost of the services they utilize is relatively weak. Moreover, patients typically do not have enough information to evaluate the true benefits of the services they receive, and have to rely on the advice of their doctors to decide what treatment they will get when they are ill. But if the provider has an incentive to supply each patient with a large volume of services, the concept of Supplier-Induced Demand (SID) suggests that the amount provided to individual patients may be larger than would be justified by the expected health benefits, or than would be in the patients' true interests; in extreme cases it may also leave individual patients impoverished.

The tendency for hospitals and specialist doctors to generate SID and supply too much costly care to individual patients may lead to inefficiency even in situations where there are relatively few doctors and limited hospital capacity. While the volume of services that will be produced in the aggregate may not be inefficiently large, the incentive on providers to supply a large volume of services to individual patients may lead to an outcome where some patients (for example, those in rural areas) will not be able to get treatment even if it is urgently needed, while others (for example, patients in large cities who go to hospitals with advanced facilities and equipment) receive more services, and more costly services, than can be justified by their condition. This dilemma may describe the situation in parts of China today.

The factors that may lead to a tendency for individual patients to be supplied with a high amount of costly care also are likely to affect the extent and nature of competition in the markets for secondary care. If a large share of the patients' costs is paid by their insurance plans, they do not have a strong incentive to search among competing providers (other hospitals and specialists instead of just the nearest one), even in a situation where they do have a choice. Furthermore, patients' lack of specialized information about the nature of their health problems and with respect to what care might benefit them makes it unrealistic to expect them to compare offers from competing providers.

By definition, in cases where buyers have neither a strong incentive to search among sellers for the best terms, nor enough information to effectively evaluate competing offers, the threat of competition will not imply a strong incentive on sellers to offer buyers favorable terms. As a result, hospital and physician charges will tend to be high and rise rapidly as new technology creates new and costly ways to treat patients, hospital capacity will tend to expand, and many hospitals will have enough revenue to acquire advanced equipment to treat even rare diseases. All these tendencies were present in health care systems such as the American one during the 1970s and 1980s — a period when health care costs were rising very rapidly — and they seem to be present in some places in China today.

Different approaches have been used to deal with the problem of weak intensity of competition in the hospital sector in systems where hospitals are funded through itemized billing for their services. One approach has been fee regulation, as in Japan, where hospitals continue to be funded predominantly by billing the social insurance plan for the services they have provided, but where individual fees are fixed, in fine detail, by the government.

In Japan, the system of detailed regulation of hospital fees appears to have been successful in keeping hospital costs under control with reasonable effectiveness.[13] However, like other forms of price control, regulation of hospital charges creates certain undesirable side effects. One problem arises because hospitals have large fixed and common costs (such as administration and finance). If these are to be covered from the revenues that the hospitals bill for their services, the fees they charge must be higher than the marginal cost of providing the services. But when the revenue from providing additional services to a patient exceeds the cost of the services, hospitals continue to have an incentive

---

[13]A recent review of the Japanese experience is Ikegami and Anderson (2012). Note that for hospitals, however, Japan now uses a form of prospective funding.

to provide a large volume of services (or a large quantity of drugs with high markups) to each patient, even with regulated fees.

In China, the fees that hospitals have charged for basic services have also continued to be regulated, sometimes at levels that most likely have been below the cost of producing them. Hence for basic services, hospitals have had no reason to supply more than what patients have needed. But what these hospitals have also had is a strong incentive to treat patients with non-basic services (or to prescribe advanced drugs) whose prices have not been regulated. A strategy under which hospitals take advantage of patients' lack of expertise to make them use more advanced services and drugs than they need can be considered as another form of SID. It appears to have been a major problem in China for a long time.

To reduce hospitals' incentive to engage in SID and to reward them for taking care of a larger number of patients would require a different funding method under which a hospital's total revenue would depend not only on the aggregate volume of services, but also on the number of patients treated. Indirectly, case-based funding methods such as the DRG do have this feature.

4.3. *Case-based funding, incentives and competition*

Another approach that has been used to counteract high hospital fees has been to promote more use of prospective payment methods such as case-based funding or capitation. In the hospital sector, this strategy was first applied in the U.S., but versions of case-based funding have been used in other countries as well, particularly the system of paying for hospitals through the Diagnosis-Related Group (DRG) method that was originally developed for the U.S. Medicare plan in the 1970s.

Clearly, the incentives on hospitals and doctors in the DRG system are quite different from those in a funding mechanism based on global annual budgets (in which the hospital's revenue does not directly depend on either the projected volume of services, nor on the number of patients treated), or on itemized billing (in which its revenue depends on the total volumes of different types of services provided, but not on the number of patients). Under the DRG system, a hospital's revenue is higher the larger the number of patients in each category that it treats, and its *net* revenue is larger the lower the cost of the services and resources it uses to treat each patient. Thus, for a given patient population, the incentives on the hospital are such as to encourage it, and its doctors, to make decisions that are consistent with the objective of the government body or private insurance plans that pay them: to treat as many cases as possible, but at a low average cost per case.

The incentive features of the DRG system are similar in important respects to those of compensation of primary-care providers via capitation, as described in Chapter 4. In both cases, providers have an interest in reducing the resources used to treat each individual patient, so as to make it possible to earn a higher total revenue by taking responsibility for more patients. While this incentive tends to reduce the total cost of resources used to treat a given population, it also implies a potential threat to the quality of care that providers offer, but there are ways of dealing with this problem (see below).[14]

Paying hospitals through a case-based funding method such as DRG also has the advantage that it can potentially create a more competitive environment. In principle, this would be true even if payment were to come from patients, rather than from their insurance plans. With case-based payment, patients would be told in advance how much they would have to pay for treatment of a particular problem in a given hospital, and could compare this amount with quotes from other hospitals. Under itemized billing, in contrast, such comparisons would not be possible, since the final bill would depend on what bundle of different services were provided for a given treatment episode, not just on the fee levels for the individual services.

In practice, however, the reason case-based funding has been associated with more competition in the hospital services markets in some countries is that it has been the basis for negotiations between hospitals and insurance plans, not between hospitals and individual patients. These negotiations have taken place as a result of an important

---

[14]Recent reviews of the evidence regarding the effects of prospective hospital funding are in Dranove (2012), and also in Christianson and Conrad (2011).

development in the market for hospital care and other health services in a number of countries — "selective contracting" between providers and insurance plans.

4.4. *Payment methods, competition and selective contracting*

The efforts by insurance plans in the U.S. and elsewhere to contain the cost of the hospital services supplied to their clients can be seen partly as a response to competition in the market for private health insurance. Some decades ago, most private insurance plans gave patients a wide range of choice with respect to which doctors or hospitals to seek care from. The plans would pay their share of the bill as long as the services were supplied by a licensed doctor or an accredited hospital. Often, the plans specified limits on the amounts that they would reimburse patients for specific services, but these limits only referred to the amounts that the patients could receive from the insurance plan, not the amounts that the hospitals or doctors could charge. In cases where the providers charged fees that exceeded these limits by large amounts, patients would discover that they had large out-of-pocket costs even though they were covered by insurance.

The approach of "selective contracting" that has changed the nature of competition in the U.S. market for hospital and specialist care was developed as insurance plans began to offer consumers a choice of plans under which they would only be covered (or fully covered) for services *from a list of approved providers*. Although they did not offer as wide a choice of providers as conventional plans, the selective-contracting plans had two offsetting advantages. First, they offered coverage that was less expensive, in terms of the monthly premiums that consumers (or their employers) had to pay for comparable coverage. Second, they implied less uncertainty for consumers with respect to their out-of-pocket costs, because the fees that providers would charge, and sometimes other terms according to which services would be supplied, had been negotiated in advance between the plans and the providers. Only providers that had agreed to the plans' fees and other conditions were included on the plans' lists of approved providers. Under such selective contracting plans, the ability of buyers to negotiate favorable fees and other terms was greatly strengthened, since the negotiations were conducted ahead of time between providers and insurance plans that represented the buying power of many existing and future clients. As a result, the negotiations typically resulted in much more favorable terms to the buyers than in cases where the terms were established on the basis of bills submitted to individual patients after they had received treatment.

The selective contracting plans that began to be introduced in the U.S. system in the 1970s have gradually transformed the nature of competition and pricing of hospital and specialist services there, to the point that most private insurance plans in the U.S. today are of this type, and many of the court cases or research projects regarding these issues now involve the nature of contracts between providers and insurance plans, not between providers and individual patients.[15]

Selective contracting between insurers and providers indirectly strengthens the market power of patients, both because each insurer bargains on behalf of many patients simultaneously, and because it reduces the significance of the information asymmetry between buyers and sellers (insurance plans can afford to pay for expert advice about costs and benefits of different procedures in conducting the negotiations, something individual patients cannot do). In the market for hospital services, it is especially likely to create a more competitive environment if it is combined with case-based payment, since that method facilitates comparisons of the terms offered by different hospitals. We will return later to the issue of how these methods could be applied in China.[16]

---

[15]The effects of selective contracting on competition in the health care sector are discussed in detail in the reviews by Gaynor and Town (2012) and Dranove (2012).

[16]Since the Medicare plan in the U.S. that covers all U.S. citizens aged 65 years or more is a government plan, the introduction of the DRG system as the basis of payment for hospital services rendered to Medicare beneficiaries can be interpreted as an example of government regulation in the market for hospital and specialist services. However, it can also be considered as a competitive innovation in the insurance market, since no U.S. citizen is compelled to be part of the Medicare plan, and, in principle, individual hospitals are not required to accept the terms offered by the plan.

5. Hospital Performance and Incentives: Additional Considerations

5.1. *Scale economies and travel costs*

A great deal of empirical research has been conducted, especially in the U.S., aimed at measuring and comparing hospitals' performance. Because hospital costs are such a large share of total health care costs, and because they had been growing rapidly over time, early studies focused mostly on measures of cost.

Interpreting comparative cost studies across hospitals is difficult because hospitals differ so much in terms of what types of cases they treat, and the cost per case (or per patient-day) will obviously vary a great deal depending on the proportion of different kinds of cases that are treated in a given hospital. Not unexpectedly, one pattern that tends to emerge from cost studies is that there are economies of scale over some range. If a hospital is too small, its costs per case tend to be high, regardless of what types of patients are treated in it. However, for hospitals that treat patients with only relatively uncomplicated problems, it is possible to attain relatively low cost even in hospitals that are not very large.

Taking into account that for patients, it is more costly, both in terms of money and in terms of disruptions for themselves and their families, to be treated in a hospital that is far away from where they live, a network of relatively small community hospitals is likely to be an element in a well-functioning hospital system. However, this conclusion is only likely to hold if the range of cases that are treated in community hospitals is relatively limited, so that they only accept patients with relatively common and uncomplicated problems. A pattern found in U.S. data is that costs tend to be very high in small hospitals, especially if they offer a wide range of services, some of which involve patients with relatively uncommon conditions or significant complications.[17]

---

[17]References to the literature on hospitals' costs and scale are in Barros and Olivella (2011). Trinh, Begun, and Luke (2008) discuss evidence on the effects when many hospitals offer a wide range of treatment technologies (sometimes referred to as the "medical arms race").

Part of the reason for this is that treatment of many types of patients requires specialized equipment, which may end up not being heavily utilized in a small hospital that treats only a small number of patients with given types of problems, implying higher cost per case treated. In the design of China's future health care system, the task of establishing the proper balance between scale economies and patient access costs will require a high degree of coordination between different levels of government so as to create an efficient allocation of responsibility for various specialized services, e.g., between rural county hospitals and tertiary hospitals in urban areas.

5.2. Scale economies, cost and quality of care

As hospitals have come under increasing pressure to contain costs, there has been increasing recognition of the fact that different hospitals may offer care of different quality. In particular, if hospitals focus too much on reducing costs per case, the quality of the care they offer may deteriorate. If too few resources are used to treat patients with various health problems, the expected outcomes may ultimately become significantly worse. To counterbalance this threat, the use of compensation methods such as capitation or DRGs must be accompanied by measures that strengthen providers' accountability for the quality of care, as well as for its cost. To some extent, this can be accomplished by administrative means, such as creation of explicit mechanisms through which patients may file complaints when they believe they have not been properly treated, and specification of appropriate sanctions for providers in cases where it can be established that the complaints are justified.

In addition, the implicit incentive to supply care of high quality that providers have because they want to behave as responsible professionals and safeguard their reputation can be strengthened through rules that make information about past outcomes more easily available to patients. In the U.S., there has been a great deal of discussion about how systematic reporting of, for example, the frequency of adverse outcomes associated with various types of operations, can be translated into a more competitive environment for hospital services to promote provider choices that strike the best balance between resource costs and quality of care.[18]

A large amount of research has been done in recent years on the extent to which there are differences across providers in terms of expected outcomes for different kinds of cases (for example, the proportion of patients who die in hospital whilst undergoing a given procedure), and what factors can explain such differences. A very clear pattern has emerged from this research, namely that the chances of a good outcome for many types of treatment increase dramatically when it is performed in a hospital that has a high volume of such cases. This pattern obviously reinforces the conclusions from the earlier literature in which it was found that the cost per case for many types of treatment tends to be higher in small hospitals that only have a small number of such cases per year. Because there is also a tendency for hospitals with a high volume of particular cases to obtain a better expected outcome, the cost *per successful treatment* is even more favorable when volume is high.

Questions with respect to the allocation of resources to hospitals will be important for future Chinese health policy, as will the issue of how to ensure that hospitals provide services of high quality with good outcomes on average. In the U.S., part of the reason for the problem of too many resources spent on providing a wide range of services in small hospitals may have been the desire of hospital managers everywhere, even in small communities, to strengthen the local reputation of their hospitals, among both patients and specialists, without too much regard for the impact on their costs or the problem of relatively unfavorable outcome statistics when volume is low. Doing so may have been relatively easy because many of the hospitals were non-profit institutions with weak monitoring of their financial results by either owners or insurance plans, and because outcome statistics were not widely publicized. While the hospital system is managed differently in China, the issue of ambitious local managers wanting

---

[18] For a review, see Dranove (2012). Porter and Teisberg (2006) stress the importance of consumer information about treatment outcomes as an important element in a strategy to improve the cost-effectiveness in U.S. health care.

to offer a wide range of services in their local hospital may be relevant there as well, and well-defined rules regarding what kinds of care will be offered in different hospitals could help accomplish more efficient use of aggregate health resources.

6. Hospital Reform in China

6.1. *China's hospital system since the 1980s*

In comparison with the pre-1980 period, China's hospital system has undergone dramatic change. While the vast majority of hospitals continue to be owned by government, the way they were funded and managed in 2010 was very different from what it had been 30 years earlier. In terms of the approaches discussed earlier, the system had moved from one similar to the global budget models in the U.K. or Canada, to a model based largely on itemized billing, the method that has been predominant in the U.S. system for many years. With respect to management, hospitals were given more autonomy. Consistent with the reforms implemented in other state-owned enterprises at that time, hospital managers were also given much more discretionary power over any surpluses that they could earn from patient charges and drug markups, giving them the ability to expand hospital facilities and acquire various types of capital equipment on their own initiative.

But while China's hospital sector had become more like the U.S. one toward the end of the first decade of the 21st century, major differences remained. First, while American hospitals still retain the right to set the fees they charge patients and their insurers — at least for patients outside the government plans — in China, the government has continued to impose strict regulations on the fees hospitals were allowed to charge for a wide range of basic medical services.[19] In contrast to the case of Japan, however, the fee controls were not comprehensive. The fees for many types of newly developed (often costly) services were not controlled; a similar pattern prevailed with respect to drug prices. As noted earlier, the distortions resulting from

---

[19] See He and Qian (2013) for a recent empirical study on the effect of administrative regulation on hospital revenue in public hospitals in China.

the fact that some fees and prices were subject to controls were part of the explanation for the problems that subsequently arose.

With respect to management, hospitals were given more autonomy in some areas, but not everywhere. Unlike many other state-owned enterprises, hospitals were not given a great deal of discretion over personnel management, so that doctors and other staff continued to be classified as state employees who were paid according to public-sector rules, and who could only be appointed or terminated by state authorities.

Another gradual change that took place in the role of hospitals in the 1980s and 1990s was their increasing role in becoming patients' first point of contact with the health care system and in delivering primary care, as the extent of primary-care provision in agricultural communes or by urban employers diminished. As more patients came directly to hospitals without first having been diagnosed and referred by a primary-care provider, there were more opportunities for hospital doctors to exercise discretion with respect to what procedures or drugs to recommend to the patients, and the rapidly rising cost per episode of treatment over this period indicates that doctors sometimes exercised this discretion in a way that responded to the increased incentives that the hospitals had to raise revenue.[20] In part, costs rose because hospital doctors increased the frequency with which they recommended treatment using newer advanced methods and drugs whose prices were not controlled. Even though hospital doctors' basic salaries were fixed by state rules, managers were sometimes able to pay incremental bonuses that were linked to the hospitals' revenues from each doctor's patients, thus giving the doctors an incentive to recommend more expensive procedures and drugs. These changes in the patterns of activity and costs in the hospital sector formed much of the basis for the sharp criticism of the earlier approaches to health sector reform that were advanced by, among others, the Development Research Center in its influential 2005 report discussed in Chapters 3 and 4.

---

[20]That is, generating SID.

6.2. Hospital reform in the 2009 guidelines

In the new directions for health system reform that were announced in April 2009, there was reference to reform of the hospital sector as one of the key elements. However, the plans outlined with respect to this element were not as clear as those referring to the new approaches to social insurance, primary care or pharmaceuticals, and by 2011, reforms in the latter areas were more advanced than those referring to the hospital sector. Two documents giving further guidelines to local authorities with respect to hospital reform were released in 2009 and 2010,[21] with the former concentrating more on general principles and the latter going into more detail with respect to concrete measures, for example, regarding the use of pharmaceuticals in hospitals, and listing the sites where certain pilot projects were to be carried out. These sites included 16 cities where pilot projects would be conducted under central government supervision (see Table 3), and 37 localities where they would be provincially managed.

Many of the sites listed in Table 3 are cities in which different approaches to hospital reform have already been tried out for some time, approaches that potentially will be role models for future hospital reform nationwide.

Evidence from the various pilot projects will only emerge gradually, and controversy over what is the best general approach will continue to rage in China for a long time to come. However, while the overall pattern of future hospital reform is still uncertain, there is one area where plans are quite clear, and where they are already being implemented, namely with respect to the use of pharmaceuticals in hospitals. Specifically, government-owned hospitals (which continue to

---

[21]For the 2009 State Council guidelines, see http://www.gov.cn/zwgk/2009-04/07/content_1279256.htm (accessed on May 29, 2012). In February 2010, five ministries including the Ministry of Health, Ministry of Finance, Ministry of Human Resources and Social Security, and the National Development and Reform Commission and the State Commission Office for Public Sector Reform released a guideline for public hospital reform; see http://news.xinhuanet.com/fortune/2010-02/23/content_13033577.htm (accessed on May 29, 2012).

Table 3. 16 cities for pilot hospital
reform announced in February 2010.

City	Province	Region
Anshan	Liaoning	Eastern
Shanghai	Shanghai	Eastern
Zhenjiang	Jiangsu	Eastern
Xiamen	Fujian	Eastern
Weifang	Shandong	Eastern
Shenzhen	Guangdong	Eastern
Qitaihe	Heilongjiang	Central
Wuhu	Anhui	Central
Maanshan	Anhui	Central
Luoyang	Henan	Central
Erzhou	Hubei	Central
Zhuzhou	Hunan	Central
Zunyi	Guizhou	Western
Kunming	Yunnan	Western
Baoji	Shaanxi	Western
Xining	Qinghai	Western

Source: Xinhua News Agency.[22]

dominate the system, accounting for over 90% of total hospital revenue in 2011[23]) will be required to supply all basic drugs to patients at no markup (although patients will be required to pay a fixed prescription fee). In compensation, the hospitals will receive more fiscal subsidies and transfers from the social insurance funds. Given the large share of hospital revenue that had previously been derived from markups on drugs, this obviously is a major, and potentially controversial, reform measure, and implementing it fully will be a task that will occupy state and local health policy authorities over at least the medium-term future. The fact that the network of primary-care clinics currently under construction also will be obliged to supply basic drugs at zero or low markups adds to the impact that this reform will have on the pharmaceutical industry, as further discussed in Chapter 6.

[22] http://news.xinhuanet.com/politics/2010-02/23/content_13033644.htm (accessed on May 29, 2012).
[23] *China Health Statistical Yearbook*, 2012.

At the more general level, the 2009 and 2010 guidelines for hospital reform list two principles that will try to address the perceived problems in the sector by making changes to the governance structure of government-owned hospitals. The first provides for increased autonomy and discretionary authority for hospitals and their managers with respect to personnel management and other employment terms. (In the document, this is referred to as a "separation" between the administrative government departments and the hospital's management.) The second principle, in contrast, refers to possible measures that will have the effect of placing stricter control over hospital managers with respect to investments and management of the hospital's finances. At the same time, the language in the guidelines also recognizes the possible usefulness of market mechanisms as increased competition among hospitals can improve efficiency and the quality of health services. If the second of these three elements (increased supervision and regulation by government) seems somewhat inconsistent with the first and the third (increased autonomy for individual hospitals and greater reliance on competition to protect the interests of the patients/buyers of hospital services), this once again may just be taken to reflect the lack of consensus in China about future directions of health care reform.

Under the switch to a more decentralized system of personnel management, hospital managers will have more control over matters relating to hiring, firing, and the terms of employment for the hospital's staff, including physicians who currently are part of the hierarchical cadre system whose terms of employment are strictly controlled by the state. Hospital managers will thus be less subject to restrictions imposed by local health bureaus and personnel bureaus, and will even be able to influence promotion decisions regarding the hospital's doctors. The guidelines also make explicit mention of the potentially useful role of performance-based incentives in the compensation of the doctors, and give hospital managers the authority to offer such contracts. The effects of such incentive contracts of course depend critically on the way performance is measured. The guidelines do not specify explicitly how this should be done in practice, and the question of how performance should be measured in practice is likely to be an important issue that will be debated as reforms are implemented. As noted earlier, bonus systems that have been used informally in the past have been mostly intended to encourage doctors to generate more revenue for the hospitals from their patients, which clearly is not the main objective that the guidelines intended in referring to the role of performance-based incentives.

Clearly, more flexibility for hospital managers in dealing with personnel issues can help them use their resources more efficiently and improve hospital productivity. This aspect of hospital reform may also make it easier for the sector to absorb the large increases in the number of physicians who will be seeking employment throughout China's provinces over the next several years, as medical students currently in the system complete their training. Although basic physician salaries may continue to be regulated, performance-based bonuses may gradually come to make up a larger share of their total compensation, giving larger scope for hospital managers' demand for new doctors in different specialties to be reflected in the offers that they receive in the respective markets. Over time, the relative attractiveness of offers in various specialties may then begin to influence medical students' choice of specialization, enabling a better balance between population health needs and the supply of new doctors.

6.3. *Government vs. market approaches in recent pilot projects*

The guidelines' emphasis on stricter regulation and supervision of hospitals' investments and financial management appears to reflect dissatisfaction with the long-term effects of the greater autonomy that hospitals have been given over time since the 1980s. It is of course widely believed that one of the main reasons for rapidly rising health care costs has been the incentive that hospitals have had to raise more revenue as they have been given greater control over what to do with their net earnings. One of the ways that many hospitals have used the money they have earned has been to invest in new, sometimes quite expensive, equipment which could be used to provide ("non-basic") services whose prices are not regulated, enabling them to raise even more revenue, and so on. As a result, the population, and the social insurance plans, have had to pay rapidly rising amounts to the hospitals, with much of the money going not to the governments that are the hospitals' owners, but to suppliers of high-end medical equipment and expensive drugs.

While the reform guidelines are not specific on the issue of how increased regulation and supervision of hospitals' financial affairs will influence this pattern, the way the guidelines have been interpreted in a number of pilot projects in some major cities provides some evidence on how local governments throughout China will react to them in future years.

One pilot project in Shanghai supplies an illustration. An institute called "Shenkang Hospital Development Center" which oversees three-fourths of all tertiary-level public hospitals was established in 2005.[24] It is designated as an institute independent of the health bureau. The duties of this institute include supervising resource allocations of public hospitals in terms of investments/loans, infrastructure building and mergers/acquisitions. For example, a hospital manager needs the endorsement of this supervisory institute if he wants to liquidate assets worth more than 50,000 Yuan. In addition, all hospitals' investment activities are required to be endorsed by the institute.[25] Hospitals should start to plan their budgets about half a year in advance, and this supervisory institute oversees public hospitals' annual budgets as well as fiscal subsidy allocation. Furthermore, the institute can procure drugs and equipment as well as bargain with insurers for public hospitals collectively. It evaluates hospital managers' performance, and managers may be fired if their performance is poor.[26] The health bureau's duty has been reduced to regulating the quality of services and entry of service providers, and planning of local resource allocation to all providers including private providers. At the same time, hospital managers are granted more power over issues such as personnel control, budget allocation within the hospital, compensation to physicians, and organizational reconstruction.

---

[24]See *Nanfengchuang*, April 28, 2009 (downloadable from http://news.sina.com.cn/c/sd/2009-04-28/092817704459.shtml) (accessed on May 29, 2012).
[25]See *Economic Observer*, January 7, 2010.
[26]Gao (2009).

A similar model has been implemented in Haidian district in Beijing.[27] An institute independent of the health bureau, called a "Public Service Administration Committee", is now supervising all public providers within the district. In both the cases of Shanghai and Beijing, these independent institutes report to the local government (i.e., in Shanghai's case, it is the city government; in Beijing's case, it is the district government). Two very similar governance patterns adopted by Suzhou and Wuxi city, Jiangsu province, are also thought to be useful models for the application of the principles of the hospital reform guidelines.

In the types of governance reform that are being tried in these pilot projects, the attempts to assert better control over rising hospital costs appear to be based principally on the government approach. The emphasis has been on redesigning the administrative arrangements governing the hospital sector and increasing the degree of centralization of the management of public hospitals, rather than on continued decentralization, competition, and incentives. It is difficult to predict how effective these methods will be. In some places, they may be successful in reducing costs, for example, by being better able to bargain with suppliers of medical and diagnostic equipment or drugs than individual hospitals are able to do. Moreover, oversight and regulation by a single central body may be more efficient than the earlier system where administrative responsibility for various aspects of hospital affairs was divided among several local agencies (the health bureau, the social insurance bureau, the personnel bureau, etc.), each one of which reported to higher-level counterparts. However, the new agencies' effectiveness will depend heavily on their composition, and on the skills and motivation of those who manage them. For example, if the agencies come to be managed by individuals who are sympathetic to the interests of the hospitals and their doctors and other personnel, they may end up negotiating arrangements with the social insurance plans that are more favorable to hospitals than what the hospitals would

---

[27] See *Medical and Pharmaceutical Economics News* ("*Yiyao Jingji Bao*"), December 1, 2008 (downloadable from http://news.91.cn/xwpd/jd/342284.htm) (accessed on May 29, 2012).

have been able to attain if they had negotiated individually with the plans.

In some other pilot projects, more market-oriented approaches that appear to leave more room for continued hospital autonomy and competition have been used. For example, in Wuhu city, Anhui province, the local hospitals organized themselves, with the encouragement of the local government, into three groups in which the hospitals in each group would be jointly managed, but where the groups are supposed to compete with each other.[28] However, as in the cases discussed above, there is a central committee, with representatives from the local health bureau, the social insurance bureau, and others, that is charged with overseeing all three groups. The head of the committee is the city's deputy mayor. All important investment, procurement, and appointment decisions in each of the groups must be endorsed by the committee, and the local government appoints the chief accountants of each group. A somewhat similar approach has been taken in Zhenjiang city, Jiangsu province, in which the local hospitals in 2009 were organized into two groups that are supposed to compete with each other. A unique feature of this experiment is that all community health centers in the city have also been allocated to one of the two groups. The purpose of this arrangement is to accomplish more efficient referral decisions between the primary-care providers in the community health centers and the units in the hospital group.[29]

6.4. *Using the evidence from pilot projects*

Since these pilot projects have only been operating for a few years, there is not yet a great deal of evidence on how well they have worked. While a model with several hospital groups that are supposed to be managed independently obviously offers more potential for competition in the sector than one with completely centralized management, whether competition will be effective depends on the extent to which local

---

[28] See *Economic Observer News*, April 19, 2010; and a report in *Oriental Outlook Weekly*, May 31, 2010.
[29] *China Economic Times*, April 14, 2010, http://business.sohu.com/20100414/n271497677.shtml (accessed on May 29, 2012).

government representatives or social insurance bureaus are prepared to reward one group over another, based on some measure of its performance. Moreover, for reasons discussed earlier, relying on competition by hospitals for individual patients as a measure of performance is not likely to give rise to effective competition as patients do not have enough expertise to judge the quality of care they can expect from different hospitals. Competition can be expected to be effective only if there is some agency (such as a social insurance plan acting as a purchaser of care) that can negotiate terms with hospitals and steer patients to those that offer the best terms.

While most hospitals in China continue to derive most of their revenue from itemized billing and drug sales, there is some experimentation with the other models of funding. The evidence that is being generated from these experiments will be carefully analyzed by future researchers. However, in doing so, it is important to recognize that the funding model that is used in a particular city or county is not the only, or even the most important, determinant of how efficiently the system operates. Of at least equal importance is the skill and determination with which local governments apply whichever funding model or management approach they are using. Thus, in evaluating the evidence relevant to the efficiency of different funding approaches, care must be taken to hold other factors as constant as possible, such as the extent to which local purchasers (county health boards or city social insurance bureaus) are effective in representing the interests of the patients on whose behalf they are contracting for services, rather than the interests of the providers who supply the services or of local government officials anxious for more revenue for investment.

One suggestion from some of the early evidence that already is available is that the progress of hospital reform and hospital costs will be influenced by the overall state of the local economy, as well as the fiscal situation of the local government. In a city like Shanghai where per capita income is high and the local government is in a good fiscal position, local government does not have a strong incentive to focus on the revenue that hospitals raise from patients. A hierarchical governance structure with carefully designed methods to monitor and evaluate hospital doctors may then be helpful in reducing profit-seeking behavior and controlling patient charges. Consistent with this, the public hospitals in Shanghai that were under the control of the managing agency (i.e., the Shenkang Hospital Development Center) achieved lower average annual growth rates of user fees for both in-patient and out-patient services every year from 2005 to 2009, compared to other hospitals in Shanghai that were not part of the project.[30] In contrast, the experience in Ma'anshan city where, before the reforms, public hospitals had been a major fiscal burden whose losses had to be covered by the local government, has been different. After a merger of five public hospitals into a single group overseen by a new management agency reporting to the local government, the hospitals' aggregate revenue increased by 11.6% in 2009.[31] In general, an important effect of the approaches to reforming the hospital system governance structure that have been used in the pilot projects appears to have been a strengthening of the control of the local government, at the expense of both the autonomy of hospital managers and, indirectly, the influence of higher levels of government. What the effects of these kinds of reform will be then depends on the relative responsiveness of local governments to various interest groups and to the public at large.

7. Conclusion: China's Hospitals in the Future

A well-functioning system of specialist and hospital care must meet two criteria. First, because treating patients in hospitals is costly in terms of resources, there must be a mechanism to ensure that the patients who are treated there could not have been treated equally effectively, but at a lower cost, in primary care, and that the only patients who are treated in hospital are those for whom the expected health benefits are large enough to justify the opportunity cost. Second, the patients who are treated in hospitals should receive care that is of high quality, but at a cost that is as low as possible.

To what extent the first criterion is met depends partly on whether or not there exists a well-functioning referral system between primary

---

[30]See *Oriental Outlook Weekly*, March 4, 2010.
[31]See *Economic Observer*, May 1, 2010.

and higher levels of care; methods for accomplishing this have been discussed previously in Chapter 4. It also depends on somehow ensuring that there are mechanisms to make certain that the only kinds of treatment that are offered at the secondary level of care are those that pass some kind of cost-effectiveness test; that is, treatment methods (or drugs) that have expected health benefits that are too low relative to what they cost should not be offered, even if many patients would like to receive them (either because they are ill-informed, or because they expect someone else to pay for them). In order for this to happen, there must be some actor in the health care system that actually performs or commissions the relevant cost-effectiveness evaluations, and is prepared to abide by them. There must also be ways of ensuring that specialists and hospitals provide truthful information about their capabilities, so that the evaluations are accurate. We will discuss these issues further in later chapters.

To meet the second criterion, doctors and hospitals in the system must have incentives to provide patients with care of high quality, but also to keep costs low. Since there is likely to be large differences among hospitals in terms of the cost and expected outcomes in treating patients with different conditions, this criterion also implies that there should be some mechanism to ensure that patients are treated in those hospitals that are most efficient at dealing with their particular problems. That is, in an efficient system, there is likely to be considerable specialization among hospitals, especially with respect to less common conditions that require advanced types of treatment.

In principle, central planning by government officials can be used to meet these criteria to a reasonable degree. However, the success of the central planning approach depends not only on highly skilled and well-informed officials, but also on a political system in which these officials are able to resist the various strong and aggressive vested interests, both from the private sector and from competing branches of the government, that are present in the health care system. Although government policy continues to have a great indirect influence on the hospital sector everywhere, in most developed countries, the trend in management of the hospital sector has been toward less centralized planning, and toward mechanisms that rely instead on various forms of decentralized decision-making in an environment where incentives and competition combine to encourage outcomes that conform to the societal objectives expressed in the two criteria above.

By definition, a decentralized model in which incentives and competition play a major role requires a high degree of autonomy for individual hospitals to manage their own affairs. As discussed above, while the process of hospital reform currently underway in China appears to move the system in the direction of more autonomy with respect to personnel management, some of the pilot projects in urban areas seem to imply a move toward *less* autonomy for hospitals with respect to financial matters, contrary to the trend observed in many other countries.

In one sense, this is not surprising, given the rapid cost increases and other problems that have resulted from the increased autonomy that hospitals have had since the 1980s. What the experience of the U.S. and other countries in an earlier era shows is that increased autonomy for hospitals and doctors on the supply side in the market for health services will not work well in unregulated markets where the terms of the transactions are established through competition among providers for individual patients. China's experience over the last several decades is an even more convincing demonstration of this. A market-based system will only work well in an environment in which there are well-informed agents with market power on the demand side, and where these agents are accountable in the sense that their principal objective is to obtain favorable terms for the patients whom they represent.

In the U.S. health care system, private insurance companies perform the role of effective purchasers when they offer plans with selective contracting, so that the terms according to which hospitals are paid are established in negotiations between the hospitals and the plans. For the Medicare plan, the terms of service have essentially been established unilaterally by the plan itself. Similarly, the model of universal health insurance that is being developed in Holland is based on markets in which consumers can choose among different subsidized insurance plans, and the terms according to which providers will be paid will be established through negotiations between the plans and the providers.

In some other countries, the agents that represent patients in negotiating the terms of hospital and specialist services are part of the government. For example, individual hospitals in Japan, both those that are privately owned and government hospitals, have considerable autonomy in managing their own affairs, but the fees that they are allowed to charge for individual services are established by an agency of the central government. In the case of the U.K., the decision to give hospitals much more autonomy than they had had before the 1980s was accompanied by the "purchaser-provider split" under which new local government agencies were created for the purpose of negotiating terms with hospital and specialist providers.

In China in recent years, there has been no agency on the demand side with a clear mandate to negotiate with hospitals so as to obtain favorable terms for the patients. While the state has regulated the fees that hospitals have been allowed to charge for certain basic health services and drugs, hospitals and their doctors have been able to circumvent those restrictions relatively easily in such a way as to enable them to raise more revenue from patients and their insurance plans. In some places, especially in large urban areas, the social insurance plans that collect state subsidies and premium revenue from enrollees have taken an active role in negotiating with hospitals regarding the terms on which their clients would be charged for treatment and drugs. However, the agencies managing these plans are part of the local government, which is also responsible for much of the cost of the hospitals. Thus, the agencies' incentive to negotiate terms of service provision that are favorable to patients has been tempered by the fact that they are part of a government that also has an interest in the revenues and financial health of the local hospitals.

In a system of health care financing that relies on private insurance plans, competition for clients in the insurance market is a force that may help ensure that patients are represented by agents with good information and market power (that is, their insurance plans) when the terms according to which they will receive services are negotiated. In a system where insurance is supplied indirectly, through government financing of health services or through social insurance plans controlled by the government, whether this happens depends on the nature of the political process. Public agencies representing patients will be able to do so effectively if they are clearly and explicitly accountable only to the potential buyers of health care, and are not influenced, directly or indirectly, by the interests of providers, or of government agencies that are linked to the providers. While China's political system at the local level may be evolving in the direction of greater accountability to taxpayers and users of public services, it is not clear that it has yet come far enough in many places to create agencies that can perform the health services purchasing function effectively. Whether the trend will continue is a critical question in itself, not just with respect to the likely performance of China's future health care system.

Chapter 6

CHINA'S NATIONAL DRUG POLICY: A WORK IN PROGRESS

1. Introduction

Pharmaceuticals constitute one of the most important inputs in the process through which the health care system produces improved population health. In China, it has been estimated that the cost of drugs has accounted for more than 40% of the total cost of health care in recent years.[1] This is considerably more than its share in most OECD countries where drug costs typically constitute 10%–25% of the total. However, drug costs have been rising more rapidly than other health care costs in other countries as well, and policy towards the pharmaceutical sector has been central to the debate over health policy in general in many countries.

We begin this chapter with a brief review of the special characteristics of the supply and demand sides of the global pharmaceutical industry, and the somewhat different policy approaches that different countries have employed to regulate the sector. We then turn to a discussion of the way the pharmaceutical sector has changed in China over the last several decades, and end the chapter with an analysis of the new policies with respect to essential drugs that were announced in late 2011 and which are still in the process of being implemented.

---

[1] Tarn *et al.* (2008).

2. Characteristics of the Pharmaceutical Industry: The Supply Side

The pharmaceutical industry is one of the most research-intensive of all major industries in the world. Rapid advances in fields such as biochemistry and molecular biology have enhanced our ability to observe and analyze the way human bodies function and hence to develop and experiment with new compounds that can help prevent or alleviate disease. Many of the drugs that we use today to combat various illnesses did not exist 30 to 40 years ago, and the development of new drugs that reduce death rates or improve patients' quality of life has made major contributions in reducing suffering and improving lives everywhere in the world.[2]

But the research and development that gives us new drugs is expensive, and a large share of the total revenue of pharmaceutical companies constitutes a return on resources they have spent in the past on developing the drugs they sell, rather than payment for the current cost of producing the drugs. A large portion of it goes to the big multinational companies that dominate the world's pharmaceutical industry. Some of them are very large indeed, with annual revenue of more than US$40 billion and more than 100,000 employees worldwide, but none of them is big enough to dominate any national market. Available statistics show around 20 firms with annual revenues of over $10 billion and more than 25,000 employees,[3] and many smaller firms. Most of the "big pharma" companies have their head offices in high-income countries (especially the U.S., U.K., Switzerland, Japan, Germany, and France), but there are also large pharmaceutical companies with headquarters in low- and middle-income countries. India and China, in particular, have firms that not only are capable of producing any of the drugs currently marketed throughout the world, but also to engage in research and development of new drugs.

---

[2]A compact survey of the pharmaceutical industry is Danzon (2011). A comprehensive reference work is Danzon and Nicholson (2012).

[3]A list based on CNN's Global 500 largest corporations can be found at en.wikipedia. org/wiki/List_of_pharmaceutical_companies.

2.1. Research and development costs and the international patent system

The R&D activities of the pharmaceutical industry are supported by the international patent system which raises the profitability of developing new products and hence helps attract the capital needed to do so. It does this by giving the patent owner a time-limited monopoly in the markets for the goods or services that make use of the technology that they have invented. Without a patent system, it would be legal for any firm to produce and sell any product without permission of the individual or firm that had invented and tested it, often at a high cost. As a result, private firms would not be willing to spend the resources to develop new products, since they would have no way of recouping their R&D costs. *With* a patent, the firm that developed a drug, for example, can charge a price that far exceeds the cost of producing it, and earn a monopoly profit on each unit sold, without fear of competition from other sellers.[4] It is the prospect of such monopoly profits that induces the private pharmaceutical firms to spend the R&D money to develop new drugs in the first place. Without this prospect, they would not do so.

While consumers (patients) benefit from the development of the new drugs, the benefit is reduced by the fact that they (or their insurance plans) have to pay the high (monopoly) price that the patent holder charges. For this reason, governments in many countries use direct regulation or other techniques to control the prices that the companies can charge on patented drugs. While lower controlled drug prices obviously benefit the country's consumers, they also reduce the patent holder's reward for having developed the drug, and hence the incentive to develop new drugs in the future.

The question of how to balance the objective of low drug prices for patients and insurers against the profits of the patent holders who have developed the drugs is answered differently in different countries. One relevant consideration is that, since most new drugs are developed

---

[4]Sometimes, the patent owner allows another firm to produce and sell the product it has developed under a licensing arrangement. The seller's monopoly profit will then accrue to the patent owner as a royalty or licensing fee.

by multinational pharmaceutical firms, the monopoly profits from a given patented drug come from many countries. The government in an individual country can then argue that a low controlled drug price in that country will only have a limited impact on the patent holders' total monopoly profit and hence on their incentive to develop new drugs in the future. Small countries therefore have an incentive to act as "free riders": that is, to benefit their own citizens by controlling drug prices at relatively low levels, while hoping that other countries will allow the pharmaceutical companies to charge high prices so as to maintain their incentive to develop new drugs. Similarly, small countries do not have strong incentives to prevent or discourage domestic firms from making profits by producing drugs that compete with those that the international pharmaceutical companies sell.

China of course is not a small country, and while it has some firms that are engaged in developing new drugs, it still does not have a major research-intensive pharmaceutical industry, so the patents on most patented brand-name drugs sold in China are owned by foreign pharmaceutical companies. Thus, the legislation that gives a monopoly to the owner of the patents on such drugs adds, directly or indirectly, to the revenue of foreign-owned firms. Other things equal, it would therefore be in China's interest to reduce or eliminate the extent of these monopoly rights. Since the seller's monopoly position typically results in a high price, allowing more competition from competing producers would result in some combination of higher profits for domestic firms and lower prices for the drugs that patients or their insurers pay for.

The legal rules that define the extent of patent protection and the way they are enforced are part of each country's national legislation, so like other countries, China has the right to formulate its legislation in a way that reflects its national interest. However, the rules that define the monopoly rights of sellers of brand-name drugs and other patented products, and how these rights are enforced, have also been an important element in the negotiations between China and other countries regarding international trade and China's membership in the World Trade Organization (WTO). In these negotiations, the United States and the European Union, which are net exporters of patented drugs, and where most multinational pharmaceutical companies are domiciled, have pushed hard for rules under which other countries would be forced to adopt rules and principles that would favor these companies. As part of the price that China had to pay for becoming a member of the WTO and getting access to other countries' markets for its exports and investment, the government has had to agree to abide by the rules formulated by the WTO regarding "trade-related aspects of intellectual property rights" (TRIPS).

The obligations that China has accepted under TRIPS imply that there are restrictions on the way China can formulate and enforce its patent laws, for example, with respect to such characteristics as the length of the patent period. But even with these restrictions, there are some measures that China can take for the purpose of reducing the cost that the patent system imposes. As will be discussed further below, the government can intervene on the buying side in the market for drugs, through regulation under which it negotiates maximum prices with pharmaceutical companies, or through the design of a drug purchasing system that creates market power on the buyers' side. Moreover, it can implement policies that strengthen the competitive position of the producers of the cheaper generic drugs that are allowed to enter the market in competition with brand-name drugs once their patent protection has expired.

2.2. *Brand-name drugs and generics*

Patent legislation in all countries contains a time limit for the duration of a patent holder's rights (typically 20 years from the time the patent was granted, which may be several years before a drug was first marketed). When a patent on a brand-name drug has expired, it is legal for anyone to produce and sell a generic version of it — that is, a drug with an identical combination of active chemical ingredients as the brand-name drug, but with a different name. Prices for generic drugs tend to be much lower than for the brand-name drug since anyone can produce and sell them, and while the brand-name drug typically continues to be sold after its patent has expired, its price will tend to come down as it is exposed to competition from generic versions.

While most of the newer drugs that are currently used in the health care system remain protected by patents, many that are used for common health problems have existed for a long time, so that legally produced generic versions exist. When they do, incentives on the demand side can be used to encourage the use of the lower-cost generics, as further discussed below. On the supply side, government can also implement policies that encourage domestic producers to enter the market quickly, when the patents on more brand-name drugs expire.[5]

3. Pharmaceuticals: The Demand Side

In Chapters 4 and 5, we discussed the potential problems that are caused in markets for health services by consumers' lack of information regarding the nature of their health problems and the likely effectiveness of different treatment approaches. In the context of the market for physician services, these problems are often characterized as stemming from an asymmetry of information between buyers (patients) and sellers (doctors) in the market, and the design of incentive mechanisms to overcome the consequences of this information asymmetry is a central issue in the analysis of markets for physician services.

The lack of patient information is obviously quite relevant in the market for pharmaceuticals as well. With few exceptions, patients do not have the specialized technical information to make good choices regarding what drugs to use for specific health problems, and hence have to rely on the providers who treat them for advice on what medication to use. As in the case of physician services, this lack of information may work against the interests of the patients, individually and collectively, if the providers have an incentive to bias their advice in ways that are advantageous to them. Whether or not they do so will

---

[5]In the U.S. and elsewhere, competition from generics has been delayed in the past by requiring them to go through trials to demonstrate that they are safe to use (even when they are chemically identical to brand-name drugs that have already been shown to be safe), and by not allowing such trials to be conducted until the patent on the brand-name competitor has expired.

depend on the policies and institutional arrangements that govern the choices and financing of the drugs that patients use.

3.1. *Prescription vs. non-prescription drugs*

One response to patients' lack of information with respect to drugs has been government regulation that prevents drug manufacturers or independent drug retailers from selling many kinds of drugs directly to patients without authorization by a doctor. Since drugs often may have severe side effects if they are used by the wrong kind of patient or with inappropriate dosage, requiring authorization by a trained professional before patients can buy and use them certainly makes sense. But it obviously is not necessary for all drugs; many that are used to treat various common health problems have little or no risk of side effects and little in the way of adverse consequences even if they are taken in the wrong dosage or by patients with different health problems than those for which they were intended. For patients, it is more convenient and less costly if they can buy such drugs on their own, without having to see a doctor first. Making the right choices with respect to which drugs fall in this category, and which ones can only be sold through a hospital or a doctor, or with a doctor's prescription, is therefore one important task for those designing government health care regulations.

The question of what drugs can be sold to patients without a doctor's prescription is also relevant to another issue that continues to be of great importance in China as well as in many other countries: to what extent professionals with less extensive training than licensed doctors can serve as less costly substitute providers of primary care. In China's rural areas, many of the barefoot doctors who lost their jobs when the agricultural communes were abolished, continued to make a living by selling pharmaceuticals, while also advising patients with respect to simple health problems or referring them to hospitals and clinics in more serious cases. Similarly, trained pharmacists serve as many patients' first and only contact with the health care system for a range of minor ailments in some of the high-income countries in North America and Europe.

The role of pharmacists and other drug sellers as substitute providers of primary care depends in part on what drugs they may provide. If drug sellers are allowed to sell a wide range of drugs, many patients with relatively uncomplicated health problems may just consult a drug seller rather than go to a doctor, implying a smaller demand for doctors in primary care. Conversely, the role of pharmacists and other drug sellers will be reduced if almost all drugs require a doctor's prescription before they can be sold legally. Getting a proper balance between the objectives of patient safety and that of giving drug sellers a larger role in supplying primary care, therefore, is also a potentially important determinant of a health care system's efficiency.

While doctors in some countries have resisted the trend toward giving pharmacists an expanded role in the provision of primary care, there are reasons to believe it will nevertheless continue. As more and more varieties of different medications are developed, it becomes increasingly difficult for doctors to ensure that they are well-informed not only regarding different diagnostic tools and the various treatment options that are available to deal with different health problems, but also regarding the full range of drugs that can be used. Important issues in choosing among different drugs include not only their relative effectiveness and proper dosage, but also their different side effects. Many patients, especially among the elderly, suffer from more than one health problem and may be taking several different kinds of drugs. As a consequence, an increasingly frequent problem in some systems is adverse patient reactions that result from interactions among the different drugs they are taking.

For all these reasons, pharmaceutical expertise is becoming more important over time as an element of primary care, so that policies with respect to the training of pharmacists, what drugs they are allowed to sell independently, and how they interact with doctors, are issues that will receive increasing attention in China and elsewhere.

3.2. *Prescribing and dispensing drugs: Should they be separated?*

As in the case of doctors' services, the consequences of the patient–provider information asymmetry with respect to drugs depend on the incentives to which the providers (doctors and drug sellers) are subjected when they advise patients. In the case of doctors' services, they are quite different when the doctors are paid through fee-for-service, as compared to salary or capitation, as discussed in Chapter 4. With respect to pharmaceuticals, doctors have the most incentive to prescribe expensive medications when their net income rises with the amounts patients pay for drugs. This will be the case when the drugs patients buy are sold to them by the doctor who has recommended them, and part of the doctor's income is a markup on the drugs he or she sells.[6]

A possible way in which this problem can be overcome is by seeking information and advice about drugs from a different agent than the one who actually sells them. Specifically, the incentive for doctors to recommend high volumes of expensive drugs is reduced if patients buy them from an independent seller, rather than from the doctor who has prescribed them. This line of argument has led to an intensive debate over one of the most critical choices that must be made in the institutional design of a health care system: whether there should be regulations that prevent the doctors who give patients advice with respect to what drugs to use from also being the ones who supply the patients with the drugs. In systems where regulations require a licensed physician's prescription before a person is allowed to obtain many drugs, this issue is often described as involving the question whether there should be a separation between the functions of prescribing and dispensing drugs, or whether doctors should be allowed to do both.

The answer to this question differs among systems. In a number of Asian countries, including South Korea, Singapore, and Japan, the choice traditionally has been to allow doctors to supply the drugs they prescribe.[7] In other countries, for example, the U.S. and Canada, the

---

[6] This incentive of course is relevant even when the person who both advises the patient and sells the drugs is not a doctor. For example, it has been noted that non-physician drug sellers in China's rural areas often recommend that drugs be administered through injection even when taking them by mouth would be appropriate, simply because they can charge extra for an injection.

[7] In the countries where prescribing doctors are allowed to also dispense drugs, there can be strong resistance against moves to restrict this right. When Korea moved in

functions of prescribing and dispensing drugs are separated: While doctors are the ones that prescribe what drugs patients should be taking, patients must go to a specialized pharmacist in order to buy them.

In addition to addressing the nature of the doctors' incentives, a system in which pharmacists are the ones who supply drugs that doctors prescribe is sometimes advocated as an indirect way of ensuring that the choice of drugs is double-checked through the participation of someone who has been specially trained as an expert on these kinds of issues. Although it is true that the doctor who writes the prescription is the one who makes the initial choice, pharmacists in this type of system are supposed to work closely with the doctors and to contact them if they discover a potential problem with the doctors' choices. In some places, pharmacists may even be authorized to modify the doctor's prescription within certain limits, for example, by supplying the patient with a generic version instead of the brand-name drug that the doctor has prescribed.

On the other hand, an obvious advantage with a model under which doctors are allowed to dispense the drugs they prescribe for their patients is that it is more convenient for patients. For many common health problems, patients can obtain both a diagnosis and the drugs they need in the course of a single visit to a primary-care provider. And while it may not be feasible for doctors to have as much information about various drugs as specially trained pharmacists, there is nothing that prevents doctors from drawing on the expertise of pharmacists in cases when they think it is appropriate, even if there is no rule that says they must do so.

To the extent that high drug costs in countries like Japan are seen as reflecting the economic incentives that doctors have to prescribe and dispense expensive drugs to their patients when part of what the patients pay goes to the doctors as a markup that becomes part of their income, or augments the revenue of the hospital where they work, a policy

---

this direction some years ago, Korean doctors mounted a strong campaign against this move, and ultimately went on strike in protest; see Kwon (2003) for a discussion. Taiwan has also moved in the direction of separating the two functions (Chou *et al.*, 2003).

of following the examples of the U.S. and Canada and separating the prescription and dispensing roles may seem like a reasonable response. An example of this approach is provided by South Korea which passed legislation to this effect, against the strong opposition of the doctors, in 2000. However, the results have been somewhat disappointing, as drug costs have continued to be a high proportion of total health care costs there, and remain high by international standards. Also, the share of drug costs in Canada is quite high in comparison with countries like the U.S. or the U.K., even though the prescription and dispensing roles are separated in Canada.

Indirectly, the incentives relating to the prescription and dispensing of drugs have been a central issue in China, as in these other countries, and as we further discuss below, the attempt at resolving it has been a key initiative in the central government's health policy in recent years. So far, China has not tried to do so by separating the prescription and dispensing functions. However, as the health care system continues to evolve, perhaps with a greater role for private provision of hospital and primary care in the future, the model where they are separated may receive more serious consideration.

4. Controlling Drug Costs: How Effective is Competition?

Other things equal, removing direct incentives for doctors to prescribe large volumes of expensive drugs by separating the role of supplying drugs from the prescribing role should reduce the upward pressure on drug costs at least to some extent. However, drug costs have continued to rise rapidly even in countries such as the U.S. and Korea where this has been done, and the question of what other policy measures can be effectively used to restrain the cost of drugs has been vigorously debated. As in other areas of microeconomic policy, some countries have relied principally on various forms of direct government regulation, while others have tried to attain better cost control (or, more generally, more efficient use of resources) through measures to strengthen market competition. While the latter approach may have shown promising results in other areas, the special characteristics of pharmaceuticals and the pharmaceutical industry are likely to make it difficult for a system based on competition to accomplish this in the markets where drugs are bought by individual patients, unless it is supported by at least some degree of judicious regulation. The argument here is similar to what applies in considering the market for physician services where information asymmetry and insurance reduce the effectiveness of competition for individual patients as a device for controlling costs and promoting cost-effective patterns of care, but it is given extra force by some of the special characteristics of the pharmaceutical industry.

On the supply side, the reliance on the patent system to provide the incentives necessary to support the pharmaceutical industry's R&D activities means that the force of competition is partially disabled to begin with. In the narrowly defined market for a single drug protected by a patent, there is, by definition, only one producer. In some cases, the price that can be charged for a newly developed patented drug may be partially restrained by competition from generic versions of older drugs, or from "me-too" drugs that exist when patent legislation is such that a technological breakthrough by one firm allows other firms to develop their own (patent-protected) drugs based on the same general technology.[8] However, for many newly developed drugs, competition from substitutes is weak or non-existent. Even if prescribing doctors do not have a direct incentive to prescribe expensive drugs, under traditional forms of compensation such as fee-for-service or salary, they also do not have any incentive to search aggressively for lower-cost substitutes for the leading brand-name drugs. As a result, the holder of the leading breakthrough drug may be able to charge a very high price unless prevented from doing so by regulation. As already noted, national patent legislation does not prevent governments from regulating the prices that sellers of patented drugs charge, and most countries do so to varying degrees.

Patent legislation is one factor that weakens the effectiveness of price competition as a mechanism for restraining prices in the markets

---

[8]The question of how similar a new drug can be to another patented one but still not be illegal, is a controversial one in the patent legislation in the U.S. and elsewhere. For a discussion, see Goldman and Lakdawalla (2012).

for some drugs, in addition to the tendency for price competition to not be very effective in situations where the patients who pay for the drugs do not have the information necessary to properly evaluate the benefits of different choices in relation to their costs. Moreover, as in the case of other health services, patients' and doctors' incentive to take prices into account when choosing among drugs is lowered when part or all of the price is paid by the patients' insurance plans, even in cases where doctors do not have a direct incentive to prescribe expensive drugs.

4.1. *Pharmaceuticals and non-price competition*

The pattern of marketing of pharmaceuticals in many countries also is consistent with a basic principle of the field of industrial organization: That sellers in industries where the degree of price competition is not very strong tend to engage intensively in various forms of "non-price" competition, such as advertising and other kinds of promotion to increase sales. Sellers of many kinds of brand-name drugs do so in ways that reflect the special characteristics of the pharmaceutical industry. While drugs usually are physically distributed to drug sellers, hospitals, and clinics through wholesalers whose margins are competitively determined, the large multinational pharmaceutical firms try to promote sales of their drugs through methods such as heavy advertising, both in specialized publications that are read by providers such as doctors and pharmacists, and, where regulations permit it, directly to potential patients through the print and electronic media. Moreover, they also often employ large numbers of representatives who travel to pharmacies, hospitals, and clinics to promote their drugs.

As activities of these kinds are costly, a substantial part of the high prices that patients and their insurers pay for drugs goes not only to the R&D activities of the companies, but also to pay the salaries and other costs of their large marketing staff.[9] Drug companies often

---

[9]In many cases, a percentage of the companies' revenue from drug sales is returned to the hospital managers and doctors who procure or prescribe their drugs, in the form of rebates or kickbacks (Yip and Hsiao, 2008; Tang *et al.*, 2007). Depending on the form they take, some payments of this kind will be illegal. In June 2013, Chinese authorities began an investigation of what was referred to as bribes by representatives of the large

argue that an important function of their marketing staff is to help disseminate the complex and technical information about things such as test results and relative risks of side effects of various drugs, that doctors and pharmacists need in order to make well-informed choices on their patients' behalf. While this argument obviously has merit in principle, it is difficult to believe that dissemination of information by representatives of competing sellers is an efficient and unbiased way of helping doctors and pharmacists keep up with changing technology.

4.2. *Competition and cost control by private or public insurance plans*

Information asymmetry and insurance weaken the ability and incentives of individual patients to act as informed buyers of health services and drugs. As a result, markets and competition will be relatively ineffective as instruments for controlling health care costs and producing cost-effective patterns of care in systems where choices of services and drugs, and the prices at which they are sold, are established mainly through transactions that are negotiated between patients and providers. The response in many countries, especially those where most health care costs are paid for by government plans, has been extensive regulation of health care markets, principally through price controls. But as discussed earlier, an alternative response in some places has been to give insurers greater influence over price negotiations and utilization decisions in health care markets. This trend has affected the markets not just for physician and hospital services, but for pharmaceuticals as well. As a result, while price competition remains a relatively weak force in markets for pharmaceuticals in most countries, it has become stronger in recent decades in some health care systems.

In particular, this has happened in places where the problem of lack of patient information has been addressed through institutional arrangements under which choices of patients' medications are made by doctors who either face restrictions on what they can prescribe, or have

---

pharmaceutical firm GlaxoSmithKline, of doctors and other drug buyers. See, e.g., "China bans Glaxo executive from leaving", *Wall Street Journal* (online edition), July 17, 2013.

incentives that push them to make these choices in a way that reflects the relative cost-effectiveness of different pharmaceuticals in improving patient health. In the U.S., these institutional arrangements have come about in part through competition among private insurance plans, while in places like the U.K. they have been introduced by managers of the publicly funded health insurance system.

Two important tools of these arrangements have been various types of "drug formularies", on the one hand, and some kind of "drug budget" for individual doctors, on the other. Drug formularies are lists of drugs that have been identified by the third-party insurer as cost-effective for various health conditions, and that are intended to imply varying degrees of restriction of the prescribing doctors' choices. By the same token, drug budgets are contractual arrangements that imply incentives on the doctors to pay attention to cost as well as expected outcomes when making these choices. In the private markets in the U.S., formularies and various forms of drug budgets may form part of the contracts that doctors have voluntarily signed in order to be included on managed-care insurance plans' lists of preferred providers from whom the insured clients are expected to obtain their health care. In the U.K., in contrast, adhering to the NHS drug formulary is compulsory for NHS doctors, and although the use of drug budgets has not been universally required so far, there is no reason in principle why it could not be made so. Another country where a drug formulary plays a major role in a publicly funded health insurance system is Australia. In both the U.K. and Australia, formal economic evaluation techniques have been used to assist the authorities in deciding which medicines should be included in the formularies. Appendix 1 briefly describes the concept of Quality-Adjusted Life Years (QALYs) that has increasingly become central to these techniques.

While formularies attempt to control pharmaceutical costs through restrictions, or at least strong recommendations, on the doctors who prescribe drugs for patients, different kinds of drug budgets try to do so by creating incentives on them to be cost-conscious in their prescription decisions. The effectiveness of drug budgets depends on a system under which prescribing doctors have responsibility for the care of a well-defined patient population (as is the case with the General

Practitioners who supply primary care to patients in the U.K. system, or the designated family doctors in certain private managed care plans in the U.S.). In such a system, the insurance plan can establish budgets that give an expected annual cost of prescription drugs for different kinds of patients, and financially reward doctors whose patients incur drug costs below the budgeted amounts, and/or penalize those whose patients in the aggregate have drug costs above the budgeted amounts. By making prescribing doctors more cost-conscious, such a system indirectly strengthens the responsiveness of the demand for individual drugs to their prices, and gives producers an added incentive to pay attention to their competition when setting their prices; that is, it tends to strengthen the degree of price competitiveness in the market. We will return below to the question of whether and to what extent China may want to make use of this type of incentive structure in its future policy with respect to the role of pharmaceuticals in the health care system.

5. Pharmaceutical Policy in China

5.1. *History: The 1980s and 1990s*

As China reformed its economy after the end of the system of rigid central planning in the early 1980s and the gradual integration of China into the international trading system, the pharmaceutical industry underwent a particularly dramatic process of change.[10]

Before the 1980s, the system for distributing drugs from importers and domestic producers of drugs to the patients who use them was a strictly hierarchical and centrally controlled one. A single agency in each province was responsible for obtaining the drugs from a relatively small number of (state-owned) producers and importers, and then distributing them to agencies at the municipal or county levels. These agencies in turn distributed the drugs to pharmacies, hospitals and clinics, for supply to the final users. While a small proportion of drugs

---

[10]Detailed accounts of China's pharmaceutical policy can be found in Eggleston (2009), which has half a dozen essays on China alone. A shorter but still very informative review that draws on some of those essays is in Sun *et al.* (2008).

were imported, most were domestically produced, with some being copies of patented drugs sold internationally. China did not adopt patent legislation similar to what applies in the West until 1984, so copying of foreign-developed brand-name drugs was perfectly legal at the time. Prices to final users were low and regulated, and state-owned drug producers, distribution agencies, and hospitals and clinics paid little attention to price since they had little incentive to create surpluses or avoid accounting losses that would in any case by covered through public subsidies.

The cornerstone of the economic reforms that took place over the next two decades was a strengthening of the incentives of firms to manage their resources more efficiently as many types of subsidies were reduced or withdrawn, and firms had to rely more on revenues raised through market transactions to finance their activities and generate income for managers and employees. In the market for pharmaceuticals, this was true for domestic drug producers who became more concerned with increasing their revenues by obtaining higher prices, and by selling more of the drugs on which their margins were not constrained by the price controls that remained for many kinds of basic drugs. As China began to enforce patent legislation, it also became much more attractive for the multinational pharmaceutical companies to become active in the Chinese market where they could now produce and sell their brand-name drugs at high prices, with less fear of competition from domestic copies.

On the providers' side, hospitals and clinics became much more dependent on revenues they could raise from patients, with markups on the drugs that they sold becoming an increasingly important part of their overall revenues, as discussed in earlier chapters. In the countryside, primary care was increasingly supplied by former employees of collectively funded clinics who now practiced privately; for many of them, the net revenue they earned from drug sales became their main source of income. In view of these strong new incentives on drug producers and health care providers to increase their drug-related revenue, and given the weak bargaining position of the patients who are the ultimate buyers, it is perhaps not surprising that rising costs of pharmaceuticals became perhaps the most important contributor to escalating health care costs during the last two decades of the 20th century.

A particularly worrisome consequence of the combination of the incentive structure and patient information asymmetry is that it has given rise to a large black market in "fake drugs", that is, pharmaceuticals that are ineffective or even harmful because they do not contain the appropriate ingredients. While reliable statistics on fake drugs are not available, for obvious reasons, there is little doubt that they have constituted a major problem in recent decades. For example, newspaper reports in 2012 cited government sources as saying that actions to combat fake drugs involving 18,000 officials had resulted in the arrest of almost 2,000 people and the seizure of counterfeit medicines worth $180 million.[11]

With more freedom for new firms to enter the market, the system of drug distribution also changed dramatically. A growing share of pharmaceuticals was sold to clinics, hospitals and drug sellers through independent wholesalers rather than through provincial government agencies.[12] As a result, there now is a much larger number of drug importers and producers than before (recent statistics suggest that there were as many as 4,600 pharmaceutical producers in the market in 2008[13]). Many multinational drug companies and domestic producers have established networks of representatives who sell directly to hospitals and clinics, but there has also been rapid growth in the number of independent pharmaceutical wholesalers which currently have been estimated to number perhaps 13,000 (in 2011[14]). Thus, the system of drug distribution has become quite complex and heterogeneous in recent decades.

A factor that has contributed to its complexity is the very rapid proliferation of the number of distinct drugs that are supplied in the

---

[11] See, e.g., "2,000 arrested in China in counterfeit drug crackdown", *New York Times* (online edition), August 5, 2012.
[12] Zhu (2007).
[13] http://business.sohu.com/20081029/n260309205.shtml (accessed on July 24, 2013).
[14] http://finance.sina.com.cn/china/20120917/033613152679.shtml (accessed on July 24, 2013).

market. Even though this has occurred everywhere in the world, the trend has been particularly noteworthy in China. As an example, it was reported that in the year 2005 alone, China's State Food and Drug Administration (SFDA) approved the marketing of 1,113 new drugs, almost ten times as many as the number that was approved by the U.S. Food and Drug Administration, its American counterpart.[15] The reasons for this pattern will be further discussed below.

5.2. *Early policy responses*

In retrospect, it is not surprising that China's move toward a market-oriented system of procurement and distribution of drugs in the three decades following the 1980s created major problems. One reason was that there was no separation between the prescription and dispensing of drugs, and markups on the drugs that they sold were major sources of income both for privately practicing rural health workers and for rural and urban hospitals and clinics. Hence, there were strong incentives on those who prescribed drugs to take advantage of patients' lack of information to recommend the use of drugs that were most profitable for those supplying them, and to charge prices for the drugs that implied large markups.[16]

Attempts to counteract the problem of high drug prices through government regulation were ineffective, and in some cases may even have made the problem worse. Part of the reason they were ineffective is due to the fact that price regulation only covered drugs in common use; for newly introduced drugs, hospitals and clinics could set whatever prices they liked. Not surprisingly, this resulted in a bias toward prescription of new drugs even in cases where older, less costly drugs would have been equally appropriate.

The agencies that were involved in regulating drug prices (the Ministry of Health, the State Food and Drug Administration, as well as the Ministry of Human Resources and Social Security and the

---

[15]Information downloaded from http://news.xinhuanet.com/comments/2007-07/13/content_6364654.htm (accessed on July 24, 2013).
[16]For a study providing evidence on this, see Currie, Lin, and Zhang (2011).

Table 1. Comparison of different essential medicine lists in China.

Name	Number of drugs	Ministry/government department	Year
National essential medicine list	2,033	MOH & SFDA	2004
National essential medicine list for health insurance and work-related insurance	1,850	MOHRSS	2004
Provincial-level NCMS essential medicine lists	N/A	Provincial governments	2009
National essential medicine list	307	MOH & SFDA & MOHRSS & NDRC & Ministry of Industry and Information Technology & Ministry of Finance, etc.	2009
National essential medicine list	520	MOH & SFDA & MOHRSS & NDRC & Ministry of Industry and Information Technology & Ministry of Finance, etc.	2012

Source: Compiled by the authors.

National Development and Reform Commission) tried to overcome this problem by expanding the lists of drugs (the "essential medicines" lists) to which price regulation applied, and by establishing lower regulated prices for newer drugs as they were introduced. As a result, the lists became longer over time. While an early list established by the MOH and SFDA in 1982 contained only 278 drugs, by 2004 the lists used by SFDA and MOHRSS included around 2,000 different drugs (Table 1).

The battle was a losing one, however, as drug sellers introduced new drugs that often were similar to existing ones, but were deemed by the authorities to be different enough so that the regulated maximum prices did not apply to them. As noted above, in 2005 alone, the SFDA approved over 1,000 new drugs to which the price ceilings did not apply. Even though some of these were generic drugs that were "new" only in the sense that they were supplied in different dosages or packaging, those prescribing drugs in hospitals and clinics quickly began to prescribe them because they could charge higher prices for them. In some cases, the ineffectiveness of the price regulation may have resulted from corruption. Over the years, a number of SFDA officials have been prosecuted for corruption involving pharmaceutical producers. In 2007, one such case even led to the execution of a former SFDA commissioner.[17]

While public or private insurance plans have implemented measures to contain the costs of pharmaceuticals in other countries, as discussed earlier, their influence in drugs markets in China has so far been limited. From the 1980s until the early 2000s, earlier forms of insurance played a diminishing role in China, as an increasing share of the cost of health services and pharmaceuticals were paid out of patients' own pockets. As the new social insurance plans have expanded in the last decade, the share of pharmaceutical costs paid by them has grown. However, contrary to insurance plans in high-income countries that typically cover part or all of the cost of any drug that has been prescribed by a physician, the practice in China's social insurance plans has been to limit coverage to only those drugs that appear on an approved list.

Prices of most of these insured drugs have been regulated by the NDRC, which has prominently announced substantial price reductions in efforts to control costs. Since 1997, it has done so on no less than 27 occasions (see Appendix 2). However, these price reductions are somewhat difficult to interpret since many of them are likely to refer to the prices of new drugs that had been recently added to the list, at high prices. More importantly, the effectiveness of these price controls in containing drug costs for those covered by the plans was reduced by the fact that hospitals and clinics were able to switch their prescriptions to new drugs that were not included on the list, and whose prices therefore were not regulated. In comparison with, for example, U.S. managed care plans that are able to restrict doctors' prescription choices to the drugs that appear in their formularies, China's social insurance

---

[17]See Yang (2009).

plans thus far have had much less ability to influence drug costs, since prescribing doctors have had neither a strict obligation nor a financial incentive to choose the drugs with regulated low prices from the plans' lists.

5.3. *2009–2011: The new National Essential Medicine System*

When the plans for a major revamping of China's system of health financing were presented in early 2009, they included reform of the system for acquiring and distributing drugs as one of their main elements, though few details about how this was to be accomplished were provided at that time. However, more detail was supplied in a follow-up guideline in August 2009.[18] Although the new National Essential Medicine System (NEMS) is built on the existing model, it will gradually change it in several important ways.

First, there will be greater coordination between different agencies in the definition of "essential medicines", and there now exists a National Essential Medicines List that has been jointly agreed on by all relevant ministries and agencies, including the MOH, SFDA, MOHRSS, the NDRC, and others. In contrast to the earlier lists issued by SFDA and used by MOHRSS in defining eligibility for social insurance plan reimbursement which included around 2,000 drugs, the new list contains only a little more than 300 items.

Perhaps the most important function of the new NEMS list is that it will form the basis for the way drugs will be supplied in the network of primary-care clinics that is one of the cornerstones of the 2009 reform plans. Specifically, the aim is to move toward a system in which all of the drugs on the NEMS list will be available in each one of these clinics, whether in rural or urban areas. While it is not realistic to expect this target to be reached quickly (many of the primary-care clinics are still in the process of being established and staffed), the year 2020 has been set as the date by which it should be attained.

---

[18] See Ministry of Health *et al.* (2009), "Guideline for implementing National Essential Medicine System", *weishengbu deng jiu bumen: guanyu jianli guojia jiben yaowu zhidu de shishi yijian* (in Chinese), http://news.xinhuanet.com/politics/2009-08/18/content_11903865.htm (accessed on May 29, 2012).

Moreover, the prices at which the drugs on the list are supplied to the clinics will be regulated and, most importantly, supplied to patients with no markup. In addition, even though doctors and nurses in the clinics will retain some degree of freedom to prescribe other drugs, they will be required to give priority to the drugs on the NEMS list, and are only supposed to prescribe other drugs in exceptional circumstances.[19]

The NEMS list is also supposed to serve as a guideline for hospital doctors when they prescribe drugs. While there are as yet no national guidelines for the minimum percentage of hospital prescriptions that are supposed to be for "essential" drugs, there are reports that some local governments have defined targets of this kind. For example, in Wuxi city, officials are monitoring prescription patterns with the aim of reaching the goal of having essential drugs account for a minimum of 15% of total health expenditure.[20] The process of encouraging the use of drugs on the NEMS list in hospitals is slow, however, as hospitals are still allowed to charge a markup of 15% on the drugs they sell. Over time, this percentage may be reduced, and the objective over the long term is to "de-couple" hospitals' revenue from drug markups, giving hospitals larger subsidies to compensate for the reduction in revenue they will face as a result.

A further measure to promote the use of the drugs on the NEMS list is contained in the regulations applied to China's social insurance plans, providing for a higher reimbursement rate to patients for drugs on the list than for other ones. Although this measure is consistent with the general objective of promoting the use of the cost-effective drugs that are included on the list, its effectiveness can be questioned since it applies to patients, not to the pharmacists, doctors, and other health care professionals whose advice is the most important factor in determining which drugs are used in the system.

---

[19]For example, only drugs in the NEMS list and the local essential drug list are allowed to be prescribed in Shanxi province, downloaded from http://www.sxws.cn/ShowAff.asp?StrAfficheAppID=1563 (accessed on July 24, 2013).

[20]See http://wx.xinhuanet.com/2011-08/06/content_23404753.htm (accessed on May 29, 2012).

The reforms also include a major change in the system of drug procurement and distribution. In a partial reversal of the decentralization process that has taken place in this market over the last several decades, the State Council in October 2010 released a detailed guideline providing for collective procurement and distribution of most drugs to hospitals and clinics.[21] Under this guideline, an agency managed by the provincial Health Bureau will act as the single central buyer in the system. The prices at which producers and importers sell the drugs to the agency will be established through a process in which competing sellers are invited to submit bids for the supply of specified drugs. This process obviously gives the buying agency a much stronger bargaining position than the individual hospitals and clinics to which drugs are sold independently in the current system. The expectation is that, as a result of this change, the cost of pharmaceuticals to the health care system will be lower than at present, reducing the burden on hospitals and clinics of supplying drugs at relatively low regulated prices to patients and their insurers. Moreover, the more centralized buying process may also result in savings to society as a whole, with fewer resources spent on marketing and promotion of pharmaceuticals.

6. China's Pharmaceutical Policy: The Future

The policy measures that have been developed during the 2009–2011 period will, if and when they are fully implemented, imply a fundamental restructuring of the system of supply and utilization of pharmaceuticals in China. The centralized provincial bargaining approach could lead to a substantial reduction in the prices at which most drugs are supplied by producers and importers, compared to what one would expect under a less centralized model. Widespread availability of the cost-effective drugs that are to be included on the NEMS list, together with incentives and restrictions to ensure that

---

[21] State Council (2010), "Guideline for establishing and regulating procurement system for essential medicines for public-owned primary-care clinics", *jianli he guifan zhengfu ban jiceng yiliao weisheng jigou benyaowu caigou jizhi de zhidao yijian, guowu bangongting, guobanfa* (in Chinese), No. 56, http://www.gov.cn/zwgk/2010-12/09/content_1761749.htm (accessed on May 29, 2012).

doctors in primary-care clinics and hospitals usually prescribe these drugs, rather than less cost-effective ones that are not on the list, could be expected to substantially reduce the burden of pharmaceutical costs on patients and insurance plans. However, even if the reform measures are fully implemented, their full effect will only occur gradually, and many questions still remain with respect to the way implementation will be undertaken.

In some respects, the attempts to control drug costs in China are similar to those that have been attempted in some other countries, as discussed earlier. In particular, the NEMS list can be interpreted as a version of the formularies that are supposed to guide the prescription behavior of doctors and reimbursement of drugs in U.S. managed care plans, or among primary-care doctors in the U.K. NHS. An important issue for the future will be how the decisions are made with respect to which drugs will be included on the list, which is to be updated every three years.

The current guidelines specify that these decisions will be made by a committee of officials of nine ministries, including MOH, NDRC, MOHRSS, as well as the Ministries of Finance, Industry and Information Technology, and Commerce. While this committee will make decisions regarding the national list, each province will have discretion to add or remove drugs from it, "according to local conditions". Clearly, the members of this committee, as well as the local authorities who decide on any modifications, will potentially be subject to a great deal of pressure from manufacturers and importers of various drugs that may be included.

In a system of competing private insurance plans, this pressure is indirectly offset by competition among the insurance plans which create the formularies that govern their reimbursement decisions, and that contracted physicians are supposed to use. In the government-funded plans that use formularies, such as those in the U.K. and Australia, the decisions are centrally made, but with major input from institutions that are charged with making recommendations regarding which drugs are to be included on the basis of formalized health economic evaluations. The National Institute of Clinical Excellence (NICE) in the U.K., in particular, has become a world leader in carrying out such evaluations, in a process characterized by a high degree of transparency so that the opportunities for the drug companies to influence the evaluations are minimized. China's ability to effectively use the NEMS list as an instrument of attaining more efficient resource utilization in the pharmaceutical industry would be greatly strengthened by the creation of a mechanism to ensure that such evaluations are made without bias or undue influence from vested interests, in a way that reflects China's situation as a middle-income country.

In addition, a model under which there would be greater opportunity for private insurance plans to compete with those funded by the public sector could also help counteract the influence of producer interests as plans compete with each other by promoting more cost-effective patterns of prescription and drug utilization. The two approaches can work together in a complementary fashion. A formulary that restricts prescription choices in the social insurance plans can also be the starting point for defining insurance coverage in private plans. At the same time, decisions by private insurers to extend coverage beyond what is in the government formulary, or to exclude older drugs from coverage when they have been replaced by newer, more cost-effective ones, can serve as signals that the government formulary should be revised. We will return to this possibility in Chapter 10.

6.1. *Essential drug lists and formularies: Flexibility vs. effectiveness*

Lists of recommended drugs can be used to restrict the choices of drugs by doctors and other professionals in situations where those who make them are employed by the public sector or have signed contracts with insurers under which they have accepted such restrictions (as in U.S. managed care plans). However, it is obviously necessary, or at least desirable, to make such restrictions flexible, in the sense of allowing for exceptions under specific conditions. While the drugs that are included in formularies are intended to be the most cost-effective choices in most cases, different patients may react differently to certain drugs, both in the sense of how effectively the drugs help them with their health problems, and in the sense that some patients may suffer serious side effects from drugs that do not affect others. Thus, in a well-functioning system, doctors, pharmacists, and nurse practitioners must have some degree of freedom to depart from prescribed formularies in individual cases, to prescribe drugs that may be more expensive than those on the list, but may be more effective and have fewer side effects for particular patients.

Once exceptions are allowed, however, it becomes important to formulate rules for when they can be made, or to create incentives for those making the choices to be conservative in making these exceptions. China's experience in recent decades provides an illustration of the importance of this. Although several lists of essential and cost-effective drugs existed, and their prices were regulated, these lists did not have much of an impact on prescription patterns in hospitals and clinics, because the hospitals and their doctors had the authority to depart from the recommended lists, as well as strong incentives to choose drugs that were not on the lists because their prices were unregulated so that the hospitals could augment their revenue by reselling these drugs at high markups.

Given the care that has gone into developing the new NEMS list, and the widespread support it will have from the different government departments that are involved in pharmaceutical policy, it seems likely that it will become a more effective instrument for containing drug costs and creating more cost-effective patterns of pharmaceutical resources than the lists that have existed in the past. The fact that all drugs on the list will be available in the planned comprehensive network of primary-care clinics will help. While it is not yet clear to what extent doctors in these clinics will have the authority to prescribe drugs that are not on the list, it seems reasonable to expect that they will be expected to do so only in exceptional cases. Moreover, the clinics will be required to supply the drugs from the NEMS list to patients at zero markup, removing the incentive to prescribe the more expensive drugs to their patients that they have had in the past.

While the intention is that the NEMS list will play a prominent role in influencing the pattern of drug utilization in hospitals as well, the task of making this happen is likely to be more difficult, given the importance that revenue from drug markups has had for the hospital sector in recent years. Although the stated objective is that hospitals' revenue will be "de-coupled" from drug markups in the future, in exchange for larger direct government subsidies, this policy is not yet fully enforced, and many hospitals continue to rely extensively on this source of revenue. Thus, how fast and effectively the new pharmaceutical policy will be able to achieve its objective of lower drug costs for patients and insurance plans will depend to a large extent on the speed and rigor with which these new rules are enforced, and with which hospitals are given access to new sources of revenue in the form of increased subsidies or, more likely, more comprehensive contracts with social or private insurance plans. More generally, therefore, the question of how effective the policy will be is closely related to the broader issue of reform of the governance and financing of China's hospital system, a topic to which we will return in Chapters 9 and 10.

Appendix 1. Methods of Economic Evaluation for Establishing Drug Formularies

The use of drug formularies is closely linked with the concept of economic evaluation, especially in publicly funded systems such as the U.K. NHS and the Australian Medicare system.[22] In economic evaluations, the cost of a given drug is assessed against evidence regarding some measure of its expected benefits. As evaluations have become more common, there has been some degree of convergence toward use of the concept of incremental Quality-Adjusted Life Years (QALYs) as the accepted benefit measure, and a great deal of work has been done on developing simpler and more reliable ways of estimating this measure for a wide variety of health improvements as a result of medical or surgical treatment. Roughly speaking, a given drug has a higher probability of being included in an insurance plan's formulary the more cost-effective it is, as compared to possible alternatives, where cost-effectiveness is measured as the cost (expressed in money) per incremental QALY. Sometimes the plan defines a critical value so that

---

[22] Recent surveys of economic evaluation in health care are in Garber and Sculpher (2012) and Walker, Sculpher, and Drummond (2011).

only drugs with a cost per QALY below this critical value are included. Generally there is some degree of flexibility in the way formularies are used, in deference to the principle of doctors' professional autonomy or to legal considerations, with procedures under which doctors may prescribe drugs that are not on the formulary in special cases. Even so, however, drug companies recognize that having drugs included in the formularies gives them a major competitive advantage, and they may adjust the prices they charge accordingly.

Appendix 2. NDRC's Efforts at Drug Price Reductions

	Time	Number of medicines affected	Average percentage of drug price reduction (%)	Projected reduction of drug expenditure (billion RMB)
1	October 1997	47	15	2
2	April 1998	38	10	1.5
3	April 1999	21	20	2
4	June 1999	150	5	0.8
5	August 1999	2	15	0.12
6	January 2000	12	10	0.34
7	June 2000	9	15	1.2
8	October 2000	21	20	1.8
9	April 2001	69	20	2
10	July 2001	49	15	0.4
11	December 2001	383	20	3
12	December 2002	199	15	2
13	March 2003	267	14	1.5
14	May 2004	3	—	—
15	June 2004	24	20~36	12
16	July 2004	18	—	—
17	June 2005	22	60	6
18	February 2006	—	—	—
19	June 2006	67	23	2.3
20	November 2006	32	14.5	1.3
21	January 2007	10	20	7
22	February 2007	278	15	5

(*Continued*)

(Continued)

	Time	Number of medicines affected	Average percentage of drug price reduction (%)	Projected reduction of drug expenditure (billion RMB)
23	May 2007	260	19	5
24	May 2007	188	16	1.6
25	December 2007	260	—	—
26	November 2010	48	19	2
27	March 2011	162	21	10
28	August 2011	82	14	—

Source: Hu, S. (2007), "Policies for national essential medicine system" in *China Health Development Report*, Social Science Press, Beijing & NDRC website.

PART III

HEALTH CARE AND HARMONIOUS DEVELOPMENT IN CHINA

Chapter 7

HEALTH POLICY
AND INEQUALITY

1. Introduction

In the 2000s, inequality has emerged as a major issue in the debate over economic policy in China. The way this issue is addressed and resolved will be very important for the future, not just with respect to economic management, but to the continuing process of modernizing Chinese society as a whole, including its political and governance system.

During the era of central planning before the early 1980s, while real per capita incomes were relatively equally distributed, they were also very low. However, the rapid economic growth that led to a dramatic increase in average real income in the subsequent three decades has changed the picture dramatically. On one hand, it has greatly benefited very large numbers of individuals at the low end of the income scale. A measure of China's economic success that is often cited is the number of people whose income has been raised above the poverty level over this period. For example, estimates by the World Bank of global poverty suggest that in China, the percentage of the population living in poverty, defined as having an income below the equivalent of US$1.25 per day, fell from 85% in 1981 to 15.9% in 2005, implying a decrease by more than 600 million people.[1]

But while real incomes rose at the low end of the scale, they grew even faster for those at the high end. As a result, there was an increase in economic inequality. For example, some estimates of

---

[1] From the article "Poverty around the world", http://www.globalissues.org/article/4/poverty-around-the-world (accessed on July 23, 2013).

the Gini index of inequality pointed to values well below 0.3 for the early 1980s, while recently released official statistics indicate that it had risen as high as 0.491 in 2008. Using a somewhat different methodology, researchers at Southwestern University of Finance and Economics have even produced an estimate of China's Gini of 0.61, well above the threshold value of 0.5 that the World Bank uses as the dividing line between "high" and "very high" inequality.[2]

A pattern of rising inequality during periods of rapid economic growth is consistent with international evidence which tends to show low values for the inequality indicators in the poorest countries, and higher values in middle-income countries. Essentially, this pattern results from the fact that when a country pursues policies that create opportunities for more rapid economic growth, different sectors and population groups will differ in their ability to take advantage of these opportunities, so that their output and incomes will grow at different rates. Deng Xiaoping's decision to accept this pattern, allowing some groups and regions to "get rich first", is consistent with the path taken in other successful countries.

But at the same time, it is clear that rapidly increasing inequality may create tensions in a country's political system, and there will be calls for policies to distribute the fruits of successful economic growth more fairly. Under the circumstances, it is not surprising that China's leaders, who consistently emphasize the importance of maintaining social stability, pay close attention to the evidence on rising inequality, and to the various proposals that emerge on possible policies that can be undertaken to modify the distribution of real income in a way that will respond to these calls.

The rest of the chapter is organized as follows. In the next section, we briefly discuss some of the data on different dimensions of real income inequality in China, and some of the programs (other than

---

[2]The official estimate by the National Bureau of Statistics was released in January 2013, as reported at http://news.xinhuanet.com/english/china/2013-01/21/c_132116852.htm (accessed on July 31, 2013). The SUFE study was briefly described in the online version of Caixin Magazine, at http://english.caixin.com/2012-12-10/100470648.html (accessed on July 31, 2013).

social health insurance) that have been developed to reduce it. We then review some of the evidence on inequality in health care, including issues relating to access to care and how the burden of health care costs is distributed across income groups. In the following section, we turn to a discussion of the way health reform can be used as a powerful tool for reducing inequality in real income, properly defined, and raise the question whether in doing so, China would do well to aim for a single universal government system of insurance coverage along the lines of those in, e.g., the U.K., continental Europe, or Japan. We conclude that for the foreseeable future, China will be better served by a mixed system with different social insurance plans for different population groups, and an expanded role for private insurance. In the Appendix, we discuss some of the reasons for this conclusion.

2. Inequality and Policies to Reduce It

A single measure such as the Gini coefficient for an entire country summarizes the inequality that results from many different factors that affect the incomes of individuals and families. In China, the most obvious explanation for increasing inequality is that it has occurred as a result of the changing roles of the state and the private sector in economic management over the past three decades. Many of those at the top end of the income scale whose incomes have grown at a faster rate than the average have been entrepreneurs and business leaders who are the owners and managers of new private firms, or privatized SOEs, that have done well and earned large profits. Among those at the low end of the scale who have lagged behind are many who lost their jobs and source of livelihood as the state ceased to support loss-making SOEs and allowed them to close down or be transferred to private ownership. Others whose incomes have stagnated or fallen are agricultural workers who were not able to earn much money under the family responsibility system that replaced the communes from the early 1980s. In order to reduce the inequality that is due to these changing roles, the natural approach is to find ways of collecting more taxes from businesses or individuals with high income, and then use this revenue

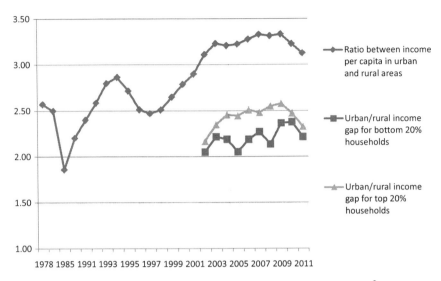

Fig. 1.   The income gap between urban and rural residents.[3]

Source: *China Statistical Yearbook*, various years.

to pay for programs that raise the real income of those at the low end of the scale.

But although the changes in economic organization have contributed to increased inequality, their effects have not been the same throughout China. Taking this into account, increased inequality can also be looked at from a geographical perspective, focusing on trends in data such as those on rural-urban income differentials or unequal regional performance.

2.1.   *Urban-rural and regional inequality*

In particular, a major reason for overall inequality in the distribution of aggregate income is the large gap that exists in most places between the average income of urban and rural populations. Figure 1 shows that on average, this gap is not only large, but has been growing over time.

---

[3]Income distribution data (in quintiles or deciles) in the rural areas are not available before 2002.

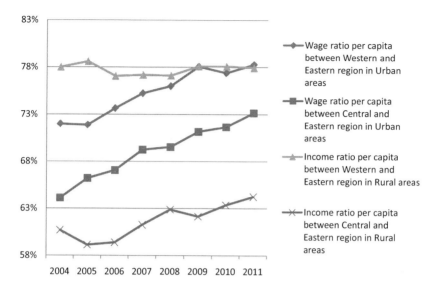

Fig. 2. Urban wage ratio and rural income ratio across regions.

Source: *China Statistical Yearbook*, various years.

A great deal of attention has also been paid in the policy debate to the large differences that exist between average incomes in China's major regions. In particular, much of the debate over redistributive policy at the central level focuses on ways in which the central government can transfer resources from the wealthier coastal regions, where growth has been especially rapid, to the poorer areas in Western and Central China. The faster growth in the coastal provinces has happened in part because much of the industry that has contributed to rising per capita GDP in China through exports to the developed countries has been concentrated there, both because of lower transportation costs and also because the Special Economic Zones that contributed a great deal to establishing China's export-based industries were first established there. Figure 2 gives an indication of the advantage that the coastal provinces have had, not only in terms of urban wages but also in terms of average rural incomes, over China's central and western provinces.[4]

---

[4]The western region includes Sichuan, Chongqing, Guizhou, Yunnan, Shaanxi, Gansu, Tibet, Qinghai, Ningxia, Xinjiang, Guangxi and Inner Mongolia. Central region

Policies that seek to reduce economic inequality by taxing businesses and individuals with high income and by supporting the poor through various targeted programs will indirectly contribute to smaller differences between urban and rural areas or between coastal and interior regions if they are applied uniformly across China. But because social policy in China is highly decentralized, there are often substantial differences in the way various programs are designed and managed, with rural areas and poorer regions having less generous programs simply because their fiscal resources are limited. To partially offset this, the central government undertakes substantial earmarked transfers to local governments, or provides larger subsidies to local programs in rural areas or in poorer regions. We will further discuss the intergovernmental dimension of China's income redistribution policy in the next chapter.

While most social programs are locally managed, they are of course also subject to restrictions and guidelines formulated at the central level. This is true not only for health policy, but also for the other programs that are gradually being strengthened as China tries to move toward improved fairness in distributing the fruits of its successful economic growth. Before returning to the issue of how the financing of health care affects inequality and how it can be reformed so as to better reflect the equity objective, we briefly summarize some of these initiatives.

2.2. *Pensions and unemployment insurance*

One important element in the effort to reduce inequality has been the development of new social insurance programs to replace the employment-related benefits that were automatically provided to almost everyone during the era of central planning. At that time, there was little unemployment and SOEs were responsible for providing their

---

includes Shanxi, Jilin, Anhui, Jiangxi, Henan, Hubei, Heilongjiang and Hunan. Eastern region includes Beijing, Hebei, Liaoning, Jiangsu, Shandong, Zhejiang, Shanghai, Tianjin, Fujian, Hainan and Guangdong. Eastern, western and central regions are defined following the definitions in the *China Health Statistical Yearbook*, 2011.

employees not only with health care, but also with a continuing income in the form of old-age pension for their retired employees.

To compensate for the fact that SOEs no longer provide guaranteed lifetime employment and may not be able to pay benefits to retirees if they close down or become unprofitable, China has established both unemployment insurance and social security schemes to which workers and their employers contribute and which provide benefits when the workers retire or if they lose their jobs. In the same way as has happened with social health insurance, these schemes initially covered mostly urban formal-sector workers, and most of the contributions were made by the employers. This continues to be the case. For example, in the Social Security scheme that provides these workers with retirement income, workers' contributions were set at 8% of their wage, while contributions from employers to the scheme may be two to three times larger on average.[5] The benefits paid at retirement consist of one component which is the same for everyone who has met the eligibility criteria for past contributions, at a rate that is specified as a fraction (often 20%) of the local average wage, and another component that depends on the amount that has accumulated in the retiree's individual account from his or her past individual contributions.[6]

From 2009 onwards, similar programs have been created to provide coverage for both urban residents who do not work in the formal sector, and also people in rural areas, whose health care costs and retirement income had been covered by the agricultural communes before they were abolished. These supplementary schemes are funded along the same lines as the URBMI and NCMS social health insurance schemes discussed in Chapter 3, from a mixture of direct government subsidies and individual contributions. Similar to the urban scheme,

---

[5]Details on China's pension system can be found in Song *et al.* (2012), which quotes a statutory employer contribution of 20%. They state, however, that in reality, many employers contribute less than the statutory rate. Also, see Qian (2013b) about institutional arrangement for the basic pension system in China.
[6]In early versions of the plan, the second component was a monthly payment equivalent to 1/120 of the amount in the person's individual account at the time of retirement.

the benefits from the rural scheme when a person retires consist of a basic component (which varies from place to place, but is subject to a minimum which was initially set as low as 55 RMB per month), and another amount that is based on past individual contributions.[7]

Enrollment in the supplementary Social Security schemes has expanded rapidly, and a recent study indicates that they have become an important source of income for many elderly people throughout China. Estimates for 2011 suggest that 300 million urban workers were covered by one of the pension schemes, while the number enrolled in a rural scheme was as large as over 325 million.[8]

In addition to the provisions for retirement income (and health insurance), China's social insurance legislation also includes schemes that provide cash benefits in cases of work-related injury, maternity, and unemployment.[9] The latter, in particular, is a significant component of China's "social safety net", providing cash benefits to employees who have lost their jobs due to involuntary layoffs, for example, when a firm goes out of business (Table 1). An important feature of the law is a rule which specifies that the amount of benefits that an unemployed person can collect must be the same for all beneficiaries within the plan's jurisdiction (that is, it cannot depend on the person's previous salary).[10] Since the contributions that must be paid to the plan are specified as a percentage (normally 2%, though it is sometimes lower),

---

[7]Although the specified minimum benefits are small, actual pensions in some areas may be much higher. For example, a study reported in Caixin Online found some pensioners in rural areas with benefits as high as 1,000 RMB per month; see http://english.caixin.com/2012-12-10/100470648.html (accessed on July 31, 2013).

[8]The estimates are from an article in *The Economist* entitled "Fulfilling promises: China is beginning to face up to its pension problem" (August 11, 2012). Since the schemes are relatively new, most of those who are enrolled in the plan have not yet retired, meaning that the number of beneficiaries who collect pensions is still fairly small.

[9]A helpful summary can be found on the website of the magazine *China Briefing*; see http://www.china-briefing.com/news/2012/02/21/mandatory-social-welfare-benefits-for-chinese-employees.html (accessed on July 31, 2013).

[10]The law specifies that a person must have contributed to the plan for a full year before he or she is eligible to collect benefits, and benefits are payable for at most 24 months.

Table 1. The number of beneficiaries of unemployment insurance in China (million).

Year	The number of enrollees of unemployment insurance	The number of beneficiaries of unemployment insurance
2001	103.55	3.12
2002	101.82	4.4
2003	103.73	4.15
2004	105.84	4.19
2005	106.48	3.62
2006	111.87	3.27
2007	116.45	2.86
2008	124	2.61
2009	127.15	2.35
2010	133.76	2.09

Source: China Human Resource and Social Security Yearbook, 2011.

this rule implies some degree of redistribution from those with high salaries to those who are paid at lower rates.

2.3. Means-tested transfers: Di Bao

In addition to developing the social insurance schemes, China has also spent very substantial resources in strengthening the equivalent of the social assistance programs that exist in all advanced countries and that are based mostly on means-tested income support targeted directly at the poor. The current system, known as Di Bao, or the Minimum Livelihood Guarantee Scheme, began on a limited scale in 1999, but it has expanded rapidly in recent years. While the central government had made efforts to alleviate poverty before Di Bao, it had done so principally by identifying especially poor counties and making cash transfers to the county government, which had considerable discretion to decide on how the funds should best be used. In contrast, the Di Bao program is based on identifying poor *individuals*, and transferring resources to them specifically. While local governments still retain a role in managing the local version of the program and setting some of its key parameters, such as the threshold below which a person will receive benefits, the central government has imposed restrictions to ensure that the same basic principles are applied in all local programs.

When the Di Bao scheme was started in 1999, it applied only to poor people in urban areas; in 2000, the program cost no more than about 2.2 billion RMB.[11] As the number of poor people in urban areas increased, partly as a result of the restructuring of SOEs, it grew fairly rapidly. However, the role of Di Bao as a key element of China's policies to alleviate poverty and bring about a more equal distribution of income increased dramatically in 2007, when the decision was made that it should be expanded to cover rural areas as well. This decision resulted both in a large increase in the number of people receiving assistance under the scheme, and in increased expenditure. By 2011, the number of recipients was around 74 million people, of which 53 million were rural residents, and total program cost had grown to 134 billion RMB, of which around 80% came from the central government.[12]

In an international perspective, the expansion of the Di Bao scheme is a major accomplishment for a middle-income country where the focus of policy in recent decades has been to accelerate economic growth, and where the policies to create effective safety nets for the poor are of relatively recent origin. As in other countries, however, issues with respect to the design and management of social assistance programs are controversial, and some aspects of the Di Bao scheme have attracted considerable criticism, especially the degree to which the objective of targeting the poor has been met in practice. Moreover, the amount of support that it offers recipients remains limited. In 2011, it was estimated that recipient households in urban areas received average benefits of no more than 287 RMB per month; for rural areas, the figure was 143 RMB per month.[13] Data on expenditure patterns suggest that these amounts are barely enough for recipient households to afford

---

[11] *China Civil Affairs Statistical Yearbook*, various years.
[12] *China Civil Affairs Statistical Yearbook* and Statistical Communiqué of the People's Republic of China on the 2011 development of social service, various years. For a general discussion of the Di Bao scheme, see World Bank (2009).
[13] *China Civil Affairs Statistical Yearbook*, various years.

a standard of food, clothing, and housing equivalent to that of the poorest 5% of urban households.[14] Nevertheless, one can expect that the Di Bao program will remain a cornerstone of China's attempts to raise the standard of living of those at the low end of the scale, and there are plans to gradually raise the support levels at a faster rate than that of average income growth in future years.

In addition to the general income support through the Di Bao scheme, Social Security, and unemployment insurance, those at the low end of the income scale also benefit from in-kind transfer programs under which the government subsidizes specific services. The most important ones, in addition to health care, are education and housing. In 2011, government expenditures on health, education and housing amounted to over 2.7 trillion RMB, the equivalent of 5.6% of GDP.

2.4. *In-kind transfers: Education and housing*

Economists generally support the principle that means-tested cash transfers constitute the most direct and efficient way to help the poor. Nevertheless, as with health care, the literature on the economics of education recognizes that subsidies to education can be effective in reducing income inequality over time, and may be justified not only because they promote a more equitable distribution of real income, but also on grounds of economic efficiency.

The argument that government subsidies to education can promote economic efficiency is based on recognition of the fact that education is an investment. The resources spent on education, including the time of the students themselves, help create various kinds of skills that increase students' future ability to be productive and earn an income higher than they otherwise would. By studying the relationship between workers' level of education and their earnings, one can estimate the return to the "human capital" that education creates, and compare this return with the cost of the resources devoted to education.

---

[14]See Qian (2013a).

If one recognizes that these resources could have been spent on investment in other types of capital instead (housing, machinery, infrastructure), the principle that applies is that in order for investable resources to be efficiently allocated, they should be divided between investments in human capital and other kinds of capital until the rate of return, at the margin, is similar. But in the absence of government subsidies, this is unlikely to happen. Without subsidies, there almost certainly would be an under-investment in education, especially in children from poor families. Even if poor families recognize the value of educating their children (as most do, everywhere in the world), without government subsidies they would not have enough resources to pay the full cost of doing so. Moreover, even if they were willing to take the risk of borrowing money to finance it, banks and other lenders would not be willing to grant them loans for this purpose without collateral security. Indirectly, therefore, government subsidies to education are efficient because they help the economy make better use of its investable resources. They also promote a more equitable distribution of income because they particularly favor children from poor families (and, later on, their parents as well, as better-educated children can give them more support when they are old).

Government programs to redistribute real income by supplying poor people with housing are more difficult to justify on efficiency grounds. In basic economic theory, a standard argument is that giving equivalent cash transfers to the poor is more effective than supplying them with particular types of benefits such as housing, since the recipients and their families can allocate these transfers in a way that best corresponds to their needs and preferences. Taken in isolation, means-tested programs of subsidized housing obviously do raise the real income of the poor, and replacing them with equivalent cash transfer programs may be administratively complicated and controversial since there would be disagreements about how large the transfers would have to be in order to fully compensate the beneficiaries. In the long run, however, the argument provides a case for moving in the direction of more emphasis on cash transfer programs over time.

3. Health Care and Equity: The Current Picture

In studying statistics about health care spending in China, the picture that emerges is one of great inequality, across different parts of the country, and among income groups.

3.1. *Inequality in health care spending: Rural-urban and regional*

Looking first at total health care expenditure (that is, including not only patients' out-of-pocket costs, but also what is paid by local governments and insurance plans), Figure 3 provides a dramatic illustration not only of how fast health care costs have risen since the 1990s, but also of the large and persistent gap between health care spending per capita in rural and urban areas. Figure 4 illustrates this gap in another way, showing the ratio between the two series. Although the trend since 2007 shows that rural per capita spending has actually grown faster than urban spending, it is still only one-third as large. While some part

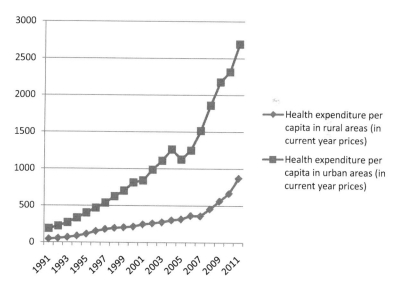

Fig. 3.   Health expenditure per capita in urban and rural areas.

Source: *China Health Statistical Yearbook*, various years.

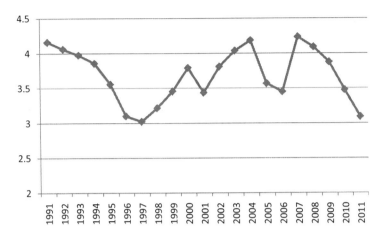

Fig. 4. Ratio of health expenditure per capita in urban and rural areas.

Source: China Health Statistical Yearbook, various years.

of the gap may be attributable to cases where seriously ill rural residents receive some of their health care in urban areas, most of the difference simply reflects the fact that rural residents have much less access to health services of good quality than people in urban areas.

Similarly, Table 2 shows the wide variation in per capita health care spending across provinces. Some of the differences may reflect differences in the per-unit cost of health services across provinces; for example, salaries of nurses and other hospital personnel may be lower in poor provinces. But again, the main reason for the large differences almost certainly reflects the fact that residents in the poorer provinces have much less access to various kinds of health services. Figure 5 shows the substantial differences that exist across China's main regions in the per capita availability of resources such as doctors, nurses, and hospital beds.

3.2. *Health care costs by income class*

The data also show that there are wide differences in health care spending across income classes. Data from *China Statistical Yearbook* show that the annual out-of-pocket spending of those in the top 20% of income earners was more than 3 times as high as for those in the

Table 2. Health expenditure per capita in 2010 across provinces (RMB).

	Total health expenditure per capita in 2010	Out-of-pocket health expenditure per capita in 2010	Government health expenditure in 2010	Social health expenditure in 2010
Beijing	4147	1033	1140	1974
Tianjin	2737	977	638	1122
Hebei	1254	539	371	345
Shanxi	1297	501	370	426
Inner Mongolia	1767	774	564	428
Liaoning	1766	696	403	668
Jilin	1654	756	448	452
Heilongjiang	1580	667	397	517
Jiangsu	1566	515	374	678
Zhejiang	2099	804	487	808
Anhui	1211	419	360	432
Fujian	1280	394	381	506
Jiangxi	992	337	404	251
Shandong	1403	543	341	519
Henan	1134	502	341	290
Hubei	1191	468	362	361
Hunan	1042	456	301	286
Guangdong	1446	586	344	516
Guangxi	1117	355	415	346
Chongqing	1501	608	417	476
Guizhou	947	293	441	212
Yunnan	1107	354	433	320
Gansu	1154	408	456	290
Xinjiang	1677	448	629	600

Source: China Health Statistical Yearbook, 2012.

bottom 20% in urban areas (about 1,700 RMB vs. 500 RMB). In rural areas, the ratio was closer to 2 (650 RMB vs. 300 RMB). However, the increases across income classes are not as large as the increases in per capita income itself. As Figures 6 and 7 show, health care costs as a percentage of total income were much lower in the high-income classes, in both urban and rural areas.

The Figures also show that there have been significant changes in some of these shares over time. In particular, the shares have fallen substantially for the higher income groups in urban areas, while in

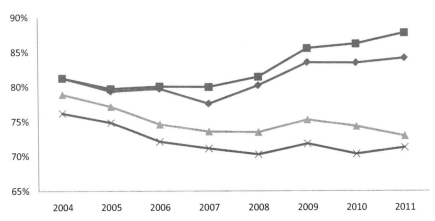

Fig. 5. Regional inequality of health care resources.

Source: China Health Statistical Yearbook, various years.

rural areas they have generally risen, especially for the low-income groups.

In interpreting the data in Figures 6 and 7, it is important to note that they refer to out-of-pocket spending only. That is, they do not include the portion of the cost of health services utilized by individuals in the respective income groups that were covered by reimbursement from social insurance plans, or by government subsidies. Although the data that would be needed to allow for this are not available, there is no doubt that a table showing the full per capita cost of the health services utilized in the different income classes would still show a pattern of higher values for those with higher income. In particular, taking into account that the out-of-pocket share of total costs that is paid by individuals covered by the urban BHI plans generally is lower than that in the URBMI and NCMS plans, would tend to produce an even

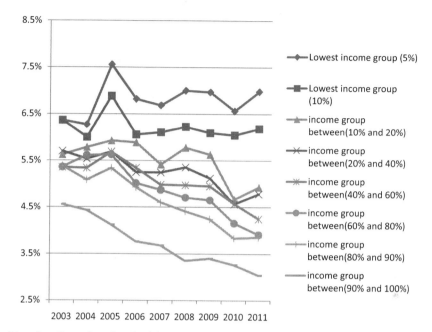

Fig. 6. Out-of-pocket health expenditure as a share of income per capita across income groups in urban areas (%).

Source: China Statistical Yearbook, various years.

stronger relationship between income and health expenditure in urban areas, since those in the BHI plans mostly are employed by government or by large firms and therefore tend to have relatively high per capita income.[15]

---

[15]The declining share of out-of-pocket health care spending in urban areas among high-income groups partly reflects the increasing extent to which urban employees are covered by social insurance, and the improvements in the degree of coverage in these plans over time. Although many urban residents with low income are now covered by the URBMI plans, the degree of coverage in these plans is generally lower, and they do not yet appear to have resulted in a significant reduction in the burden of out-of-pocket costs for low-income groups in the cities.

The increase in out-of-pocket costs as a percentage of income in rural areas is harder to explain, since it coincides with expanded health insurance coverage in rural areas through the NCMS plans that now cover a majority of rural residents. In part, the trend is likely to just reflect increased availability of health services and drugs in rural areas, leading to rapid increases in total spending. However, Wagstaff and Lindelow

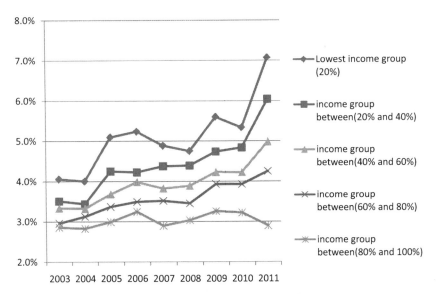

Fig. 7. Out-of-pocket health expenditure as a share of income per capita across income groups in rural areas (%).

Source: China Statistical Yearbook, various years.

When these data on health care spending by income class are interpreted against the background of the literature on health care and equity, they suggest that health care resources in China continue to be allocated and paid for in ways that would be considered relatively inequitable.

First, an implicit assumption in much of this literature is that in an equitable system, the amount of health care services that people with different kinds of illness should receive should be determined according to need, not by ability to pay. But there is no reason to expect that the need for health services rises with income. If anything, the evidence from other countries suggests that people at the low end of the income scale have more health problems, and hence greater need for health services, than those with high incomes. Based on this reasoning, an

---

(2008) suggest that it may also reflect the fact that insurance coverage encourages people to seek care when they otherwise might not have, and to seek care from more expensive high-level providers.

equitable allocation of health services would therefore require higher per capita spending on those in the lower income groups, or at least not a pattern of higher expenditure in the higher income groups.

Second, evidence that out-of-pocket spending on health services constitutes a higher share of per capita income in the lower income brackets than among those with high income is interpreted in much of the literature as an indication that health care is financed in an inequitable way. In reaching this conclusion, the literature uses terminology drawn from the theory of taxation, where taxes for which larger amounts relative to income are paid by those in lower income brackets are classified as regressive, in contrast to progressive taxes that imply a redistribution from the rich to the poor since they reduce the disposable income of the rich proportionately more than that of the poor.

But if the distribution of health care and its costs in China cannot currently be considered equitable by conventional standards, this mostly reflects the fact that the reforms in health care that have been undertaken in the past decade have not been in effect for a long enough time such that their effects are evident in the data. As the process of reform continues and implementation moves forward, the picture is likely to improve. Indeed, reform of the health care financing system may be one of the most powerful methods through which the government can advance its agenda of a more equitable society.

4. Health System Reform: Moving Toward Equity

While Chinese citizens only had access to very simple and basic health care before 1980, the system under which health services were produced and financed in the centrally planned economy could nevertheless be classified as being quite equitable. There was relatively little difference in the standards of health care that was offered across income groups, and most of the cost was paid for out of general government revenue rather than out of patients' pockets. By the same token, the changes in the health care system toward more financing from revenues raised from patients in the form of fees and markups on drugs that took place during the 1980s and 1990s made the system less equitable. With a larger share of financing coming out of patients' pockets, the system became more regressive, both in the sense that the disposable income of poor people was reduced by a larger proportion than that of the rich if they received given kinds of treatment, and in the sense that the poor suffered more than the rich from not being able to afford needed care. Moreover, it also became less equitable in the sense that a larger share of health services were used by the rich, as poor people either could not afford costly treatment or drugs, or had to make do with very basic care, while those with higher incomes could afford to pay for more advanced treatment or drugs.

The reforms that have been undertaken since the turn of the century and especially in the last few years have, however, begun to gradually reverse the trend and make the system more equitable, and can be expected to do so even more as the recent reforms are implemented on a wider scale. Indeed, one can argue that the reforms that call for strengthening China's social insurance programs and primary-care sector have the potential to serve as instruments that will very significantly contribute to a less unequal distribution of real income, broadly defined. It can do so in several ways.

First and foremost, a system that reduces the share of health care costs that come directly out of patients' pockets improves welfare because it implies a higher degree of redistribution of real income from those who are well, to those who are ill. Paradoxically, this redistribution will only be reflected to a limited extent in the usual measures of income inequality, such as the Gini coefficient. The reason is that these measures are computed using a conventional definition of income that does not take into account the fact that individuals' welfare depends in a significant way on their health status, not just on their income as conventionally defined. Most of the welfare gains that occur within income classes through improved risk pooling when patients pay a smaller share of their health care costs out-of-pocket are not reflected in the way real income is measured, since the standard way to define real income does not depend on how the income is spent.

While redistribution of income from the well to the ill can be accomplished through private insurance as well as by government policy, markets for private insurance are affected by problems (discussed in earlier chapters) that limit the extent to which they are able to accomplish this without government regulation. In practice, therefore, deliberate policies to strengthen risk pooling are required to accomplish this type of redistribution, and continued efforts to further reduce the out-of-pocket share in financing health care in China represent one of the most promising approaches to distribute rising real incomes in a more equitable way.

Although reducing the patients' out-of-pocket share of health care costs promotes equity in the sense of redistributing real income from the well to the sick, it may nevertheless be costly if the reduced cost causes patients to demand and utilize substantially larger amounts of health services. In the health economics literature, the possibility of losses of economic efficiency from this effect, referred to as the "moral hazard" effect, has been extensively discussed. However, the significance of the moral hazard effect depends on the extent to which the health care system allows the utilization of health services to be determined by decisions made by patients and the incentives to which they are subjected. As discussed in earlier chapters, most decisions about health care utilization, or about pharmaceutical use, are effectively made by doctors and other health personnel, since patients must rely to a great extent on professionals' advice in making such decisions. For this reason, the incentives that govern the advice, prescriptions, and referrals that health professionals make are likely to be much more important than the incentives on patients in determining aggregate health services utilization and cost, reducing the significance of the moral-hazard effect and weakening the argument against a low degree of patient cost-sharing.

Developing the health financing system in such a way that it strengthens the degree of risk pooling by reducing the share of out-of-pocket payments by patients can thus be seen as promoting equity because it increases the extent of redistribution of real income from the well to the sick. Moreover, this can be done in such a way that it also reduces the degree to which the system is regressive, in the sense described earlier. Specifically, when the share of out-of-pocket payments is reduced, the system can be said to become less regressive if the revenue that is raised to finance the increased share of third-party financing is derived from taxes or social insurance contributions that rise with income.[16]

The social insurance plans that have been developed in China in recent years already do so, at least to a limited extent. For individuals who are covered by an urban BHI plan, the benefits to which they are entitled from the social pooling account when they are ill are the same for every enrollee, but the contributions to the BHI plans are typically fixed as a given proportion of the individual's salary (that is, neither regressive nor progressive). Enrollment in an URBMI or NCMS plan normally requires payment of a fixed individual premium which does not depend on income (and therefore is regressive), but there is also a government subsidy which is financed out of the general tax system (which is progressive, at least to some extent). The development of a network of primary-care clinics in which all citizens will be entitled to subsidized care will accelerate this trend, since the part of the cost that is covered by government will be raised through the general tax system. Moreover, plans to gradually increase the government subsidy for enrollees in the URBMI and NCMS plans will have the same effect, as it increases the share of financing that comes out of general tax revenue.

Compared to the uniform universal systems in countries like the U.K. or continental Europe, China's system of health care financing still makes a relatively limited contribution to the redistribution of real income from rich to poor. However, the trend toward a more progressive model is firmly established, and there is every reason to believe that it will continue to develop in this direction.

4.1. *Is a single plan for everyone the ideal?*

The universal systems in places like the U.K., Japan, and continental Europe are seen by many as the most equitable among the health care systems across the world. If China wants to continue in the direction

---

[16]The data discussed earlier on out-of-pocket health care costs as a percentage of income show that there is still a long way to go before the effects of the current reforms will clearly show up in the data, especially for rural areas.

of using health policy to reduce the inequality in real incomes, should the government move toward a model of uniform universal coverage similar to the one in those countries?

Doing so would require merging the three different social insurance plans that now cover different segments of the population. Moreover, a single universal government plan similar to that in these countries leaves little room for individuals who are able and willing to do so to acquire private insurance that substitutes for, or supplements, the coverage that all citizens have in the public plan. Should China also aim for an equity target that discourages private health insurance alongside the public system?

Though many health economists would answer "yes" to these questions, our view is that for the foreseeable future, China will be better served by continuing to improve the existing plans, rather than work towards merging them.[17] Moreover, we also believe that private insurance can have a very useful role to play alongside the public plans. Indeed, for reasons that we further discuss in the Appendix, we would argue that China might be better served, even in the long run, through a system that allows some diversity and choice in health insurance, rather than through a strictly universal model.

5. Conclusion: Income Distribution, Equity, and Health Policy

China's rapid economic growth over the last 30 years has benefited broad segments of the population, lifting hundreds of millions out of poverty. But as in other fast-growing middle-income countries, standard measures of inequality in the distribution of income, such as the Gini coefficient, have been rising, and in the middle of the first decade of the 21st century, had reached levels that were internationally regarded as a cause for concern.

In the very long run, continued economic growth is, by itself, likely to produce a trend toward reduced inequality, as increased investment

---

[17]As further discussed in Chapter 9, however, we think a good case can be made for a unified set of rules to cover the URBMI and NCMS plans.

raises the ratio of capital to labor, causing real wages to rise relative to the returns to capital, and as an expansion in the proportion of educated workers shrinks the earnings gap between educated and unskilled workers. International evidence points to lower degrees of income inequality in high-income countries, even when income is measured before taxes and transfers to the poor. But in high-income countries, there is also a substantial amount of additional redistribution through the tax-transfer system, and through various social programs that also are designed in part for the purpose of reducing inequality in real incomes.

During the first two decades of rapid growth, the focus of the central government's economic policy was on the gradual dismantling of the system of central planning, the transition to a market economy, and the opening up of China to international trade and investment. Since the turn of the century, however, and especially since the last several years of the Hu–Wen era, the issue of economic inequality and the importance of reducing it through various forms of redistribution and social policy have received much more attention. In comparison with other middle-income countries at a similar stage of development, today and in the past, China has already made great progress in this regard.

Programs such as Di Bao and provision of retirement income through social security have begun to raise the cash income of the poor in both urban and rural areas, and subsidies to education at all levels are creating better opportunities for children from poor families as well as helping the growth process. There is every reason to believe that the new leadership under Xi Jinping and Li Keqiang will continue to emphasize the importance of reducing inequality and improved social policies. In doing so, a reasonable initial focus can be on ensuring that these programs are effectively established everywhere in China, and are strengthened by offering enhanced cash benefits and more resources and better trained teachers for students, respectively.

Reducing the inequality of income through redistribution through the tax-transfer system will indirectly help reduce the inequality in the access to health services to some extent, since it helps individuals with low income to pay for health services, or private health insurance, out of their own pockets. However, private health insurance markets are unlikely to be effective in ensuring access to essential health services for poor people. Given the potentially devastating consequences of serious illness for uninsured people with low income, government programs to ensure that they do have such access potentially represent one of the most effective ways of indirectly redistributing real income toward the poor.

While some health economists advocate going further and setting a target of providing the same kind of health services to all people with given health problems, regardless of willingness and ability to pay, we believe this would be an unrealistic approach at China's current state of development, and that the government would do better to focus on promoting equality by building a system that guarantees access to at least a basic menu of health services and drugs to everyone, including the poor.

Appendix. Equity, Utilization of Health Services, and Ability to Pay

As noted earlier, a common view in the health economics literature is that in an equitable system, the health care services used by sick people should depend only on their need for such services, not on their ability to pay. While we believe that the high correlation between health services use and ability to pay that is indicated by the current data in China will diminish over time, we do not share the view that equity in this sense is a reasonable goal for China in the medium term. Moreover, we are also of the view that an attempt to attain equity in this sense can be costly in terms of reducing the degree of economic efficiency, even in the long run.

The principle that health services utilization should be based on patients' needs rests on the assumption that it is possible to define, for each type of illness, a set of health services that are needed or necessary, and that everyone with this illness condition should have access to these services. It is also implicit in this principle that any health services that a person utilizes beyond those that are needed are of little or no value in terms of improving the patient's health; by definition, they are not needed or necessary. In contrast, the services that are needed are of very high value; if a patient does not have access to them, he or she will suffer severe consequences in terms of ill-health.

A question that must be asked, however, arises when the data from most countries show that in fact, the amount of health services that individuals with different illness conditions actually do use are different, with high-income individuals using more services than those with low income. Specifically, does this mean that in order to achieve equity in the use of health resources, we would have to ensure that per capita use of health services in every income class would have to be as high as that among those in the highest income class? Or does it mean that in order for the allocation to be equitable, one would have to prevent individuals with high income from utilizing health services beyond those that are needed, even if they are willing to pay for them?

Both of these alternatives raise problems. The first one implies that achieving equity in the utilization of health services would be prohibitively costly, since the data show that per capita health care use in the highest income bracket is much larger than in the lower brackets. The other alternative, that of bringing about equity by reducing health services utilization by those in higher income brackets, would logically mean that in order to accomplish this, policies must be found to identify which of the health services that they were using should be classified as unnecessary, and prevent them from using these services.

In reality, it is not possible to make a clear distinction between health services that are needed and those that are not. In general, the outcome of any one illness episode is unpredictable, so that a good outcome can never be guaranteed; at best, utilization of health services increases the probability of a good outcome. Moreover, in many situations, individuals are faced with choices where the expected benefits of additional diagnostic tests, more advanced interventions, or costly drugs may increase the probability of a good outcome, but only by a small amount. It is not clear whether these services or drugs would be classified as necessary or needed. For a high-income individual with substantial ability to pay, spending the additional money for such services or drugs may seem worthwhile, whereas a person with lower ability to pay might choose not to do so. In such cases, it would be inefficient, as well as unrealistic, to insist on the principle that people with given illness conditions should receive the same services, regardless of their ability and willingness to pay.

On balance, therefore, we believe that it would be unproductive for China's policymakers to pay a great deal of attention to the inequalities in patterns of health services utilization between rich and poor that will continue to exist in the foreseeable future. At the same time, we do believe that the government does have an important role to play in establishing what constitutes a basic set of health services to which everyone, even those at the bottom of the income scale, should have access. In particular, persons at the lowest end of the income scale will benefit greatly from the establishment of a network of primary-care clinics where every resident will have access to a menu of basic health services and essential drugs at low, subsidized rates. The ability of local governments to ensure that this planned network can be established and function as intended depends to a large extent on exactly how these menus of services and drugs are defined, and we believe that systematic attention to the value of different types of health services and drugs in improving health at low cost could be of great help in deciding on which ones should be included.

While financing of these clinics might be easier if they are allowed to also supply other drugs and services to those who are willing to pay for them, in practice this might result in diversion of their resources toward high-income patients. A case can be made, therefore, for restricting these clinics to supply only those services and drugs that have been evaluated as essential in a package to which everyone should have access, and letting those who wish to buy more advanced services or costly drugs do so in private hospitals and clinics.

Chapter 8

DECENTRALIZED GOVERNMENT, CENTRAL-LOCAL FISCAL RELATIONS, AND HEALTH REFORM

1. Introduction

In this chapter, we discuss an issue that ultimately will be critical in determining the way China's health care system will evolve: how the responsibility for reform and management of health care is divided between governments at the central and local levels.

Normally, the assignment of responsibility for various functions between the different levels of government in any country is determined by its constitution. From the viewpoint of constitutional law, China is a unitary state, rather than a federation like the U.S., Germany, or Canada. In a federation, subnational units, such as the U.S. states, Canadian provinces, or German Länder, are given certain specific powers in the country's constitution, and constitutional changes cannot be made unilaterally through a central body, but only after negotiations with representatives of the subnational units. In unitary states like the U.K. or China, in contrast, constitutional changes can be made through the highest central political authority alone (Parliament in the U.K., the National People's Congress in China), in accordance with specified procedures.

In the U.S., the process of constructing a model that guarantees universal health insurance coverage is complicated by the fact that of the two largest government programs, Medicare (which provides coverage for the elderly) is a federal (central) government program, while Medicaid coverage for the poor is the responsibility of the individual states. In Canada, the constitution explicitly specifies that health care is the responsibility of the provinces, so that while there is universal government health insurance coverage in Canada, this is accomplished through the existence of a set of similar insurance plans in Canada's ten provinces and three territories. However, even though the constitution clearly allocates responsibility for health care to the provinces, the federal government nevertheless plays a central role in health policy because it makes large transfers of tax revenue to the provinces that are conditional on certain restrictions that the provincial programs must meet. In the U.S., too, the central government makes revenue transfers to the states subject to conditions that their Medicaid plans must meet.

As discussed in Chapter 2, health policy and health reform can be highly controversial and difficult processes, partly since they typically involve negotiations between government and powerful special interest groups. The history of health policy in countries like the U.S., Canada, and Germany also provides evidence that reform can be even more difficult in federal systems because they then involve governments and politicians at both the central and subnational levels, with often conflicting priorities and a desire to appeal to different constituencies. In contrast to the near-stalemate that sometimes seems to characterize the debate over health reform in these countries, some countries with unitary systems (for example, the U.K. and Japan) seem to have had more success in creating and managing health care systems with universal coverage that function well and appear relatively cost-effective.

But although China, like the U.K. and Japan, is a unitary state in a legal sense, in practice it is a country whose economy is managed in a highly decentralized fashion, as the central government has delegated a great deal of authority over economic management to provincial and lower levels of government. While the orientation of economic policy in the last several years has shifted from an almost exclusive focus on increasing the rate of growth to a more balanced approach with more emphasis on the creation of a "harmonious society" through enhanced social programs, the principle of decentralized management has continued to be applied. Accordingly, local government officials have considerable discretion not only with respect to how they implement reform initiatives that have originated at the center, but even in terms of important characteristics of the programs and their management. This certainly applies to management not only of the health services production sector, but also of the social health insurance programs that now cover some 95% of China's population. In previous chapters, we have already seen how this has led to a great deal of variety across provinces, cities, and counties in the nature and scope of coverage of the social insurance plans, in the incentive structures to which hospitals and clinics are subjected, and even in the way the essential drugs system has been implemented.

The rest of the chapter is organized as follows. In the next section, we describe in more detail the role of local governments in managing the health care system, both with respect to the financing function, and the production of health services. Following this, we turn to a discussion of the reasons why China's leadership continues to favor a high degree of decentralization of the economic system generally, even though there may be some reason to believe that this approach may have made it more difficult to reform health care in such a way that it contributes more effectively to the objective of greater equality in real income broadly defined.

An important reason why decentralization has had this effect is that China is still in the process of reorganizing its public finances, including the system of intergovernmental fiscal relations which currently may have the unintended consequence of biasing local decision-makers against using public funds to pay for a higher standard of health care for the population at large, and against reducing the share of health care costs that patients have to pay out of their own pockets. Moreover, the incentives to which local officials are subjected may not yet be effective in reflecting the increased emphasis that the central government now places on reducing inequality, as opposed to the objective of bringing about a high rate of economic growth. We conclude the chapter with a brief discussion of the way the system could be improved in these respects.

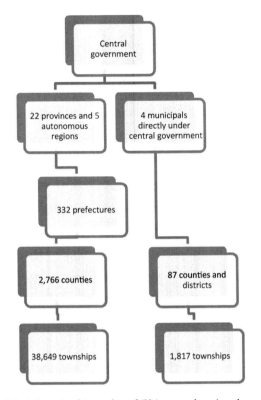

Fig. 1. Administrative hierarchy of Chinese subnational government.
Source: China Statistical Abstract 2012.

2. The Role of Local Government in China's Health Care System Today

China's system of government involves several levels, and decentralization of authority regarding economic and social policy has taken place not only from the center to provincial authorities, but further down to prefectures, counties, and townships as well. (Figure 1 provides a stylized representation of China's different levels of government.)

As discussed in previous chapters, the government's role in the health care sector includes that of organizing and subsidizing the three major sets of social health insurance plans in China: Basic Health Insurance System for Urban Staff and Workers (BHI), the new rural Cooperative Medical Scheme (NCMS), and Urban Resident Basic

Medical Insurance (URBMI). In addition, it is planned that a large number of publicly owned and subsidized local health service facilities will be established in order to supply primary (out-patient) care. For each township, there would be at least one publicly funded health center, and for urban areas, networks of clinics in each community are being built most of which are publicly funded. The tasks of funding the construction and operating costs of these provider clinics as well as higher-level hospitals, and subsidizing the health insurance plans, are largely falling upon governments at the subnational level, from the provincial ones and downward, although lower levels of government may generally receive some amount of transfers from higher levels.

In health policy and reform, the prefectural governments in the large cities and the county governments in rural areas have especially important roles since they are the owners of most of China's hospitals, and are responsible for management of the social insurance plans discussed in Chapter 3.

2.1. *Local government as service provider*

Local government decisions have a major influence on the way hospitals operate. Although there were large-scale hospital reforms in the 2000s, the majority of hospitals in China are publicly owned. Thus, the operating costs of most hospitals, including basic salaries of the hospitals' staff, are to a large extent paid from county and city governments' budgets.[1] In 2010, about 13% of total revenue of all service providers came directly from government. For primary-care providers, the share was over 20%. Also, local governments can influence hospital managers' behavior by the conditions according to which they allocate these grants, and through their control over the personnel appointments in publicly owned hospitals, as discussed in Chapter 5.

Hospital salary budgets are large in relation to total expenditure of local governments, and may be inflated when higher-level governments

---

[1]Gu *et al.* (2006) discuss the ownership structure of China's hospital system. Around 9%–12% of hospital expenditure including basic salary of physicians was financed from government budgets in the early 2000s. In 2011, the number was about 8.4% (*China Health Statistics Yearbook*, 2012).

require them to hire redundant civil servants who otherwise would be unemployed.[2] The pressure from these expenditure requirements makes it very attractive for local governments to induce hospitals to raise as much revenue as possible from the patients that they treat, and the data show that revenue from public service units such as hospitals is one of the important sources of "off-budget" revenue (we will discuss this concept further below).[3]

2.2. *Local government as insurer*

As we further discuss below, local governments in China have for a long time been subject to a high degree of fiscal pressure. This has affected the way they have operated the social health insurance plans for which they are responsible, since the net expenditure or revenue from these plans also has a negative or positive effect on their budgets.

An important factor in this context is the matching grants that are given to local governments from central and provincial governments when they enroll members in the social health insurance plans. The government grants are at least four times as large as individual enrollees' premium contributions. The ratio between the matching grants from the central government and the contributions from subnational governments for the NCMS plans and urban residents' plans (in central and western provinces) is determined according to local conditions. For example, in Nanning city, Guangxi province, the grant from the central government was 124 RMB and from local governments 109 RMB for

---

[2]This continues a long existing practice; see World Bank (2002), Liu *et al.* (2009), Qian and Do (2012). In a recent interview, a hospital manager stated that only around 300 out of 2,000 employees in a city hospital had been recruited publicly (*Southern Weekend*, November 22, 2007).

[3]Wong and Bird (2008) mention briefly the importance of hospital revenue as a source to cover local governments' expenditure. Qian (2011b) discusses the fiscal relations of local government and public hospital reform in China. A recent interview with an official source (the vice president of the health bureau of Guangdong province) also reveals that some local governments could pay for other local civil servants' salaries and various investment projects from local hospitals' accounts; see http://news.xinhuanet.com/politics/2006-01/04/content_4008375.htm (accessed on August 2, 2012).

the URBMI plan in 2011[4] (i.e., a ratio of 1.1:1). In Tongchuan city, Shanxi province, the grant from the central government was 156 RMB and from the local governments 94 RMB for its URBMI plan in 2011[5] (i.e., a 1.6:1 ratio). The amount of social insurance funding that will be managed by local government is expected to increase further as government grants are expected to increase to 360 RMB per enrollee by the end of 2015.[6]

2.3. *Local government as regulator*

Thirdly, as briefly noted above, local government also has another potentially important role in China's health financing system (especially in urban areas), namely as the regulator of the private health insurance market (e.g., regulation of conditions of entry of private plans in the health insurance market, regulations that affect the scope for opportunistic behavior of physicians toward patients in private insurance plans, or restrictions on the extent of integration between hospitals and private insurers).

Local government also regulates the quality of health care services. For example, in medical malpractice disputes, the local health bureau is the major agency who selects experts to sit in an authentication committee to determine whether there has been malpractice. Also, the local health and justice bureaus are in charge of mediation processes for medical malpractice dispute resolution.[7]

2.4. *Local governments and the form of decentralization*

A health care system such as China's in which local government simultaneously functions as insurer and health services provider is similar in some ways to the publicly owned and managed regional

---

[4]Nanning Social Security Bureau, 2011, Document 125.
[5]Tongchuan Social Security Bureau, 2011, Document 390.
[6]See a recent Xinhua report, at http://news.xinhuanet.com/society/2012-03/23/c_111691764.htm (accessed on August 2, 2012).
[7]Disputes of this type have become more common in recent years; see Qian and Leong (2012).

monopoly National Health Service (NHS) system in the U.K. or the Veterans Health Administration (VHA) system in the U.S.[8] However, there are several institutional features that are unique to the Chinese system.

First, the way that officials manage the local departments and agencies of the NHS and the VHA in the U.K. and the U.S., respectively, is subject to detailed rules and regulations that have been formulated by the central government, and that are strictly enforced. Local officials have little or no role as regulators of the system, and have relatively limited discretion with respect to the principles they use as managers. In comparison, county and city officials in China have considerably more autonomy.

Second, under the U.K. NHS and the American VHA, the budgets for the local health authorities or branches are provided through allocations from the central (federal) government. In other countries (such as Canada, and in the U.S. for the state Medicaid plans that cover those with low income), responsibility for funding is more decentralized, but only to the second level of government (Canadian provinces or American states). In China, in contrast, local governments at the third or fourth level from the top are responsible not only for managing the health services system, but also for raising a large part of the funds that the local health agencies need.

These institutional differences are potentially very important, both in terms of predicting how the system will function, and also in assessing the prospects for success of the efforts currently underway to reform the system. In particular, we will argue that to the extent decentralized management with a high degree of autonomy allows local managers to experiment with innovative methods and approaches, this is an important strength of the Chinese system that in the long run will enhance the prospects of successful reform. However, under the arrangements that currently govern intergovernmental fiscal relations in China, local officials typically face a very high degree of fiscal pressure, and are subject to incentives that are likely to cause them to put too

---

[8]The U.K. NHS system is discussed in Chapter 2 as one of our reference cases. A description of the VHA system is in Oliver (2007).

little emphasis on social spending, including on health care, relative to spending on investment projects that raise the local rate of economic growth. While the central government tries to correct for this bias through issuing new directives and imposing various restrictions, the effectiveness of the approaches it has been using so far is uncertain, and needs reinforcement in order to more fully realize the objectives of the reform efforts that now are underway. We discuss these issues in the next two sections.

3. Diversity, Innovation, and Decentralization

Given that China's political system is usually regarded as a highly hierarchical one that is dominated by the central leadership of the Communist Party, and given that during its first three decades the People's Republic adopted a Soviet-inspired model of central planning for economic management, the fact that it now is highly decentralized may seem surprising. However, there are several reasonable explanations. First, China is a very large and heterogeneous country, and economic and social policy must be adapted to local conditions — something that obviously can be accomplished more efficiently under decentralized management.

Second, somewhat paradoxically, it has been suggested that delegating certain types of authority to the local level may in part have the effect of offsetting a tendency toward conservative and risk-averse decision-making in a hierarchical one-party society. Decentralization makes it possible for local officials to experiment with different models of economic and social management without directly associating the outcomes with specific individuals in the central leadership.[9] This idea is consistent with the cautious approach to reforms that has been practiced since the early 1980s, and which was famously described by Deng Xiaoping as "crossing the river while feeling the stones".

In the area of health system reform, the government has been quite explicit in its encouragement of local experiments. In particular,

---

[9]Xu (2011) makes this point.

this principle was highlighted in the guidelines for health reform that were released in 2009.[10] The rationale is that experiences from local experiments can be very helpful in indicating directions for nationwide reform. Such local experiments can happen in many policy arenas including the design of the social health insurance plans, in establishing the network of primary-care clinics, and in deciding what drugs will be included in the list of essential medicines, and how the list will be used within the system. A particularly important area of reform where there still is considerable uncertainty about future directions is with respect to management of public hospitals and the role of private providers. Evidence from local experiments in this area, and with respect to different approaches to the relationship between providers and the social insurance plans, is likely to play an important part in shaping China's evolving health care system in the coming years. The great variety of local experiments in this and other areas has been referred to in many places in earlier chapters of this book.

But while the freedom of local managers to experiment can potentially be regarded as a strength of a decentralized system, the way these managers use their autonomy also depends on the incentives they face. In the Chinese model of governance, these incentives depend both on the fiscal relationships between the central and local levels of government, and on the objectives of the central leadership and the methods it has used to exercise its influence over the decisions that are made at the local level. We will argue below that the intergovernmental fiscal arrangements that are in place today, as well as the incentive structure on local managers that is implied by the existing model of decentralization, may not yet fully reflect the objective of increasing the focus of economic policy on reduced inequality, including inequality that is related to health and the cost of health care. Indirectly, this may have the effect of slowing down the process of health reform, and to some extent channel it in less promising directions.

---

[10]A summary is at http://www.gov.cn/jrzg/2009-04/06/content_1278721.htm (accessed on August 2, 2012).

3.1. *Intergovernmental fiscal relations in China*

While China's central government has for some time been clear in its desire to reorient economic policy toward more attention to income distribution and reduction of economic inequality, it has continued to respect the principle of decentralized management. While there has been considerable debate at the central level with respect to the major programs that are central to this new direction, decisions at the central level have taken the form of relatively general guidelines, with considerable freedom for local officials to implement them in the way they see fit and suitable to local conditions. This applies not only to health policy, but also to education, retirement income security, and redistribution through general social assistance (the Di Bao program), as discussed in Chapter 7.

But implementation of pro-equality policies in these areas is expensive, putting a heavy fiscal burden on local government. Figure 2 shows that the share of local government expenditure in GDP increased from 8% in 1995 to over 20% in 2012, while the share of government expenditure in general had reached 24% in 2012. The expenditure on various social services as a share of local budgets

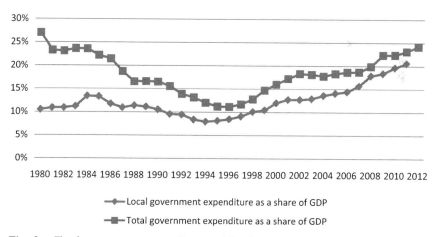

Fig. 2. Total government expenditure and local government expenditure as a share of GDP.

Source: Financial Yearbook of China, various years.

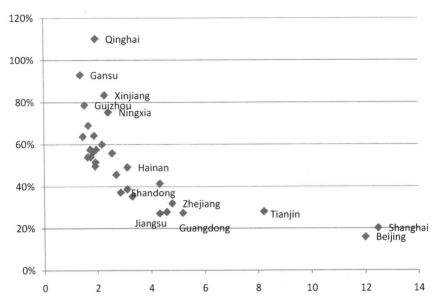

Fig. 3. Expenditure on education and health as a share of local government revenue in 2010.

Note: Horizontal-axis refers to local fiscal revenue per capita (in RMB 1,000).
Source: *China Statistical Yearbook*, 2011.

is increasing. Capital and operating expenditure for services such as health, education, and social safety net programs, as well as urban and community affairs at the local level, constituted 42% of local government expenditure on average in 2010, while expenditure on these services only accounted for about 32% in 2002. Expenditure on health and education accounted for more than 50% of total government revenue in 17 provinces in 2010, including Qinghai, Gansu, Xinjiang and Guizhou. The burden on local authorities in these relatively poor regions to provide public goods such as education and health is huge (Figure 3).

Local governments may still be able to pursue the policies mandated by the central government if given access to enough sources of tax revenue. But it is widely recognized that the current intergovernmental fiscal relationships in China, as a legacy of the central planning system and the piecemeal reforms that have taken place since the 1980s, have not given very strong revenue-raising capability to the county/city levels of government.[11]

Since the major centralization of revenue resulting from the reform in the mid-1990s, the subnational governments' share of government budgetary revenue has continued to be less than 50% of the total, while its share in expenditure remained at roughly 70% of the total, a pattern sustained till today (see Figure 4).

The result has been a large and growing fiscal gap. Figure 5 shows that, while local governments' revenue had increased to more than 6 trillion RMB in 2012, the fiscal gap still amounted to over 70% of their revenue in that year. In the circumstances, it is not surprising to see that 791 out of 1,635 rural-based county governments did not have enough

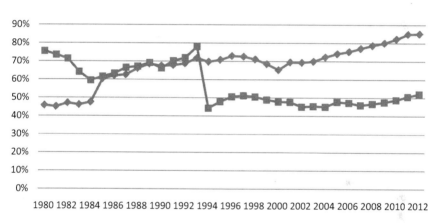

Fig. 4. Local government expenditure/revenue as a share of total government expenditure/revenue.

Source: CEIC and Ministry of Finance, budget report 2013.

---

[11] An early comprehensive study of public finance issues in China is World Bank (2002). More recent discussions that emphasize central-local fiscal issues are Whiting (2007), Wong and Bird (2008) and several of the essays in Lou and Wang (2008). Zhou (2004) is a detailed field study on the organization and day-to-day operations of a county government in northern China.

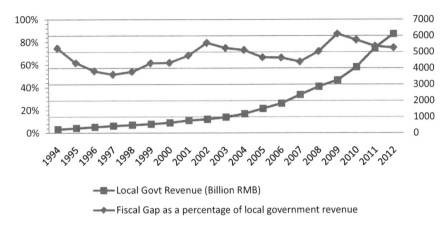

Fig. 5. Fiscal gap between local government's expenditure and revenue.
Source: Financial Yearbook of China, various years.

revenue to cover their expenditure in 2004.[12] Given this, many local governments must rely significantly on revenue outside of the normal budget system as well as on transfers including general purpose and earmarked transfers from upper-level governments, in order to maintain day-to-day operations.[13]

There are several reasons why local government's own revenue is relatively low. First, under the current intergovernmental fiscal system, subnational and central governments are sharing tax revenue on terms

---

[12] The numbers are from *China Reform* (2007). It is widely reported that local government's debt is extremely high. Much of it has been incurred in order to finance public projects. Estimates by the National Audit Office suggested that the total amount of local debt was 10.7 trillion RMB in 2011; see http://news.xinhuanet.com/fortune/2011-07/11/c_121651516.htm (accessed on August 2, 2012). Tong and Yao (2011) discuss the dangers posed by this indebtedness.

[13] Off-budget revenue includes extra-budgetary funds and off-budget funds. Extra-budgetary funds are defined as "levies and user charges collected and spent by government agencies in performing duties delegated to them by higher levels" and "[all] resources managed directly or indirectly by administrative branches of the government outside the normal budgetary process" but which are overseen by the Ministry of Finance. Off-budget funds refer to funds/revenues which are not subject to Ministry of Finance's supervision (Whiting, 2007).

that are not very favorable to the former. Most of the tax revenues from major taxes, such as the value added tax which accounted for about 30% of aggregate tax revenue in 2010, are allocated to the central government. For instance, the central government receives 75% of value added tax revenue.

In principle, data showing a large fiscal gap do not necessarily imply that local governments are under a high degree of fiscal pressure, if transfers from higher-level governments are large in relation to the local governments' expenditure responsibilities. In China, however, there is no well-defined set of rules to provide for large general-purpose transfers, partly because the central government needs to keep a tight grip on spending in order to avoid an overheated economy and maintain macroeconomic stability with limited inflation. While the central and provincial governments make substantial earmarked transfers for specific initiatives and programs, this only partially relieves the fiscal pressure on local authorities since such transfers do not always correspond to the increased expenditure responsibilities that have been passed down to local governments in recent years. On the whole, therefore, the evidence does suggest that fiscal pressures at the local level may slow down the strengthening of the social programs that is needed in order to make significant progress in building a more harmonious society. Moreover, this tendency may be reinforced by the incentives to which local decision-makers are subjected under China's system of government.

3.2. *Incentives on local decision-makers in China*

In federal systems that are multi-party democracies, local decision-makers are politicians who are accountable to local voters. In a unitary one-party form of government, in contrast, local decision-makers are directly accountable only to the officials in the higher levels of government from whom they derive their authority. The way they will use their discretionary powers in making local decisions, therefore, will depend both on what objectives the central authorities want them to pursue, and on the incentives and restrictions that are used to make local officials pursue policies that agree with these objectives.[14]

In China, the main tool that the central government has been using to influence local decisions has been its control over official appointments which have been highly centralized and controlled by the party. Officials from provincial governors and below are appointed for time-limited terms, and reappointments and promotions depend critically on performance evaluations that are regularly carried out. One important principle in the system is that high-level officials typically are moved between large cities and provinces, partly to reduce the tendency for them to identify more closely with regional rather than nationwide objectives.

Consistent with the overriding objective of accelerating China's economic growth, the most important criterion according to which officials were evaluated in the first two decades starting in the early 1980s has been the rate of economic growth in the jurisdiction for which they were responsible. Local growth rates have been closely monitored by the center. Indirectly, therefore, local officials have been subject to a powerful incentive to promote high rates of growth by whatever means they had, since their prospects for career advancement depended on success in that dimension.

To do so, they have aggressively sought to increase investment in local production facilities in various ways. In some of the coastal provinces and big cities, many local officials were successful in bringing about increased investment by pursuing policies to attract foreign investors, through tax concessions and in other ways. In rural areas and in provinces where there was relatively little foreign investment, efforts to produce a high rate of economic growth required domestic financing. While some financing came from the banking system, the amounts were limited by rationing as the central government sought to stabilize aggregate demand by asserting increased control over bank lending. Moreover, local governments have had very limited power

---

[14]Xu (2011) is an important survey of research relating to the interaction between the center and local officials in China's economic policy. Another interesting recent paper on this topic is Kung and Chen (2013).

to issue debt of their own, in the form of municipal bonds or other instruments. Consequently, local governments therefore often resorted to investing their own resources in local firms (township and village enterprises), or reducing the revenue they collected from government-owned firms. Either way, the result was increased pressure to raise revenue through local taxes or through fees, land sales, and other extra-budgetary or off-budget sources.[15]

The strong incentive on decision-makers to channel local resources toward investment is likely to have led to a slower development of social programs in areas such as health, education, or social assistance, given that local decision-makers had considerable discretion about where and how to spend their resources. Perhaps in recognition of this problem, the central government has introduced an arrangement referred to as the "target responsibility system". Under this system, the performance of local cadres is evaluated to a large extent on the basis of their ability to raise enough funds to deliver a defined range of social welfare and other public services. But the local GDP growth rate continues to play a large role in the evaluation of cadres, and hence their chances for promotion.[16] Local government decision-makers still have a strong incentive to devote their resources to investment of all kinds (in infrastructure, government-owned firms) to increase local GDP, rather than spending on social programs.

4. Local Incentives and Health Care Reform

The incentives to which the officials of local governments have been subject have influenced their decisions in all three of their roles in the health sector, as listed above: as owners and managers of the clinics and

---

[15]Tong and Yao (2011) also discuss this problem. Li (2008) argues that new rules permitting local governments to issue debt could be beneficial, and suggests a regulatory framework that would facilitate this. In an interesting contribution, Gordon and Li (2011) analyze a model in which local officials are assumed to simply try to raise as much net tax revenue (total revenue less expenditure on public programs) as possible, and argue that the model's predictions are broadly consistent with the evidence.

[16]See Whiting (2007), Tsui and Wang (2008), and Shih *et al.* (2012).

hospitals where health services are provided; as managers of the social insurance programs; and as regulators of public and private providers and insurers.

4.1. *Incentives and patient payments*

In the context of their role as providers, local officials' incentive to raise resources for investment is likely to have been a major contributory factor to the rapid increase in the amounts that hospitals and clinics have been earning from patients in recent decades, as discussed in earlier chapters. Since local governments are the owners and are responsible for managing hospitals and clinics, they have had an incentive to encourage doctors and hospital managers to raise more revenue from the services they supply, or from markups on the drugs they supply to patients, since increased earnings from these sources become available to the governments who are their residual claimants; more realistically, these increased earnings reduce the deficits that local governments might otherwise incur by being responsible for paying hospital salaries and other costs. Although leading local officials may not themselves make the decisions that influence provider earnings, they can indirectly encourage doctors and hospital managers to raise more revenue, for example, by paying them annual bonuses that depend on hospitals' and clinics' revenue.

4.2. *Incentives and social insurance*

Governments at the municipal and county levels have also been responsible for managing the social insurance plans that have been the source for an increasing share of health care financing since the late 1990s. Although there may be rules that stipulate that all the plans' revenues should be used only to pay for insured health services and the costs of administering the plans themselves, local governments may be able to draw on any surpluses in the plans, at least temporarily, for other purposes, such as financing investments in infrastructure or other activities that generate revenue. The evidence cited in Chapter 3 that the plans have indeed generated large surpluses in recent years certainly is consistent with the idea that they have been managed with this intention.

To some extent, there is of course a conflict between the incentives that local officials have to produce surpluses under the social insurance plans, and to reduce the net costs of operating hospitals and clinics, since payments of insurance benefits increase when hospitals provide more services or prescribe more drugs. However, this conflict may be minimized by more restrictive rules regarding what the social insurance plans will cover, or by tighter upper limits on annual benefits. Moreover, hospitals and clinics can be encouraged to concentrate more on supplying advanced services and newer drugs that are not covered by the insurance plans, as seems to have happened in some places. Strategies to jointly manage the social insurance system and the government-owned providers in such a way as to minimize the net cost to the local government will be easier to implement if the same officials are involved in both activities, as often happens. It is a common practice that the same local health bureau manages the social health insurance fund and public health service providers, particularly in rural areas.[17]

4.3. *Incentives on local government as regulators*

Finally, the incentives to which local decision-makers are subjected may also influence the way they exercise their authority as regulators. For example, provincial officials with an incentive to demonstrate high growth rates in their jurisdiction have created barriers favoring producers in their own province and making it hard for firms elsewhere to compete for various kinds of contracts.[18] In the area of health care, local authorities with an incentive to increase the revenue of the hospitals and clinics that they own may use their regulatory authority to make it difficult for private hospitals and primary-care providers to attract patients (for example, by not allowing the social insurance plans to reimburse patients for costs of care from private providers). Similarly, when local authorities regulate insurance markets, they may

---

[17] Gu *et al.* (2006, p. 230) and Han and Luo (2007, p. 44) note this point.
[18] Xu (2011) cites this as one of the undesirable consequences of the governance model.

do so in a way that takes into account the impact on the net revenue they expect to generate under the social insurance plans they manage. As China's health insurance markets are still in a relatively early stage of development, there are not yet, to our knowledge, any studies showing that this has been a problem; but as we discuss in Chapter 10, it may become a more significant issue in the future if China gradually moves toward a model with a greater role for private providers of health services, or an insurance system with more competition between the social insurance plans and independent health insurers.

4.4. *Realigning local incentives*

The examples discussed above suggest that the incentives on local officials may cause them to make decisions that hamper the implementation of the central government's objectives of better protecting patients against the high cost of serious illness and reducing health-related inequality. The central government can attempt to offset this bias, at least to some extent, through the guidelines it provides for local decision-makers, or by imposing various restrictions on them.

One method that is extensively used is to earmark transfers from higher to lower levels of government — that is, to specify that they can be used only for specific purposes. But enforcing such guidelines and restrictions can be difficult and costly. For example, making sure that earmarked funds are used as intended requires that local governments maintain detailed accounts. Even if they do so, it may be difficult to effectively enforce earmarking restrictions without devoting considerable resources to extensive audits, as local governments can evade these restrictions by practices such as using transfers for specific programs to cover the payroll of employees who spend much of their time on other tasks, or to contribute more than their fair share to general infrastructure costs.[19]

---

[19]Lin *et al.* (2006) and Liu *et al.* (2009) discuss these issues. In principle, matching grants are likely to be more effective than simple earmarking in influencing local spending patterns, since with earmarking only, local officials typically can offset its effect simply by reallocating the way they spend their own revenue.

As another example, when the central government decided to encourage local officials in rural areas to revive the Cooperative Medical Schemes, it also decided that the new version of the schemes would, in principle, be voluntary, and that coverage by NCMS plans would be conditional on individuals having elected to pay an individual premium. By making the scheme voluntary, the central government intended to prevent local officials from using compulsory enrollment in an NCMS plan as a form of taxation, and to give them an incentive to design their plans with a sufficiently comprehensive and generous benefit structure, so that most rural residents would find it worthwhile to pay the stipulated minimum premium and enroll in the local plan. To further encourage enrollment, the central government also undertook to pay a subsidy for each person who enrolled in the plan. But this subsidy also meant that, provided the amounts of benefits paid out under the plan were low enough, it was in the interest of local governments to increase the number of enrollees in the social health insurance plans in order to take advantage of these matching grants to improve their fiscal situation. Consistent with this idea, it has been observed that some local governments actually paid for individuals' required premium contributions to the social health insurance plans in order to achieve a high enrollment rate and gain access to the matching-grant subsidies from higher level governments.[20]

The incentive on local government decision-makers to increase enrollment in the social insurance plans has also been strengthened by the fact that the central government views this as a valuable objective in itself, and lets local decision-makers know that their ability to accomplish a high rate of NCMS enrollment will be viewed as a favorable performance indicator for promotion, etc. Given these incentives, it is perhaps not surprising that NCMS enrollment in rural areas increased as rapidly as it did (see Chapter 3). At the same time, it is also not surprising that many NCMS plans were designed with restrictive provisions with respect to what costs would be covered,

---

[20]See Gu *et al.* (2006, p. 180), and Wagstaff (2007). Han and Luo (2007, p. 138) and Zhou (2004, Chapter 5) also discuss the incentive effects of matching grants of this type.

high degrees of patient cost-sharing, and low limits on the maximum benefits that could be paid annually. While the central government subsidy per enrollee, and the desire to get a favorable performance evaluation, gave local officials a strong incentive to achieve high rates of NCMS enrollment, they also had an incentive to generate incremental government revenue by restricting the average cost of the benefits they had to pay per enrollee.

5. Decentralization and Intergovernmental Fiscal Relations: The Future

Issues with respect to decentralization of governance and intergovernmental fiscal relations raise complex and difficult problems in large countries, whether they are federations or unitary states. On the one hand, decentralization is necessary in order to enable decision-makers to adapt to local conditions. On the other hand, restrictions must be placed on local policies so that they do not interfere with nationwide objectives, such as maintaining a competitive environment with no restrictions on domestic trade and ensuring free mobility of factors of production, in countries where economic management relies on markets and competition to a large extent. The need for decentralization and adapting policy to local conditions also extends to the area of social policy, raising questions with respect to how responsibility for redistribution of resources to achieve more equality should be divided between the central and subnational levels of government.

The task of establishing an effective model of decentralized decision-making in China is further complicated by its form of government. Without regular competitive elections at the local level, it is more difficult for the central authorities to gauge the extent to which local populations are satisfied with local governments, as it has to rely on information from various forms of administrative monitoring, and on imposition and enforcement of various guidelines and restrictions on local officials. As noted above, restricting and monitoring of local officials is likely to be difficult and costly, and can often be done only with limited effectiveness.

In the context of social policy generally, and health policy in particular, the preceding discussion suggests that attention should be focused on two major problems with China's current approach to decentralized management: on the one hand, the imbalance between local governments' expenditure responsibilities and their access to tax revenue; and on the other hand, the strong incentives on officials to increase local investment and economic growth rates.

Neither of these issues can be easily addressed in the short run. With respect to the incentive problem, it is not possible to formally specify in advance precisely how local officials' performance will be evaluated. While a shift in priorities from raising the rate of economic growth to achieving greater economic equality can be signaled through guidelines and directives, such as through the target responsibility system referred to earlier, it is only one input among many in performance evaluations, and managers will only be convinced that it will be consistently applied once they have seen it reflected in a number of actual promotions.

Moreover, attempts at specifying concrete measures of progress in social policy that will influence performance evaluations may be counterproductive if they cause managers to focus excessively on decisions that can be easily observed and measured.[21] For example, in the health policy area, managers may make strenuous efforts to meet targets with respect to building a specific number of health clinics or installing a specific number of hospital beds, while at the same time not devoting enough resources to ensure that patients in hospitals and clinics receive high-quality care. Further distortions may be induced if imperfect proxy measures are defined for characteristics that are difficult to measure, such as quality. How to design measures that weaken the incentives on local officials to increase net revenue and over-emphasize investment over current expenditure on social programs remains one of the big challenges for China's leadership in the years to come.

Similarly, softening the effects of the fiscal imbalance between the central and local levels of government is likely to be accomplished in a gradual process over time. Some analysts have identified a pattern

---

[21]This point is stressed in the classic paper by Holmstrom and Milgrom (1991) and further developed in Baker (1992). See also Qian and Do (2012).

in China's public finances consisting of major initiatives to centralize control over government revenue and expenditure, followed by periods of increased decentralization.[22] The last major such episode was in the mid-1990s, when the revenue collection system was redesigned in a way that dramatically raised the central government's share of revenue, partly in order to strengthen its ability to use fiscal and monetary policy to achieve macroeconomic stability.

Increasing the central government's share of tax revenue need not necessarily create problems for the management of public finances in a decentralized system, if it is accompanied by an offsetting increase in the amount of revenue that is transferred from the central to local governments, or by the central government's assumption of a larger share of the public sector's expenditure responsibilities. However, the incentives on local governments in China today still favor high rates of investment expenditures, at the same time that local governments are expected to carry a large share of the costs for strengthening social programs. While the central government has increased its transfers to local governments, it does not appear to have done so on a large enough scale to significantly reduce the need for local governments to raise revenue in other ways, through land sales and sometimes heavy user fees for public services, or to reduce expenditures through restrictive rules under their various social programs. Thus, continued progress in constructing a rules-based system that will gradually achieve a better balance between local authorities' revenue and expenditure responsibilities will indirectly help the central government achieve its objective of refocusing economic management toward more emphasis on redistribution and equity, both in the context of health system management and more generally.

---

[22] See Lin, Tao, and Liu (2013).

PART IV

CHINA'S HEALTH SYSTEM
IN THE FUTURE

Chapter 9

HEALTH SERVICES IN THE FUTURE: SOCIAL INSURANCE AND PURCHASING*

1. Introduction

As earlier chapters have made clear, it is still difficult to predict what role markets and private firms will be playing in China's future health care system. The uncertainty relates both to the system of production of health services, and to the private sector's role in the financing of health care through insurance. In this chapter, we focus on the former issue. With respect to financing, we assume that government subsidies and government-organized social insurance plans will account for most of the third-party financing, with private insurance playing a limited role; the alternative under which private insurance plays a major role on the financing side is discussed in the next and final chapter.

In the debate that preceded the publication of the major health policy guidelines in 2009, many participants argued strongly in favor of a continuation of the trend toward increased reliance on decentralization, markets and financial incentives in the health services sector. Most observers of the remarkable success of the Chinese economy in recent decades ascribe it at least in part to the dismantling of the earlier system of centralized economic management and the greater reliance that is now placed on the market mechanism for allocation of economic resources. The changes that took place in the health services industry between 1980 and the mid-2000s were consistent with this trend.

---

*Portions of this chapter have previously appeared as Chapter 3 in Zhao and Lim (2010).

With reduced government subsidies, hospitals and clinics, like most other kinds of firms, became increasingly dependent for their resources on the revenue they could earn from selling their services to buyers (patients) in the market. Although this method of financing implies higher charges to patients and hence a larger risk of financial hardship for them, those who favor the market-based approach argued that this problem can be substantially overcome through social insurance programs of the kind that are being introduced in China.

However, not everyone supported this approach, as we discussed in earlier chapters. In particular, many of those participating in the debate argued that a better option would be to return, at least partially, to a system in which there would be larger direct government subsidies to health service providers, and less reliance on charges to patients for financing them. Supporters of this view include representatives for the state Ministry of Health, many of whom also believe that hospitals and other providers should be more actively managed by the state than they have been during the last several decades.[1]

In concrete terms, those who supported more direct state funding and management of health care focused on two state initiatives. The first initiative involves the supply and pricing of pharmaceuticals for hospital patients. Following the earlier reforms, many hospitals were earning large amounts of revenue through the markups that they charged patients on the drugs they received. In the new system, these markups will be strictly controlled and will be much smaller. In return, there will be increased direct state subsidies to the hospitals, and the state will also take greater responsibility for supplying hospitals with pharmaceuticals at low prices. The second initiative will consist of state subsidies to local governments for the purpose of establishing and operating a network of rural health centers and urban community clinics that will produce "basic" health services at low controlled prices for all residents.

While these initiatives were the cornerstones of the new health policy guidelines that were announced in 2009, the central government has so far not given detailed prescriptions to local governments with

---

[1] Gu (2008) gives a succinct description of the conflicting views of the two camps. Also see Qian and Blomqvist (forthcoming).

respect to the way the new primary-care clinics will operate and be managed, but pilot projects are underway, and it is clear that these reforms have the objective of re-establishing a strong role for the government and the Ministry of Health in deciding on issues relating to the funding and operation of the institutions that supply health care.[2]

Predictably, critics of the new initiatives have characterized them as a move back to the earlier "command and control" approach to managing the health care sector, and claim that they will make the system both wasteful and less responsive to patient needs if they are fully implemented. What they favor instead is continued decentralization and privatization of health services provision, and a strengthening of the social insurance system under which patients are reimbursed for part of the cost of the health services they use.

1.1. *Social insurance vs. direct subsidies to providers*

The question of how the clinics and hospitals that provide health services will be managed is closely related to the methods that are used to fund them. Specifically, government funding of health services production can either come through social insurance, or via direct subsidies to providers.

The main purpose of the social health insurance plans is to help protect patients against the financial impact of the high cost of serious illness, like private health insurance. They do so by partially pooling the risk associated with illness: Part of the cost of the health services that patients use in cases of serious illness is paid for from a fund to which all plan members have previously contributed. But social insurance is of course not the only method through which the government can pool risk. In one sense, direct government subsidies to health service providers can be thought of as an alternative way of accomplishing the same thing. When subsidies to providers are used to pay for much of the cost of operating hospitals and clinics, they in turn can lower the charges to patients and still balance their budgets. The shift of part of

---

[2]As discussed in Chapter 6, considerable progress has been made with respect to implementing the new policies concerning pharmaceuticals.

the burden of paying for health care to taxpayers and away from patients implies an increased degree of risk pooling as it reduces the financial risk associated with illness, just as a social insurance does.

However, the two approaches differ in one very important respect. Under social insurance, the revenue that providers use to cover their costs consists of what they can earn by "selling" their services to the patients they treat, in the markets for health services.[3] In contrast, when providers receive much of their funding through direct government subsidies, there typically is no direct link between the amount of subsidy they receive and the services they provide. In the view of those who support the social insurance alternative, the lack of incentives on providers is a critical weakness of the direct subsidy approach. When much of the providers' revenue is independent of the services they supply, the result may be low productivity in the sense that relatively few services will be produced, or that the quality will be low. Moreover, attempts at compensating for the lack of incentives on providers through administrative measures are unlikely to be effective, in the view of those who are critical of the direct subsidy approach.

Those who supported the direct subsidy approach in the pre-2009 debate did so in part because they have more confidence that careful bureaucratic management of health service providers can raise productivity and maintain a high quality of health services. They also argue that in reality, the incentives that providers have to earn high revenue under a social insurance system do not benefit consumers/patients. Instead, they lead to high fees and markups on hospital drug sales, as well as provision of many services that patients do not really need but which earn high revenue for providers. A major shortcoming of the current Chinese health care sector, in some of these critics' views, is that too many resources have been channeled to hospitals where doctors can earn relatively higher incomes, and not enough have gone to lower-level

---

[3]Gerdtham and Jönsson (2000) refer to this as the "public reimbursement" model, since risk pooling is accomplished through subsequent payments to patients of part or all of what they have been charged. They refer to the model in which government directly manages the production of health services and pays for it out of general tax revenue as the "public integrated" model.

clinics that provide important public health services (such as control of contagious diseases) and basic primary care. While this has happened in both urban and rural areas, the problem has become especially acute in the countryside. For these reasons, this camp felt that government subsidies to establish clinics that would both strengthen the supply of public health services and offer basic primary care, should be a policy priority.[4]

1.2. *A compromise: Government purchasing of health services*

In our opinion, there is some merit in the arguments of both sides in this debate. We agree with those who see an urgent need for devoting more resources to strengthening the provision of public health and primary-care services in China, and for promoting more cost-effective utilization of pharmaceuticals. We also share the view that the trend toward decentralization of health system management and greater reliance on charges to patients for financing health care providers has produced highly undesirable side effects, including a tendency for health care costs to rise rapidly, as they have done in other countries that have followed such policies, most notably the U.S. At the same time, we also believe that it would be a mistake to return to the earlier "command and control" approach to management of health services providers. Both China's own experience in an earlier era, and that of other countries (such as the U.K. and Sweden), provide evidence of the difficulties of centralized top-down management of health services production in the absence of incentives on those that supply them.[5]

This leads to the question: Is it possible to imagine a system which preserves some of the incentives inherent in market-based health services production, but which gives better protection for patients

---

[4]As discussed in earlier chapters, the case for a change of direction in Chinese health care reform along these lines was forcefully made in the important collection of essays by scholars associated with the Development Research Center of the State Council (Ge *et al.*, 2007).

[5]Helpful descriptions of the U.K. and Swedish health care systems are in European Observatory on Health Systems and Policies (1999, 2001). A discussion of the more recent reform approaches in the U.K. is in Talbot-Smith and Pollock (2006).

and society against the high cost of health care than what a largely unregulated market for health services does? In the rest of this chapter, we discuss how such a compromise system could be constructed, based on the principle of government as a "third-party purchaser" of health services from decentralized or private producers of health services.[6]

2. Why is Third-Party Purchasing Needed in Health Care?

In an economic sector governed by the market mechanism, profit-seeking firms compete with each other in selling their goods and services to consumers who are free to buy from whichever seller offers the best alternative (combination of price and quality). For many types of goods and services, the market system works well for consumers, as China's experience in the past quarter-century has demonstrated. However, there are some types of goods and services for which competitive markets are unlikely to work well on their own, so that they give rise to a need for an institution such as a third-party purchaser. For reasons that we discussed in Chapter 1, health services belong in this category.

2.1. *Why market competition in health care may not be effective*

To recapitulate, one instance when competitive markets may not work well is when the goods or services being bought and sold can only be understood and evaluated by someone with highly specialized knowledge, something that is very much the case in health care. When there is "information asymmetry" in the sense of sellers having much more knowledge about what is being sold than buyers do, the effectiveness of competition is reduced.[7] In particular, sellers may be able to increase their revenue by advising buyers (patients) to pay for

---

[6]The third-party purchasing model we propose is a particular form of what Gerdtham and Jönsson (2000) call the "public contract" model. Yip and Hsiao (2008) also suggest that the idea of third-party purchasers should be further explored in the context of Chinese health system reform.

[7]Propper and Leckie (2011) discuss how the effectiveness of competition in hospital services markets will be different depending on how informed the buyers are.

services that they do not really need, given the nature of their health problem. Moreover, it is difficult in the case of health services or drugs to tell whether a particular patient was given proper medical advice even after treatment has taken place. Patients who recover might have done so even if they had received less extensive treatment or drugs; conversely, even patients that have been properly treated may get worse or die.[8]

The effectiveness of competition as an instrument to promote lower prices and better quality also depends on how costly it is for consumers to search for alternative offers from different sellers. For patients who need health care, search costs may be very high, explicitly or implicitly. In rural areas, there may only be one provider within a reasonable travel distance. For patients with acute illness, delaying treatment may be dangerous and painful, effectively making it necessary to be treated by the first available provider. In other cases, the process of getting an accurate diagnosis of the patients' health problem may be time-consuming and expensive, making them less likely to look for an alternative provider even when they believe they might be able to find one that would charge a lower fee.

Because of factors such as information asymmetry and high search costs, competition among providers cannot, by itself, be expected to be very effective in keeping medical fees and drug prices at reasonable levels if health services and pharmaceuticals *are sold directly to patients*, with no involvement by a third party. If patients are insured so that insurance pays part of the costs of services and drugs, they have even less incentive to try to find a provider that will treat them at lower cost. For all these reasons, it is not surprising that in countries where there is widespread insurance and where medical fees are not regulated, the aggregate cost of health care tends to grow very fast. The clearest example of this process has of course been the U.S., where the cost of

---

[8]In economic theory, a good whose quality can be inferred after it has been used is sometimes referred to as an "experience good". In contrast, goods such as health care are sometimes referred to as "credence goods" to signify that it may not be possible to ascertain their quality even after they have been used, so that effectively they are bought "on faith".

health care currently is approaching 18% of GDP.[9] By the same token, however, it is also not surprising that it is in the U.S. that the model of third-party purchasing has developed most actively as a response to these problems.

2.2. *Third-party purchasers in the private sector: Prepaid care and competition for contracts*

In the U.S., the upward pressure on health care costs has been the principal reason for the development of new forms of health insurance based on some version of the principle of "managed care". Private managed care plans can be interpreted as examples of third-party purchasers of health services. While there are many types of such plans, they all have one feature in common: They only cover the services of providers with whom the plan has a contract regarding the fees that providers can charge, and perhaps also regarding other aspects of the care they supply.[10]

By restricting fees and imposing rules on the services that providers are allowed to charge for, the plans can control costs more effectively than conventional plans that do not have such restrictions and rules. The reason they are able to do so (that is, are able to make providers agree to these restrictions) is that providers can only get access to the patients in the plan if they agree to the plan contracts. That is, in a system with managed care plans, providers do not compete directly for patients. Instead, they compete for the contracts that give them the right to treat (and be paid for treating) the patients covered by the plans.[11]

Negotiations of the terms of such contracts are much less affected by the problems of information asymmetry and high search costs that make competition for individual patients relatively ineffective. Because they represent many patients, managed care plans can afford to hire

---

[9] See, e.g., the 2013 edition of the OECD health database (http://www.oecd.org/health/health-systems/oecdhealthdata.htm).

[10] Surveys of managed-care methods include Glied (2000) and Baker (2011).

[11] Put differently, the plans can be said to act as purchasers of care *on behalf of* their patients.

medical experts that negotiate in advance regarding the terms of care that all the plans' patients will receive. Because they have medical expertise, and because the cost of searching for competitive providers is born collectively by many insured patients, the plans can act much more effectively as buyers of health care than individual patients can.

From the viewpoint of patients, being covered by a managed care plan may in some ways be less attractive than being in a conventional plan, since it restricts their choice of provider, and may place restrictions on what treatment they can receive in specific circumstances. However, the cost of their care on average is likely to be lower, and most people may be willing to accept restrictions on the way they can be treated as long as they have confidence that doing so is not going to significantly increase the risk of adverse health outcomes.

2.3. *Purchasers in publicly funded systems*

In a system with private managed care plans, each plan plays the role of the third-party purchaser of health services. In some countries where health care is paid for by the government, various government agencies may play the role of third-party purchaser if health services are supplied by private or decentralized producers. In Canada, for example, government pays for all physician and hospital services, but physician practices and hospitals are privately owned and supply their services on terms that are negotiated with government insurance plans or provincial health ministries or regional authorities.

Another example is the U.K. whose system we briefly reviewed in Chapters 2 and 4. The GP practices that supply primary care are private firms who are paid for their services under contracts with the NHS which in that sense acts as a third-party purchaser. While the government owns and operates most hospitals, since the 1980s, however, there has been a trend toward more autonomy and decentralized management, with agencies such as the District Health Authorities or (under the Labour government) Primary Care Trusts acting as third-party purchasers of their services. Thus, although the hospitals are publicly owned, they are subject to the same market-like incentives as private providers would be.

The term "internal markets" was used for a period of time to signify the fact that the providers that participated in the reform experiment were not for-profit firms but publicly-owned entities. While the term later disappeared from public use for political reasons, it was a useful one in that it drew attention to the fact that markets and competition may have a useful role to play even in situations where the main actors are not corporations whose main objective is to make a profit for shareholders. Another expression to capture the idea of an arrangement that involved markets in which both the purchaser and the sellers were government agencies was "purchaser-provider split". At the time this arrangement was introduced, the government employees that had previously been involved in managing the health care system were divided into two groups: one that was supposed to act as purchasers of health care on behalf of the tax-paying public, and another that consisted of those who were responsible for managing the government hospitals and other agencies from whom health services were "purchased".[12]

The role of purchasing agencies in publicly funded systems is similar to that of managed care plans in that they also negotiate with physicians and hospitals about methods and rates of reimbursement for the services they supply to the insured. However, it is also different in some respects. First, in countries such as Canada and the U.K. where the public plans are financed out of general tax revenue and cover every citizen, the public-sector purchasers are automatically allocated their revenue from the government, and do not have to rely on insurance premiums paid by clients, as managed care plans must do. Secondly, because the publicly funded plans cover every citizen, they are, effectively, the only third-party purchaser of health services in these countries, giving them a very dominant market position. (In contrast, when there are many managed care plans, as in the U.S., they must compete for the services of doctors and hospitals, since the providers can choose with which plans to contract.)

---

[12] An excellent summary of the reform approaches that have been used in the U.K. is Brereton and Vasoodaven (2010).

3. Health Services Markets with Government Purchasers in China: A Proposal

In China, introducing a role for government as a purchaser of health services might open up the field for a possible compromise between the views of those who favor a significant continuing role for decentralized management of health service resources based on markets and incentives, on the one hand, and those who support a return to a system in which government takes a greater role in managing the institutions that provide health services.

Under a purchasing system, providers would still be financing their activities based on selling the services they produce for their patients, rather than on the basis of direct government subsidies, giving them incentives to be productive and reduce costs, along the lines supported by adherents of the market view. At the same time, the government agencies acting as purchasers would be in a better position than individual patients to protect the public against high prices and fees, and overutilization of expensive services and drugs. Although they would not directly manage the service providers, they could indirectly influence them through the contracts that would be negotiated between the providers and the public purchasing agencies. In particular, the contracts can be designed in such a way as to preserve the incentives that providers have to be productive in a purely market-based system. At the same time, the right of the purchasing agencies to monitor the way the providers fulfill their obligations would indirectly enable them to ensure that providers serve the public interest, in a way similar to what government managers in a system of direct public management would try to do. A system with government purchasing agencies can therefore be seen as one that preserves major advantages of both the pure market-based and government-managed alternatives, and thus as a potential compromise between the competing views in the debate.

The history of health policy in a number of the world's high-income countries in recent years lends support to the idea that this type of compromise represents a reasonable approach to health system organization. In most countries in continental Europe (France, Germany, the Netherlands), as well as in Canada and Japan, most health services are produced by private providers, with governments acting as the major purchasers either directly (Canada), or through government-regulated social insurance plans. In the U.S., health services are largely produced by private firms, and private insurance has played a larger role on the financing side in that country than anywhere else. But in the U.S., too, the government has long had a major role as purchaser of health services for specific population groups (the elderly and the poor), and it has moved to strengthen this role further under the reforms that have been passed during Obama's presidency. Moreover, some of the countries where health services have been produced by government have been experimenting with an increased role for markets and competition; the most important example has been the U.K., but similar approaches have also been taken in the Nordic countries, particularly Sweden. At the same time, while a number of countries have been strengthening the role of government in the financing and purchasing of health services, we can think of no examples of countries where the government's role as a *producer* of health services has been significantly expanded in recent decades.

3.1. Creating a coherent purchasing model for China

As discussed earlier, the 2009 guidelines for health care reform in China foresaw both a major expansion of the social insurance system and a stronger role for government in producing health services (the network of primary-care clinics). Expansion of the social insurance system can be seen as consistent with the model of government as a purchaser, since local governments are the managers of the social insurance plans, and since the plans can, in principle, negotiate regarding the terms according to which health services will be supplied to those who were covered by the plans. As observed in earlier chapters, while the social insurance plans have so far mostly functioned as conventional insurance that simply pays a share of the bills submitted by providers, in some places they have been experimenting with more active approaches to their purchasing functions.

With respect to the increased role of government in the provision of primary care through the network of publicly-owned clinics, the 2009 guidelines were not very specific with respect to the way these clinics should be managed or funded, beyond the principle that they would be the responsibility of the local government. In particular, there was little discussion of the way the care provided in these clinics would be integrated with that supplied in hospitals to those who were covered by the existing social insurance plans.

In retrospect, this was perhaps not surprising. As we have seen, the proposals for a stronger government role in primary care originated principally from people who did not favor the insurance-based approach to managing the health care system, and some of them probably would have argued for an expanded role of direct government funding and management in secondary and tertiary care as well. In our view, however, it seems both likely and appropriate that China's future health care system will be moving in the same direction as elsewhere in the developed world — toward an enhanced role for government and social insurance as purchasers of health services, but with a relatively high degree of decentralization and reliance on incentives and markets in the production of health services. In the next several sections, therefore, we discuss in some detail how such a system could be designed. In particular, we consider how the government-owned primary-care clinics can be funded and managed in a way that makes them an integral part of a health care system where most of the resources are channeled through a social insurance system through which the government purchases care in decentralized markets.

3.2. Weaknesses of a mixed system

As discussed in Chapter 3, the three types of social insurance plans that now exist in China — namely Basic Health Insurance (BHI, for urban employees), Urban Resident Basic Medical Insurance (URBMI, for other urban residents), and the New Cooperative Medical Scheme (NCMS, for rural residents) — now cover over 95% of China's population. However, there is great variability in the coverage of these plans across cities and counties. In particular, as also discussed in Chapter 3, the degree of coverage in the URBMI and NCMS plans is often reduced as a result of relatively low limits on maximum benefits per year or episode, and also because patients may be charged for drugs and services that the plans do not cover. Strengthening the degree of coverage in these dimensions, and making it more equal across plans, will therefore be important tasks for local health policy in future years. Another shortcoming of the social insurance plans has been that, like the health care system at large, they have been focused on care supplied through hospitals. In some cases, coverage has been limited to episodes of in-patient care, so that patients have had to pay for any out-patient care or drugs out of their own pockets, or from the individual accounts in which some of their premium contributions to the plans have been kept.[13]

The plans to create a nationwide network of primary-care clinics that would offer basic care for "common and frequently occurring diseases" can thus be seen not only as a much-needed strengthening of the primary-care sector, but also as a way of increasing the effective degree of coverage of the existing social insurance system. Since care in these clinics will largely be paid for through direct government subsidies, with patients only being required to pay low fees, some members of the existing social insurance plans will have better coverage in the sense that they will have access to care that previously was not available, or that they would have had to pay for out of their own pockets.

Thus, a system in which government directly pays most of the cost of primary care, while social insurance reimburses patients for a share of the cost of higher-level care, can be interpreted as providing enhanced risk-pooling, with all taxpayers sharing most of the cost of primary care while the members of the social insurance plans share the rest. But this way of improving the degree of risk pooling in the system has a major drawback: It will substantially reduce the ability of the social insurance system to reduce costs and promote more efficient resource use through its actions as a purchaser of health care.

---

[13] Since the amounts that are available to pay for health services from the individual accounts are limited to what the insured person has contributed in the past, these accounts involve no risk pooling, just "forced savings".

As purchasers, private or public insurance plans try to reduce the cost of the care that their members receive, or improve its quality, by negotiating contracts that give providers an incentive to be efficient in the sense of supplying care at low cost and of high quality. From the viewpoint of the health care system as a whole, one of the most important determinants of efficiency relates to the interaction between primary care and the rest of the system.

As we have discussed in earlier chapters, primary-care doctors have an important influence over aggregate health care costs through their decisions with respect to what drugs to use. More significantly, in the present context, their decisions on when to refer patients to higher levels of care can make a big difference. In systems where too many patients are referred to hospitals in cases when they could be treated at less cost in primary care, the hospital sector is likely to be relatively large and aggregate costs high. On the other hand, if primary-care doctors are reluctant to refer patients to higher-level care, health outcomes may be worse as patients' health problems are not accurately diagnosed or they are treated using the wrong kind of intervention. In the long run, a tendency to delay referring patients to specialists may also increase aggregate health system costs if the delay leads to a worsening of their condition.

In Chapter 4, we discussed the issue of how primary-care doctors could be given incentives to make their referral decisions in a way that would reduce aggregate system costs and promote efficiency. Approaches that have been tried include the U.K. experiments with "fundholding", and compensation models that contain bonuses that are inversely related to the costs of patients' hospital care in U.S. managed care plans where primary-care doctors are paid via capitation. In principle, these methods can also be applied in a primary-care system that is managed by government and is financed separately from the social insurance system, out of general government revenue. But the officials managing the primary-care system do not have strong incentives to do so.

Strategies that are designed to avoid referrals to secondary providers require resources and efforts by the doctors and other personnel in primary care as they try to be more careful in evaluating patients before referral, or to manage their symptoms in order to not have to send them on to hospitals or specialist clinics. That is, these strategies imply additional costs that must be borne out of the primary-care system's budget. The benefits, on the other hand, consist of reduced utilization of the services of hospitals and specialists. But the costs of those services are mostly covered by the social insurance system, and hence do not benefit the budgets of the primary-care managers. On balance, therefore, these managers have little incentive to reserve part of their budget for these kinds of schemes, or to collect accurate information about the costs of different kinds of hospital and other secondary-care services in order to identify where the best opportunities for cost savings are. This is the main weakness of a system under which the funding that flows through the social insurance plans is managed separately from those that flow as direct subsidies to providers. To overcome it, the system has to be designed in such a way that the two flows are managed together, through a single agency whose responsibility it is to get the most value from the total amount of funds spent in health care.

3.3. *An integrated approach*

Creating a model that combines the advantages of a decentralized purchasing approach with the objective of integrating the funds spent on primary care with those that flow through the social insurance system is not difficult in principle. It can be accomplished simply by channeling the government funds that go to finance primary-care clinics through the same agency as the one that is responsible for the social health insurance plans. In China today, most of the responsibility for management of the social insurance plans and the primary-care clinics lies with local government agencies at the city or county levels, working under the supervision of ministries in provincial and central governments. At the local level, therefore, a more integrated system in urban areas would merely require that the branches of the Social Insurance Bureaus that are responsible for the urban social insurance plans (the BHI and URBMI plans) should also be responsible for the funds that flow as subsidies to providers, especially the primary-care clinics. In rural areas, the NCMS plans are already the responsibility of the county Health Bureaus; in an integrated system, the same agency within the Bureaus would jointly manage the funds flowing through these plans and those flowing as direct subsidies to hospitals and rural primary-care clinics.

While the administrative changes that would be required at the local level may seem relatively straightforward, more difficulty may arise in ensuring that the higher-level branches of government that are involved in managing the system also exercise their authority in a way that is consistent with the integration objective. As discussed earlier, the state-level ministry responsible for supervising the social health insurance plans is the Ministry of Labor and Social Security, while ultimate responsibility for supervising the budgets of the providers that receive direct government subsidies lies with the Ministry of Health. Ensuring that there will be no conflicts arising from the way these ministries discharge their responsibilities clearly is a necessary condition for an integrated approach to work effectively at the local level. Given the differences of view regarding the direction of health policy that have existed in the past, this may not be an easy task.

4. Elements of an Effective Purchasing Model

In a purchasing model, the basic idea is that a specialized agency negotiates for the supply of health care services to a specified population in markets where decentralized producers are subject to incentives through the way they are funded, and compete with each other for the purchasing agencies' contracts. The experience of managed care plans in the U.S. shows that the model can compete effectively in private insurance markets with conventional plans that simply reimburse a portion of patients' health care costs. Although attempts to use this model in the context of health care systems that are dominated by government financing (especially the U.K. and the Netherlands) have been going on for some time, there is less agreement regarding how effective it is likely to be in such a system, and progress in implementing it can at best be described as slow and fitful. Nevertheless, it is our view that the logic underlying the model is compelling, and that for China, there is a good possibility that it could serve as the cornerstone for an efficient health care system in the future. Whether it will do so depends partly on factors related to politics and partly on the techniques that would be used to implement it. We will discuss each in turn.

4.1. *Purchasing in health care and the role of the state*

In a situation where a single public agency such as a city Social Insurance Bureau or a county Health Bureau is the single purchaser of health services in a local market, it plays a role that in some ways is similar to that of a regulatory agency that sets restrictions on many aspects of what the firms in a particular industry are allowed to do. Because it essentially is the single monopoly buyer in the local health services markets, a public purchaser is in a very powerful position relative to the providers; like a regulatory agency, it can to a large extent control the prices and other conditions under which firms supply services.

But (as we discussed in Chapter 2), while regulatory agencies are supposed to act in a way that reflects the interests of society at large, experience in other countries suggests there is a risk that in practice they will come to partly represent the interests of the producers they are supposed to regulate. The phrase "regulatory capture" has been used to refer to situations where the interests of private producers have had an undue influence on public agencies that were supposed to restrict producers' pricing and other actions on behalf of society at large.

The experience with public purchasing agencies in places like the U.K. and Sweden suggests that they may be subject to a similar effect when they negotiate contracts with health services providers. The risk that the purchasers may pay too much attention to the interests of providers may exist even when the providers they negotiate with are government-owned. This was typically the case in the experiments with a "purchaser-provider split" in the U.K. and Sweden, where the purchasing agencies were staffed by people who previously had been employees of the local departments that were responsible for managing the government-owned hospitals and clinics. Under a model in which the local Social Insurance Bureaus or Health Bureaus would act as purchasers in China, this potential conflict of interest would have to be taken into account in designing the system, since these bureaus are closely linked to the same city and county governments that are responsible for managing local government-owned hospitals and clinics, and for paying their employees' salaries. Paradoxically, an effective resolution of this potential problem may require relatively close supervision and regulation by higher-level governments of the actions of the local purchasing agencies.

The role of the state in setting the rules that would help create an effective system of health services purchasing at the local level cannot, of course, be separated from the more general question of fiscal relations between the central and local levels of government in China, or indeed from the issue of how its future political system will evolve. For example, the extent to which decentralization of economic management to the local level is appropriate, and what form it should take, depends in part on whether or not local officials will be held accountable to the population in elections, or whether they will be appointed by the state, as they are at present. Rather than speculate on what the future directions of China's system of local governance will be, however, in the next section we consider the more narrowly defined question of what general rules and guidelines might be used by the state to increase the likelihood that a system of decentralized purchasing at the local level will work well in the sense of making the purchasers more responsive to the interests of their local populations at large, rather than to the local officials that manage the government-owned hospitals and clinics.

4.2. *Setting the rules for local purchasing agencies: The revenue side*

The most important principle that should govern an effective purchasing model is that the purchasers should have control over *all* the funding that flows to health services providers from all levels of government, and through the social insurance plans. That is, under a purchasing system, no funding for the operating costs of providers would flow directly from any level of government directly to providers; all such subsidies would be channeled through the purchasing agencies. This would apply not only to funding for secondary and higher level hospitals, but also to primary-care clinics and local public health agencies. Ideally, budgets for the purchasing agencies should be kept separate from those of local government in general, so that, for example, a surplus in an agency's budget in a given year could be carried over and used for increased provider funding in future years.

One important set of issues arises from the fact that in many places, local purchasing agencies will negotiate with providers on behalf of patients in more than one social insurance plan. While the entire population in some rural areas may belong to the local NCMS plan, in urban areas the agency that acts as a purchaser will represent both patients covered by the more generous BHI plan and those covered by URBMI, and the boundaries in some large cities may also include adjacent rural areas in which the population is covered by an NCMS plan. Moreover, since the URBMI and NCMS plans are voluntary plans, there are a few jurisdictions with at least some individuals who do not yet belong to any social insurance plan, and the local purchasing agency would still be responsible for negotiating with providers for basic care for this population as well. Two questions therefore arise. First, would purchasing agencies negotiate with providers for different terms for patients with different (or no) social insurance coverage? Second, would the agencies be required to balance the revenue and expenditures for each plan (population category) separately, or could they pool the revenues of the different plans, being required only to balance their total revenue and expenditure in the aggregate?

We discuss the question whether the terms negotiated with providers should be different for patients in different plans in the next section, and argue there that the terms should be similar. The question on pooling of revenue and expenditure is more controversial. Comparing the three types of plans currently in force (see Chapter 3), urban employees who are covered by the BHI plan make substantially larger contributions (in the form of deductions from their pay) than those in the NCMS or URBMI plans who only have to pay small individual premiums out of their own pockets. In places where the same purchasing agency manages both the BHI and other plans, those contributing to the BHI plans can reasonably argue that most of their contributions should go to pay for the health care costs of BHI members, rather than to subsidize benefits of those covered by the other plans. Based on this logic, they would prefer that the purchasing agencies be required to balance the revenues and costs of each type of plan separately.[14]

On the other hand, however, one can also argue that the urban employees that are covered by the BHI on average have substantially higher income than those covered by the NCMS and URBMI plans, and therefore should pay a larger share of their income as taxes that go to finance public expenditures. The fact that BHI members make larger contributions than those in other social insurance plans can then be interpreted as simply reflecting their higher average income, so that some degree of subsidy of the benefits to those in NCMS and URBMI plans can be considered as part of the system of taxes and transfers through which China, like other countries, accomplishes some degree of redistribution of real income from rich to poor. With this interpretation, it is reasonable to allow the purchasing agencies to subsidize the benefits of those in the less generous plans from the contributions of those in the BHI plan at least to some extent.[15]

Under the purchasing model proposed here, the revenues of the purchasing agencies would include not only the contributions, subsidies, and individual premiums paid under the existing social insurance plans, but also the amounts that are paid as direct subsidies to clinics, hospitals, and public health agencies in the current system. Part of this revenue would come from city or county government budgets, but part of it also comes, directly or indirectly, from the provincial and state governments. One of the requirements for creating a well-functioning purchasing model would be to formulate clear rules for determining how large these revenues should be, and how the responsibility for raising them will be divided between the different

---

[14]An important issue in this regard is whether employees who are insured under the BHI plan continue to be covered by this plan after retirement. If they are, the case against allowing BHI contributions to subsidize deficits in the other social insurance plans is even stronger.

[15]In countries with universal social insurance coverage through multiple plans (such as Japan, for example), it is common for plans that cover population groups with high average health care costs to receive subsidies either from government revenue, or from other plans that cover populations with low average costs.

290 Health Policy Reform in China

levels of government. These are clearly issues that cannot be separated from the more general question of how fiscal relations between the state and local government in China will be defined in the future, and how the state will use intergovernmental transfers to help reduce inequality by making larger per capita transfers to poorer regions than to wealthy ones.

One issue that complicates setting the per capita amounts that purchasing agencies in different jurisdictions will receive is the fact that some of the health services that patients in many places utilize are produced in a different jurisdiction. In particular, many patients with complicated health problems who live in rural areas will seek treatment in higher-level hospitals in large cities. This means that some of the subsidies that currently are paid directly to hospitals in large cities indirectly benefit not only local patients, but also patients from surrounding jurisdictions.

In a model where the purchasing principle is used, hospitals would no longer receive such subsidies directly, but would derive all their revenues from services supplied under contracts with purchasing agencies. Consistent application of this principle, therefore, would require that the funds that currently flow as any direct subsidies to large urban hospitals would have to be part of the revenue of the purchasing agencies not just in the cities where the hospitals are located, but also in surrounding areas from which some of their patients come. To design a purchasing system that would satisfy this requirement, governments in both urban and rural areas must have accurate information not only about the volume of different kinds of services that these hospitals normally supply, but also about where their patients come from. Clearly, collecting this information will be a major task in designing a purchasing system, and doing so will involve some amount of trial and error.

4.3. Rules for purchasing agencies: The expenditure side

On the expenditure side, the mandate of each local purchasing agency is simple in principle: It would be to negotiate the terms according to which all providers of health services would supply different kinds of care to members of the population in the agency's jurisdiction. These providers (public health agencies, primary-care clinics, and hospitals) would receive no direct government funding for their operating costs. Instead, they would only receive funding from government, including the social insurance plans, as revenue earned under the contracts they had negotiated with the funding agencies.

As noted above, a fundamental requirement for a well-functioning purchasing system would be that its decisions would be guided by the interests of the population on whose behalf it was negotiating, not by the interests of the owners, managers, or personnel of the clinics and hospitals that supplied the services. The agencies' incentive to act in this way could be strengthened in various ways.

One approach would be to require them to report periodically, in a standard format, to supervisory agencies at higher levels of government. For example, they could be asked to report not only on the amounts they had paid to different providers, but also on the nature of the contracts between the purchasing agencies and the providers that had been negotiated between them, and that would be the basis for the payments.

It would also be reasonable to make branches of the purchasing agencies responsible for collection and reporting of many kinds of local health statistics, including not only mortality and morbidity statistics, but also data on the success rate of different kinds of major interventions in hospitals. Ultimately, the objective of health care spending is to improve population health, so that the evaluation of purchasing agencies' success should depend at least in part on measures of their success in that respect. Moreover, collection of such information would be useful not only for those evaluating the purchasing agencies' success, but also for the agencies themselves in terms of identifying emerging health problems and patterns of practice that might guide future changes in what types of care to purchase, or in selecting which providers to contract with, in cases where they have more than one option.[16] The agencies' sense of accountability to their populations

---

[16]In the U.S., requirements that providers supply accurate statistics on the outcomes they have achieved in treating patients with various health problems (for example, in the form of "report cards") have figured prominently in proposals to create a more

could also be strengthened by requiring them to report on their activities not only to the provincial and state ministries that supervise them, but also directly to the public, through the press and other media.

One of the main arguments for a unified purchasing system encompassing both universal subsidized primary care and the existing social insurance plans is that it can be used to promote a more cost-effective pattern of care by discouraging the utilization of hospital services for health problems that can be treated at lower cost in primary care. As discussed below, this can be done both through referral requirements (e.g., through restricting reimbursement of patients' hospital costs to those patients who had been treated in hospital following a referral from a primary-care clinic), and through economic incentives on primary-care providers to avoid hospitalization of patients under their care.

But the objective of promoting a cost-effective pattern of care also suggests another important principle: that a local agency should be allowed to negotiate for the purchase of certain kinds of care from hospitals outside its county or city if outside providers can supply those kinds of care at lower cost. Implementing this principle may not be easy, and may be resisted by local providers and governments, but it is a potentially important one from the viewpoint of making certain types of advanced care more generally available at reasonable cost. For purchasing agencies in rural areas, negotiating with tertiary urban hospitals about various forms of advanced treatment may also be difficult as they may not have the requisite expertise regarding their cost. However, provincial or national guidelines can help them do so more effectively.

As noted above, we believe that the terms purchasing agencies negotiate for funding providers should be the same, regardless of whether or not the patient is covered by a social insurance plan, and if so, which one. From the viewpoint of society as a whole, the purpose of the purchasing system is to encourage cost-effective provision of health care for the entire population, and since the cost of treating a patient for a given health problem is independent of the patient's insurance status,

---

competitive environment in the market for health services. For discussion, see, e.g., Dranove (2012), or Porter and Teisberg (2006, Chapter 4).

there is no reason why providers should receive different amounts of revenue for treating patients in different insurance plans. From the viewpoint of the patient's out-of-pocket costs, of course, insurance status does make a difference, being lowest for those in the most generous plans (typically BHI), and highest for those not covered by social insurance.

How the principle that providers should receive the same revenue for given types of treatment of all patients would be implemented depends on the way providers are paid for their services. One method that would have the advantage of simplicity would be for the purchasing agency to be the "single payer". Under this approach, providers would receive all their revenue from the purchasing agency, and would not charge patients anything out of pocket, either for services or for drugs; patients would then pay the out-of-pocket fees required under their plan to the purchasing agency, not to the provider. A major advantage with this method from the providers' point of view is that they would incur no costs associated with collecting fees from patients, as those costs would be borne by the purchasing agency.

Under an alternative method, providers would receive all or part of their fees and drug charges from the patients, who would then be reimbursed by their insurance plans, at rates that would differ from one plan to the next. In order for this to be consistent with the principle that providers are paid the same amount for a given type of treatment of any patient, they would have to charge every patient the same amount, regardless of his or her insurance status. Implementing this principle would therefore require the purchasing agencies to negotiate contracts under which providers agree to charge all patients at the same negotiated rates, and to monitor providers to ensure that they abide by these contracts.

5. Purchasing: How Should Purchasers Pay Providers?

One purpose of an approach under which funding of health care providers is delegated to local purchasing agencies is that these agencies are familiar with local conditions and providers, and hence are better able than central planners to negotiate for patterns of care that take these factors into account. Other things equal, there is therefore a case for giving local purchasing agencies considerable freedom to decide on what the content of these contracts should be, including the methods that should be used for paying the providers. At the same time, however, experience from other countries shows that considerable time may be needed before local officials acquire sufficient skills and expertise to negotiate effectively with providers, and before they are able to develop sufficient independence from providers and other local officials to do so in a way that reflects the interests of patients and society at large. In the initial stages, therefore, they are likely to benefit from relatively detailed guidelines on how an effective purchasing system can be set up, including advice on payment methods and other features of the contracts under which providers will be funded.

5.1. *Prospective vs. retrospective funding*

We have already discussed different funding methods, for both primary and higher levels of care, in Chapters 4 and 5. In that discussion, we stressed the advantages of methods based on capitation for funding primary care, and some form of case-based payment such as that in the Diagnosis-Related Group (DRG) model for hospital care. To recapitulate, both are examples of *prospective* funding methods, under which the amounts providers receive for treating particular patients or cases are determined before it is known precisely what services patients will receive in the course of treatment. In contrast, *retrospective* funding methods, such as fee-for-service in primary care, or itemized billing in hospital care, are based on bills that are submitted after it is known exactly what services the patient received.

The major difference between the two types of methods is in the incentives they create for providers when they make decisions with respect to how a patient will be treated. Under prospective funding, supplying additional services to a given patient does not increase the provider's revenue, since the revenue is predetermined. Under retrospective funding, on the other hand, the revenue earned from treating a given patient is increased if additional services are supplied. As a result, prospective funding has a tendency to produce less costly patterns of care.[17] It is, of course, also possible to use mixed ("blended") models that contain elements of both prospective and retrospective funding. For example, primary-care providers can be paid partly on the basis of capitation, partly on the basis of fee-for-service, and similarly for hospitals.

5.2. Capitation in primary care

If China were to move toward a system of local purchasing agencies in its future health care system, we believe that funding of primary care, which will be supplied principally by the network of basic care clinics that has been under construction since 2009, should be through a model with a significant capitation element. There are several reasons why we think capitation is the best option.

As we already discussed in earlier chapters, an advantage of capitation over fee-for-service is that the latter implies an incentive on providers to supply a large volume of services, and sell large quantities of drugs, to each patient, as this raises the provider's revenue. The tendency for "supplier-induced demand" to exist under fee-for-service may exist even if the doctors who treat patients in primary-care clinics receive most of their compensation through salary, since even salaried doctors are likely to be under pressure to pay attention to a clinic's revenue if its financing is mostly through fee-for-service.

Although capitation can imply an incentive on providers to "under-treat" patients (that is, supply them with fewer or less advanced services than their health problems would warrant), this incentive is at least in part offset by the professional ethics of physicians, which emphasizes their duty to provide the services that patients need, and can also be counteracted by outside monitoring of the quality of the care provided. In contrast, medical schools typically do not emphasize doctors' responsibility to save health care costs in their training; that is, there are no strong professional norms to offset the tendency toward supplier-induced demand under fee-for-service.

---

[17]But as Propper and Leckie (2011) note, there is some evidence to suggest that another consequence may be some reduction in the quality of care that is provided.

A second reason we believe that funding of primary-care clinics should be on the basis of capitation is that it can be used to create incentives for primary-care providers to play a role in controlling health care costs more generally. As discussed in Chapter 4, in other countries such as the U.K. and the U.S. (in many managed care plans), incentives have been created for primary-care doctors to control both the cost of drugs used by patients under their care, and their patients' use of specialist and hospital services. For example, in some American managed care plans, part of the primary-care doctors' revenue is a year-end bonus, the size of which depends on the cost of their patients' prescription drugs and the services of specialists that the patients have used after referral from their primary-care doctors. But incentives of this kind can only be created if each patient has a single primary-care provider who is responsible for his or her care during the year. A capitation system does create such a relationship between each patient and a single designated provider. Under capitation, each patient must register with one (and only one) primary-care provider, who will then receive the capitation amount for this patient, and who will be the only provider from whom the patient receives subsidized services during the year.

Even though a capitation system is based on the principle that patients can only be registered with a single provider at a given time, it is possible to design it in such a way that it allows for at least some degree of competition among primary-care providers. To accomplish this, patients must have a choice between several primary-care providers. In a model under which patients are only allowed to sign up with a designated local clinic, there is, of course, no effective competition. In practice, the effectiveness of competition in the market for primary care in many places will be inherently limited by geography, especially in rural areas where it can be very costly and time-consuming to travel to any clinic other than the local one. In urban areas, however, competition may be more effective, and even in rural areas some of the population will live in communities within reasonable distance of more than one provider. If patients are given a choice among several providers in a capitation system, one issue that must be decided is when and how often patients will be allowed to switch their registration.

In principle, a capitation contract between a purchasing agency and a primary-care provider will start with a specification of exactly what services the provider is responsible for supplying to registered patients. These need not be exactly the same for each provider; for example, in places where some clinics have more advanced diagnostic equipment, their contract will specify that they are responsible for tests that otherwise are performed in hospitals. When the range of services for which clinics are responsible are different, the capitation amounts will be adjusted accordingly. In capitation models in other countries, it is also common for the amounts that are paid for different patients to be differentiated according to certain patient characteristics, including sex and age, reflecting differences in the expected average use of different health services and drugs. While it clearly is desirable to allow local purchasing agencies considerable leeway in the way they design the contracts, and in determining the capitation structure and amounts, the complexity of the tasks involved will be great and local officials in many places would need help in the form of guidelines from higher levels of government.

While we believe that capitation payments from purchasing agencies should be the main component in the funding of primary-care providers, the funding model could have other elements as well. One such element would refer to public health functions. While some public health functions can be related to individual patients, others (such as monitoring various environmental determinants of health) are for the benefit of the community as a whole, and might best be paid for separately, so that those providers who were made responsible for them would receive additional funding beside capitation.

Moreover, even though the capitation models elsewhere (for example, in the U.K.) specify that patients will receive contracted services at no out-of-pocket cost, others are mixed models in the sense that the providers receive some payments directly from their patients as well. We think a mixed model of this type is the only reasonable option in most places in China today. It would not be realistic to ask local governments to take responsibility for paying the full operating costs of an expanded primary-care system, even with support from higher levels of government. The out-of-pocket fees that primary-care providers would charge, however, should be set at levels negotiated with the purchasing agencies, and should not be so high as to effectively negate the desirable incentive effects of a capitation system as compared to fee-for-service.

5.3. *Funding hospitals*

As we discussed in Chapter 5, China's hospital sector continues to be dominated by secondary and tertiary hospitals that are owned by the government. The decades since 1980 have seen a trend toward giving these hospitals more autonomy in managing their personnel and other resources as they received less funding in the form of direct government subsidies and had to raise more revenue through charges for their services and markups on drugs; but as noted in Chapter 5, in some places it appears that the system has been moving back toward a more centralized approach with stricter government control over their investment and other operating expenditure. If China is successful in gradually creating a model with a strengthened role for local purchasing agencies, the need for a return to an approach that relies on direct government management would be reduced, with purchasing agencies becoming more effective in controlling the cost of hospital care and creating incentives for hospitals to earn their funding in ways that would be more consistent with society's objectives than in the recent past.

Put differently, with more effective purchasing agencies, the advantages of a more decentralized system relying on markets could be exploited in the hospital sector in much the same way as they have been in other sectors. This could be accomplished through administrative changes even if most hospitals continue to be government-owned. However, another advantage of a strengthened purchasing system would be that there could be a greater role for privately owned hospitals who could compete on equal terms with the government-owned ones, indirectly promoting more efficient operation of the sector as a whole.

The general arguments in favor of prospective vs. retrospective funding of health services providers that were noted above apply to funding of hospitals as well as to primary-care providers. The performance of China's hospital sector in the last two decades offers perhaps a better illustration of the disadvantages of the fee-for-service model in health care than almost anywhere else in the world. But as also discussed in Chapter 5, prospective funding has taken a somewhat different form in the hospital sectors in the countries that have moved in this direction than it has in primary care, with some form of case-based funding, particularly the DRG model, having been the most frequently used one.[18]

5.4. *Hospital costs and gate-keeping*

Case-based prospective funding of hospital care can be seen as a natural complement to the capitation model in primary care. This is so especially if there is strict enforcement of a requirement that hospital treatment is only allowed after referral from primary-care providers that have a "gate-keeping" role and an incentive to control the hospital costs of their patients (for example, through some form of extended capitation or "fundholding" as discussed in Chapter 4).[19] The cost per capita of hospital care in a given patient population does, by definition, depend on two factors: the average cost per case of hospitalization, and the rate at which its members are treated in hospital. With consistently enforced referral requirements, the rate of hospitalization will be determined by primary-care providers' decisions, which in turn can be influenced by the incentives to which they are subjected in a capitation system. The average cost per case, in contrast, is mostly determined by decisions of the doctors who treat patients in the hospitals. With a prospective case-based funding approach, the hospital's (and therefore, its doctors') incentive is to treat each patient at the lowest possible cost.

As in the case of capitation, one may worry that the incentives to reduce cost in a pure prospective approach are so strong that it may lead to a reduction in the quality of care that is provided. This problem can be addressed either by opting for a mixed system under

---

[18]Dranove (2012) includes a good review of the evidence on the effects of the DRG method in the U.S.

[19]Brief discussions of the gate-keeping and fundholding concepts are in Scott and Jan (2011) and Barros and Olivella (2011).

which hospitals are funded partially through a fixed payment per case and partially through retrospective charges, or by direct monitoring of the outcomes of the cases they treat. When funding is through a mixed system under which patients have to pay for some part of the services they receive out of their own pockets, the rates that hospitals are allowed to charge should be negotiated between the hospitals and the purchasing agencies. As in the case of primary care, patients would be reimbursed for part of their out-of-pocket charges, with the rate of reimbursement depending on what social insurance plan they belong to.

5.5. *Hospital out-patient departments and primary care*

In designing a model based on capitation in primary care and case-based funding (for example, some form of DRG model) for hospital care, an issue that would arise in many places is whether hospitals should be allowed to supply primary care in competition with the independent government-owned clinics. There are a number of arguments in favor of letting them do so. One is based on the example of Japan. Competition between hospitals' out-patient departments and independent family doctors has been cited as a factor that has had an important influence on the performance of Japan's health care system, which appears to compare favorably with those in other countries in terms of cost and quality of care.[20] Another reason is that it is likely to take some time before the Chinese public in many places will gain confidence that the quality of care they will receive in primary-care clinics is comparable to what they expect from hospitals. Until this happens, people may resent a requirement that they must have a referral from primary care before they can receive hospital care.

    If hospitals are allowed to operate out-patient departments that offer primary care, however, attention must be paid to the role that these departments would have in referring patients for secondary care in the same hospital. Even if hospitals' out-patient departments were

---

[20] Ikegami and Campbell (1998) remains an informative source on the Japanese health care system; see also Ikegami and Anderson (2012).

separately funded via capitation with incentives to control the cost of their patients' hospital care, these incentives might be offset by the incremental net revenue that the hospital would earn by admitting its own primary-care patients for hospital treatment.[21] Dealing with this problem might require special rules for the funding of hospitals that offer both primary care and various kinds of in-patient services, as we discuss further in the next chapter.

A further issue that would arise under a purchasing system would be to what extent hospitals (and perhaps even primary-care clinics) that have contracts with purchasing agencies should be allowed to also treat patients outside of the social insurance system (that is, patients who pay for care out of their own pockets, or under a private insurance plan). In some countries (Canada, for example), hospitals that receive funding under the provincial government insurance plans are not allowed to also treat patients who pay out of their own pockets; in some Canadian provinces, independent doctors who bill for services under the provincial insurance plans also are not allowed to treat private patients.

Valid arguments can be made for either side of this issue. On one hand, allowing hospitals to treat outside patients might create the risk that they focus most of their resources on such patients, causing waiting lists or a reduction in the quality of care for patients treated under the contracts with the purchasing agencies. On the other hand, not allowing them to do so might lead the most skilled and experienced doctors to go to private hospitals outside the public purchasing system, with similar results. On balance, we believe that allowing providers to treat patients outside the system is the better option, provided that there is effective monitoring to ensure that hospitals and clinics live up to their obligations under their contracts with the purchasing agencies, with respect to both the quantity and quality they have agreed to supply to patients covered under these contracts.

---

[21] In the Japanese system, regulators have tried to avoid this problem by setting relatively low payment rates for in-patient procedures, but paying out-patient primary-care providers relatively well.

6. Social Health Insurance in the Future: A Scenario

Any prediction about the future of China's health financing system clearly must involve a high degree of speculation, as it depends not only on the choices that are made with respect to the alternative policy approaches that have been discussed here, but also on developments in economic policy and governance more generally. Nevertheless, we conclude this chapter with an outline of how we think the system might evolve in the future if China chooses a model of health financing with a purchaser-provider split, along the lines discussed here, and assuming also that the economy in general will continue to grow and the political system evolve in a stable fashion.

As discussed earlier, the central element in the system will be local purchasing agencies, growing out of the urban Social Insurance Bureaus and rural Health Bureaus that currently manage the existing social insurance plans. A key assumption is that these agencies will also be given control over the funding of the network of primary-care clinics that is now being established throughout China. With this assumption, one can think of the subsidies that the government will pay for the operation of these clinics as part of an expanded social insurance system, as we have done in this chapter, and interpret the current system as one under which all Chinese residents are covered by one or more of four different plans. First, every citizen will have the right to receive care at highly subsidized rates in these clinics; we interpret this as a partial form of universal government insurance. Second, most citizens in rural areas and many in urban areas belong either to a voluntary but subsidized NCMS plan or to a URBMI plan, respectively. Finally, urban government employees and employees in large firms (state-owned or private) are covered under a local BHI plan in which membership, in principle, is compulsory.

With continued economic growth and modernization, the standards of coverage in the social insurance system will gradually improve. If the local purchasing agencies become responsible for the funding of universal primary care as well as the other plans, it seems reasonable to expect that they will want to move toward a simpler system with fewer differences between different individuals and plans. A nationwide commitment to a policy with greater emphasis on reducing economic inequality is also consistent with working toward a model in which differences across individuals in publicly financed health insurance become smaller.

At present, there is a big gap between the standards of benefits in the urban BHI plan and those in the other, less comprehensive plans. We believe it is unrealistic in the short and medium term to envisage a system in which this gap is completely eliminated, but we believe it is reasonable to expect a trend under which the relatively modest current subsidies under the NCMS and URBMI plans are merged with those going to primary care into a modified low-cost plan that covers everyone that is not covered by a BHI plan. In the following, we will refer to this as the G+ plan (with G signifying government subsidies for primary care). Thus, under the scenario we have in mind, China would have reached a form of universal coverage, with everyone covered by one of two government plans, BHI or G+.

The purchasing agencies in the Social Insurance Bureaus in urban areas and the Health Bureaus in the countryside would form the core of the health financing system, as managers of both the G+ and BHI plans. All health care services eligible for complete or partial coverage under the two plans would be supplied to citizens on terms that had been negotiated with the purchasing agencies, and all government subsidies for health care, as well as premiums and contributions paid by individuals and employers, would flow through the purchasing agencies.

A key feature of the model would be that funding of primary care would be through a system under which everyone would have to register with a single provider, typically a government-owned primary-care clinic, but possibly a privately practicing doctor or private clinic. Patients would be free to choose with which local primary-care provider to register, and each provider's revenue would consist mainly of monthly capitation payments from the purchasing agency, computed on the basis of the number of patients registered with the clinics. As further discussed in Chapter 10, capitation payments could be risk-adjusted, to reflect the fact that some types of patients (the elderly, those with various types of chronic diseases) have higher expected use of health services than others.

Patients would be eligible for services in hospitals and by specialist doctors only on referral from their primary-care provider, and most of these providers would be subject to incentives to refer patients only when their health problems could not be adequately handled at the primary level. Hospitals and specialist doctors, whether government-owned or private, would also provide services to insured patients on terms negotiated with the purchasing agencies. Patients might be required to pay part of the cost of their care out of their own pockets. Patients' out-of-pocket costs could differ, depending on whether they were covered by the low-cost G+ plan or by the more generous BHI plans, but the fees that the providers would be allowed to charge patients under both plans would also be governed by their contracts with the purchasing agencies. The use of pharmaceuticals, whether in primary or higher levels of care, would be governed by essential drug lists, with incentives on providers to control costs by prescribing less expensive drugs from among those available to deal with a given patient's health problems.

If China's health financing system were to evolve along the lines of this scenario over the next few decades, it would gradually come to resemble the U.K. system in many respects. The main principles on which the scenario is based are to a considerable extent drawn from the current U.K. model and the ideas that have been the basis for the various reform efforts that have been made there over the past 30 years. A major difference, of course, is that in the U.K., the universal coverage offered by the government plan is the same for every resident, while the universal coverage in the scenario we have sketched is based on two different plans. Although the idea of universal coverage through a single government plan is appealing from the viewpoint of equity, we believe the less ambitious version we have proposed is more realistic as a medium-term goal, for reasons similar to those implicit in Deng Xiaoping's support of the idea that successful economic development in China was more likely if some people were allowed to get rich first.

Even in a health financing model of this kind in which government subsidies or compulsory social insurance contributions supply a large share of health care financing, there can still be a substantial role for the private sector. First, even when health services are supplied under government insurance plans, on terms that have been negotiated with public purchasing agencies, the sellers can be private hospitals, clinics, or individual doctors. Second, some individuals may choose to obtain private insurance to pay for health services that are not covered under the public plan, or to obtain reimbursement for their share of the costs under it. Some wealthy individuals may also choose to get their health services privately, rather than under the government plan, and even pay for private insurance that helps pay for such services. Nevertheless, in a system of subsidized universal coverage of this kind, the role of private insurance and service production is likely to remain limited. In the next chapter, we turn to a discussion of an alternative model under which the private sector can play a more central role, not only in the production of health services but also in health financing.

Chapter 10

CHINA'S FUTURE HEALTH CARE SYSTEM: A MIXED PUBLIC-PRIVATE MODEL?

1. Introduction

For the reasons discussed in Chapter 1, health care is a sector in which unregulated markets will not function well in the sense of allocating economic resources in a way that accords with the interests of consumers or society. The tendency toward various forms of market failure in health care is present not only in private markets for health care services, but also, and perhaps even more so, in private markets for risk pooling through health insurance. As a result, governments in all countries have intervened heavily in these markets, either through direct financing and production of health services, or through extensive regulation of the private firms that supply health services and insurance in them.

In Chapter 9, we sketched a model for China's future health care system under which the government would respond to the potential market failures in health services production and health insurance principally through strengthening the social insurance plans that have gradually been introduced and developed during the first decade of the 2000s, and through the activities of the local government purchasing agencies that would negotiate with hospitals and primary-care clinics concerning the way health services would be supplied to the population. While the model we sketched there would rely on decentralized decision-making and market-like arrangements between purchasing agencies and providers, the transactions between them would take place in what the British have referred to as "internal markets": on the buying side, the purchasers would be government agencies, not private consumers or firms; while on the selling side, providers would be mostly government-owned hospitals and primary-care clinics, not privately practicing doctors or privately owned hospitals.

In principle, the internal-market model may be made to function well. It has been the basic model underlying the way the U.K. health care system has been managed since the 1980s, and in spite of considerable controversy over the way it has been implemented, it looks set to continue as the foundation for the U.K. system (though perhaps under a different name) for the foreseeable future. However, as was also discussed in Chapter 9, successful use of the internal-market model requires a strong commitment by the government to ensure not only that the officials in charge of the purchasing agencies act in ways that correspond to the interests of the patient population they are supposed to represent, but also that they maintain an arm's-length relationship with the managers of the government-owned hospitals and primary-care clinics.

In the U.K., the difficulty in attaining an effective "purchaser-provider split" between the branches of the NHS District Health Authorities that were supposed to act as purchasers, and the managers of the NHS Hospital Trusts, has been part of the reason why the purchasing role is now being transferred to primary-care practices, and it is still too early to tell how well this will work, or whether there will be further changes. In China, even though there has been considerable discussion about the idea that the local government agencies that manage the social insurance plans should act as purchasers of health services, local governments in many places seem to have been reluctant to give them full control over the social insurance funds and to let resource use in the hospital sector be determined by negotiations between hospital managers and purchasers. Whether an effectively functioning model of a purchaser-provider split of the kind outlined in Chapter 9 can be successfully used in China in the future is thus likely to depend on whether there will be a clear set of guidelines to that effect from the state.

A model based on a purchaser-provider split and internal markets tries to accomplish some degree of decentralization and exploitation of the advantages of a market mechanism indirectly, by trying to use administrative measures to make government employees behave in ways similar to private agents. While this approach is inspired by the example of the U.K., in Chapter 2 we argued that there is an alternative European model that also contains potentially useful ideas for China, namely the one that is gradually being introduced in the Netherlands.[1]

In the Dutch model, too, the allocation of resources in health care is supposed to be determined in a decentralized fashion, through negotiations between providers and insurance plans acting as purchasers. However, in the Dutch model, the split between purchasers and providers is not one that has to be enforced by administrative means. In part, this is because providers in the Dutch system are not government-owned: Primary care is supplied principally through privately practicing doctors, and most Dutch hospitals are private (though operated as non-profit firms).

Moreover, although about half the financing of acute health care in the Netherlands is through a common pool to which all Dutch residents must contribute, there is in fact an insurance market in which they can choose among several competing government-sanctioned sickness funds or private insurance plans. Thus, although Holland has a universal health insurance system that is largely funded through compulsory contributions[2] (that is, they are equivalent to taxes), health care resources in Holland are allocated in a decentralized fashion, on the basis of contracts negotiated between purchasers and providers in real markets for health care services. In this chapter, we consider the question of how China might organize a system similar to the Dutch model, with a role not only for private health services providers, but also for private insurance plans.

---

[1] Although we focus on the case of the Netherlands, other countries, including Belgium, Germany, Israel, Switzerland, Slovakia, and the Czech Republic, are using the same basic approach; see van de Ven and Schut (2011).

[2] Before 2005, the common pool paid for as much as 85% of the premium cost of the plans to which Dutch residents belonged. After 2005, the share has been 50%, with the rest coming from individual premiums. However, to compensate for the higher individual premiums, the government introduced an income-related transfer to all individuals with incomes below a given threshold; see van de Ven and Schut (2008).

Somewhat paradoxically, a mixed model with major roles for both private provision of health services and private health insurance may constitute a policy approach that would be less controversial in China than the U.K.-inspired version of a purchaser-provider split and internal markets outlined in Chapter 9. Superficially, the latter model may seem like a reasonable compromise between the two camps in the health policy debate — those who advocate a return to greater reliance on direct government funding and management of health services production, and those who want to rely more on competitive markets in health care as in other sectors. But at the same time, it may be a compromise that is hard for both sides to accept.

From the viewpoint of those who favor a return to more centralized management, the distinction between the purchasing and provider function may seem like a needless administrative complication, and they are likely to argue that the incentives on providers who have to rely on revenue they earn in the market can lead to behavior that is not in society's interest. Those who favor markets, on the other hand, may lack confidence in the ability of government to consistently make purchasing agencies act on behalf of the patient population, and to give government-owned providers the same incentive to manage their resources efficiently as they would have in privately owned firms. A mixed policy, in contrast, could be perceived by the two camps as giving both of them an opportunity to show that their approach would work better than the other side's. We will return to this idea later on.

The rest of the chapter is organized as follows. In the next section, we briefly describe the role that private health insurance currently plays in China. We then turn to a discussion of various policy issues that would have to be addressed if China were to move in the direction of a mixed system in which private insurance would play a more substantial part, including the question whether it would serve as a complement/supplement to social insurance, or as a substitute, and measures that could be used to overcome the well-known problem of adverse selection in private insurance markets. In the following section, we discuss how a greater role for private health insurance could indirectly serve to promote greater participation of the private sector in the production of health services as well. The chapter ends with a

Table 1. Revenue and reimbursement of private health insurance, 2001–2012.

	Premium revenue from private health insurance (RMB Billion)	Reimbursement from private health insurance (RMB Billion)	Net underwriting revenue (RMB Billion)
2001	6.16	3.35	2.81
2002	12.25	4.99	7.26
2003	24.19	6.99	17.20
2004	25.99	8.91	17.08
2005	31.23	10.79	20.44
2006	37.69	12.51	25.18
2007	38.42	11.69	26.73
2008	58.55	17.53	41.02
2009	57.4	21.70	35.70
2010	67.75	26.40	41.35
2011	69.17	35.97	33.20
2012	86.28	29.82	56.46

Source: China Insurance Regulatory Commission.

description of a hypothetical scenario under which a modified version of the Dutch approach would be used as a model for China's future health care system.

2. Private Health Insurance in China Today

Private health insurance has been growing rapidly in China in recent years; the data in Table 1 show premium revenue growing at more than 25% per year over the last decade, and a recent estimate suggests that as much as 7% of China's population now has some form of private coverage. Nevertheless, private insurance still remains something of a niche product. In 2012, it financed less than 2% of total health expenditures.[3] While many foreign insurance companies are active in the Chinese market, most of the over 1,000 private plans that existed in 2012 belonged to the large domestic companies, including China

[3]The data come from a brief article on the market for private health insurance published in March 2012 by two analysts from L.E.K. Consulting in the magazine *China Economic Review* (Chen and Lin, 2012).

Life and Ping An. Central government guidelines to local governments on health financing policy have generally been supportive of private insurance, and much of the private insurance that has been sold has been marketed in collaboration with the agencies responsible for managing the local social insurance plans. However, the companies have also offered health insurance of the type that is known in the West as "dread disease" plans. Under such plans, which are often marketed in conjunction with life insurance, the benefits consist not in payments to reimburse part of the insured's health care costs, but instead, in lump-sum amounts that are paid if he or she is diagnosed with one of a specified set of diseases.

In some major urban areas, private insurers have coordinated their marketing with the social insurance plans, and offered plans that simply extend the latter's coverage by reimbursing patients for costs above the upper limits under the social insurance plans. In the BHI plan in Xiamen, for example, private coverage has been offered with an upper limit of 150,000 RMB per year, almost a tripling of the limit of 53,000 RMB under the basic BHI plan.[4] In other cities, local governments have been working with private insurers to market plans that reimburse the costs when patients are treated in specific hospitals, reducing the amounts that even patients with social insurance coverage have had to pay out of their own pocket. Finally, many local governments have entered into contracts with private insurers to help the local Social Insurance Bureaus or Health Bureaus manage the basic social insurance plans. In such cases, the insurers may be paid simply to help these agencies with administrative tasks such as designing the rules under which benefits will be paid, marketing the voluntary social insurance plans, and administering premium collection and payment of reimbursement, without participating in the risk-pooling function. However, the private insurers may also function both as managers of the basic plans *and* as providers of extended insurance; they may also combine their role as managers of a social insurance plan with marketing of their own life insurance plans, or "dread disease" plans.

---

[4]Chen and Lin (2012, p. 25).

3. Mixed Private-Public Insurance: Policy Issues

In the analysis of government policy toward health insurance in countries where government pays for a large portion of health care costs, either directly or through social insurance plans, a sharp distinction is made between cases where private insurance plays the role of a *complement* or *supplement* to government plans, on the one hand, and cases where it can be a *substitute* for the government plans.[5]

In the conventional terminology, supplementary plans are those that are offered in systems where the coverage under the government plans excludes certain kinds of health care costs, and private plans are offered to cover those costs. A typical example would be plans that cover the cost of out-patient drugs in the Canadian health care system. In Canada, many provincial government plans typically only cover the cost of out-patient drugs for the elderly, but not for the general population.[6] Since the cost of drugs that patients take on doctors' prescriptions can be quite high, many people have therefore joined private insurance plans that cover the cost of such drugs. In most cases, they have acquired coverage through employment, as most employers offer it as a fringe benefit under group insurance contracts that they have negotiated with private insurers on behalf of their employees.

Plans that are described as complementary to the government plans, in contrast, are those that are offered in cases where the government plans have deductibles or patient cost-sharing, so that those covered by the government plan have to pay a significant share of the cost of covered services. In the U.S., for example, the standard Medicare plan that covers all U.S. citizens over age 65 requires patients to pay part of the cost of both out-patient and hospital care. Some of the so-called Medigap plans that exist in the U.S. offer to reimburse patients for out-of-pocket payments they have had to make under these provisions, and therefore serve as "complements" to the Medicare plan,

---

[5]We follow the terminology of the OECD here; see Colombo and Tapay (2004).
[6]In Canada, in-patients do not have to pay anything for the services or drugs they receive; all hospital costs, including pharmaceuticals used by in-patients, are paid by the provincial governments.

in the conventional terminology. In many cases, private plans serve as both complements and supplements. Before the U.S. Medicare plan was expanded to offer coverage against the cost of out-patient drugs, most Medigap plans included both (supplementary) coverage of out-patient drug costs, and (complementary) reimbursement of patients' out-of-pocket costs for physician and hospital care, as part of their benefits.

Supplementary and complementary private insurance are plans that strengthen the degree of coverage that the public plans offer. Most private health insurance in China so far has served this function, and it is the most common form of private insurance in many other countries as well. Substitute private insurance, in contrast, refers to private plans with coverage that, partly or completely, overlaps with the coverage in plans offered by the government directly or through social insurance. Not surprisingly, it is a less common form of private insurance than the former types, since coverage through government plans is mandatory in most advanced countries. With mandatory government coverage, the only reason to sign up for a private plan that offers similar benefits would be a belief that the private plan offers coverage of higher quality in some dimension; but since the public coverage is already paid for, few people find it worthwhile to pay the full cost for a private plan even if they believe its quality is somewhat better. That is, with mandatory coverage by a government plan, private insurance is not competing with the government plan on equal terms.[7]

But even though competition between mandatory government coverage and substitute private insurance is not common, there are a few countries where deliberate policy measures have been implemented to create a mixed system in which the two do compete. One such case is the U.S., where citizens over age 65 may either accept highly subsidized coverage through the basic Medicare plan, or sign up for a private substitute plan. If a person chooses the latter option, he or she is no longer eligible for the benefits under the basic Medicare plan, but in

---

[7]The expression "duplicate insurance" is sometimes used with reference to the case where people are privately insured under a plan that covers the same kinds of costs as those for which they already have coverage through a public plan.

return, the Medicare plan contributes a fixed amount to the premium cost of the private plan.[8]

Another country which has implemented a version of this approach is Australia, where everyone is automatically covered by a government plan that pays the cost of most physician and hospital services, but where many citizens have opted for substitute private hospital insurance. Coverage through a private plan goes beyond that of the public plan in that the private plan will pay for the cost of care in a private hospital (which the public plan does not), and a patient who pays privately for care in a public hospital can choose his or her doctor (while "public patients" are treated by a doctor to whom they have been assigned). However, private insurance can compete reasonably effectively with the public plan because it is subsidized by the government: To reflect the fact that the government does not have to pay for the hospital costs of patients who pay privately, it subsidizes patients' premium costs if they buy private insurance.[9]

But the clearest example of a country in which policy deliberately favors competition on equal terms between public and private insurance is Holland, as already discussed in Chapter 2. To recapitulate, Holland has a universal social insurance system to which everyone has to contribute, and every resident must be enrolled in a health insurance plan that meets specific requirements for minimal coverage. In choosing among plans, residents can choose a plan offered either by a private insurer, or by one of the non-profit sickness funds that originated out of the earlier social insurance system.[10] From a resident's point of view, what is important is the quality of the coverage offered by the fund, and the out-of-pocket premium it charges. Once he or she has chosen in which plan to enroll, the plan receives a subsidy from the central government insurance fund which is the same whether the

---

[8]A thorough recent description of this so-called Medicare Advantage plan is Medicare Payment Advisory Commission (2012).

[9]A recent and detailed analysis of the Australian health care system is Duckett and Willcox (2011); see also Colombo and Tapay (2003).

[10]Descriptions of the Dutch system are in van de Ven and Schut (2008), and Enthoven and van de Ven (2007).

plan is offered by a private insurer or by a sickness fund. In addition to being treated equally with respect to the amount of subsidy they will receive for covering a given person, private insurers and sickness funds also are subject to the same restriction with respect to the out-of-pocket premium they can charge: it has to be the same for every person enrolled in the plan. All plans also must agree that they will enroll anyone who is willing to pay the out-of-pocket premium; they cannot refuse to enroll anyone based on factors such as age, sex, or previous illness history.

In our view, private insurance could potentially play a useful role in China's future health financing system, both as an element that would supplement and complement the public plans, and also as a substitute for public coverage. In the next several sections, we discuss various policy measures that could be used to facilitate this.

3.1. *Private insurance as supplement or complement to social insurance*

In the health economics literature, considerable attention has been paid to an unintended side effect of complementary private insurance when consumers are covered by a public plan under which they are required to pay a share of the cost of the health services they receive. Specifically, if patients have complementary private insurance that covers their share of costs under the public plan, there may be a tendency for them to utilize more services than they would without the complementary private insurance, since their out-of-pocket cost of health services has been reduced. Readers familiar with the literature will recognize this argument as a form of the "moral hazard" problem, which suggests that it may be efficient to require insured consumers to pay a share of their health care costs, since health insurance implicitly subsidizes their utilization of health services, creating a tendency for inefficiently large utilization and contributing to high health care costs.[11]

Although the logic of this argument is correct, its practical significance is reduced by the fact that most of the decisions that affect

---

[11] A classic exposition of this problem is Taylor, Short, and Horgan (1988).

health services utilization and aggregate health care costs are made not by patients, but by the doctors who treat them once they have made the decision to seek treatment. Thus, making sure that doctors and other health professionals have an incentive to treat patients in a cost-effective manner is generally more important than creating incentives on patients through cost-sharing. Nevertheless, since it does make sense to require patients to pay a fee when they first seek treatment so as to discourage them from seeking care for minor problems, and at least a share of the cost of services they subsequently receive, so as to retain at least some incentive for them to accept the simplest and least expensive way to deal with their problems, we believe there is a case for retaining such provisions in government insurance plans. However, incentives on providers are more important, and we do not believe that a concern for incentives on patients is a sufficient reason to pursue restrictive policies toward complementary private insurance.

As noted above, many of the private insurance plans currently offered in China are intended to protect patients whose health care costs are sufficiently high so that they exceed the upper limits on the benefits that are payable under the social insurance plans. The standard arguments in favor of risk pooling suggest that such plans are efficient. Only a small minority of patients are likely to have health care costs that are high enough to reach these limits, so the premiums on the plans should be relatively low; at the same time, the financial consequences for patients without complementary private insurance could be disastrous, implying that the benefits of such insurance would be high. Moreover, the moral hazard argument is particularly unimportant in this case: Persons who have incurred health care costs that are high enough to exceed the limits in government plans have not done so by choice.

In a health care system in which government insurance restricts coverage to specific sets of health services and drugs, private insurance may also serve a supplementary role by covering services and drugs that the government plans do not. From patients' point of view, plans that serve this supplementary function can clearly be beneficial, as it may protect them and their families from very difficult financial problems if they have received advanced and expensive drugs and services that are not on the lists of the government plans. However, this supplementary private insurance may not be consistent with economic efficiency. In principle, the drugs and services that are excluded from coverage under the government plans should be chosen from among those that have low cost-effectiveness, in the sense of offering relatively low incremental health benefits in comparison with less expensive alternatives, in spite of their high cost. From the viewpoint of economic efficiency, the use of such drugs or treatment methods should be discouraged, even if doctors or hospitals find it attractive to recommend them to patients because they increase providers' revenue.

Private insurance that pays a set amount of money when a person has been diagnosed with one from a list of specified serious diseases can also be regarded as a form of supplementary health insurance. Because the benefits payable under insurance plans of this type are independent of the cost of the health services or drugs that patients have used, the issue of moral hazard does not arise. The benefits that consumers expect from coverage through plans of this kind obviously depend in part on the degree to which their government insurance plans are expected to cover the costs of the health care they need if they contract one of the listed diseases, so the demand for plans of this kind will vary from place to place and depending on what kind of government plan is available to the individual. However, even for people who are covered by a relatively complete social insurance plan with limited cost-sharing and a high upper limit, plans of this kind may be attractive in cases where the insured person is the family breadwinner or contributes a significant portion of its income, and the person becomes unable to work as a result of the illness. In such cases, the plan serves partially as a form of income replacement insurance, a form of insurance that is part of the social insurance system, or is offered as a fringe benefit of employment, in many advanced countries.

In general, our conclusion is that private supplementary or complementary insurance can play a useful role even in a country where most people are covered through government social insurance plans. We believe its role can be particularly useful in the system of health care financing in China today, where the government's role in health insurance and health financing is still evolving. Even though there may be a tendency for private insurance to be bought mostly by relatively well-off individuals, there is no reason to deny them the benefits of extended insurance coverage if they are willing to pay for it, and transactions in the private insurance market may provide useful signals for government officials with respect to ways in which they can strengthen the government insurance plans. If, for example, private insurers offer plans that cover the cost of health care beyond the upper limits in the government plans, the premiums charged for such plans can give governments an implicit estimate of the expected cost of raising these limits, something that might be desirable in any case.

Moreover, policies that encourage private insurers to enter the health insurance market may help develop professional expertise in the management of health insurance, and hence create opportunities for mutually beneficial contracts between government purchasing agencies and private insurers for the administration of the government plans, as has happened in many places in China. As we will discuss in the next section, allowing a strengthened role for private insurers in the market may also, over time, create conditions for an expanded role for the private sector in offering substitute insurance that competes with the government plans.

3.2. *Private insurance as a substitute for social insurance*

In contrast to complementary and supplementary private insurance, substitute private insurance consists of plans with benefits that overlap those for which patients are eligible under government insurance. In order for private substitute insurance to be able to compete effectively with government plans, the contest between them must be on a "level playing field". That is, the rules that govern the consumer's choice between private and public coverage must be such that the implicit subsidy consumers receive when they choose the public plan is available also when they choose the private alternative.

In a place like the U.K., the playing field is not level in this sense. While private plans are available that cover the same services as those offered under the NHS at little or no out-of-pocket cost to the patient, a person who signs up for such a plan receives no subsidy toward the premium that the plan charges. While some people nevertheless pay for private substitute insurance (for example, because they prefer to be treated by privately practicing doctors, or in private hospitals that are not part of the NHS), they tend to be individuals with very high income who are willing to pay for what they believe is coverage of somewhat higher quality than what is available under the NHS, even though they are eligible for NHS coverage at no out-of-pocket cost.

In contrast, the private insurance plans that compete with the sickness funds in the Dutch system compete on a strictly level playing field. As previously noted, the government's role in health care financing in the Netherlands essentially consists of collecting compulsory contributions to a national risk-pooling fund which then pays a subsidy toward the premium cost of the insurance plan that the consumer has chosen. This subsidy is the same, regardless of whether the consumer chooses a private plan or a sickness fund plan.[12] Similarly, retired persons in the U.S. who are eligible for the government Medicare plan can choose a substitute private plan under the Medicare Advantage program; if they do, the government pays a subsidy toward the premium cost. The amount of the subsidy is set so as to enable private insurers to compete on equal terms with the public plan: It is designed to approximate the expected savings to the government as the government is no longer responsible for the future health care costs of persons with substitute private coverage.

In principle, it is possible to formulate policies that would make it easier for private insurance to offer substitute health insurance plans that could compete with government insurance on reasonably equal terms in the Chinese system. Two of the social insurance plans in the current system, the URBMI and NCMS plans, are technically voluntary plans that receive well-defined government subsidies. Competition between these plans and private insurance on equal terms could be created simply by allowing eligible consumers to use the subsidy to pay for a private plan, instead of joining the government plan.

---

[12] Some analysts have stopped making the distinction between private and government plans in the Dutch system, since the non-profit sickness funds that previously were considered part of the government system now compete on equal terms with private for-profit insurers.

Under the BHI plan (which is compulsory for urban employees), there is no explicit government subsidy, but in each city, there are well-defined rules that specify the amounts that are paid into the social insurance system on behalf of each employee. Competition between each BHI plan and private substitute plans could be created by simply specifying that employees could use these contributions to pay for an approved private plan as a substitute for the BHI plan, along the same lines as in the Dutch system.

The implicit insurance coverage that will be provided to each Chinese resident through the direct government subsidies that are paid to the network of primary-care clinics that is being developed can also, in principle, be integrated into a model with competition from private insurance. For example, if the government subsidies to these clinics are paid to them on the basis of specified capitation amounts for each patient registered with the clinic, as suggested in the previous chapter, the government could offer to pay this subsidy toward the premium cost of a private plan under which consumers receive their primary care from another provider.

However, while these relatively simple measures would create some degree of competition between government insurance and substitute private plans, experience in other countries has demonstrated certain problems that are likely to arise in mixed systems of this kind. In particular, the task of ensuring that the competition takes place on a level playing field is complicated by the fact that there are large differences across individuals in their risk of illness, and hence in the expected cost of insuring them. Unless safeguards are created to take such differences into account, major distortions are likely to arise that will prevent the system from functioning as intended.

3.3. Risk differences, equity, and adverse selection

In general, competitive markets are based on the principle that the terms according to which transactions in them are made are mutually beneficial: Whenever a transaction is made, it is on terms acceptable to both the buyer and the seller. In most markets, this principle leads to sellers quoting the same prices to all buyers: If the seller is prepared to offer a commodity at a given price to one buyer, he or she is generally happy to offer the same price to any other buyer, since all that matters is the price the seller receives for the commodity. But in insurance markets, this principle does not hold. If potential buyers of insurance differ in terms of their risk of illness, and hence in the expected cost of insuring them, sellers will only be happy to insure high-risk buyers if they pay a higher premium than low-risk buyers. That is, in unregulated competitive insurance markets, buyers who can be identified as being at high risk — for reasons such as age, sex, or previous illness history — will generally have to pay higher premiums for a given insurance coverage than others.

But this effect makes it more complicated to design a competitive system in which individuals are allowed to choose between government insurance, on the one hand, and a substitute private plan, on the other. If the government pays the same subsidy to everyone who chooses a private plan, there will be a selection effect: Substituting a private plan for public coverage will seem most attractive to individuals at low risk of illness (with low expected health care costs), since private insurers will offer them coverage at a relatively low premium. That is, the benefits of that type of mixed system will go disproportionately to people such as the young, or those with no history of major illness. Conversely, the old, or persons who have had high health care costs in the past, will tend to remain in the government plan.[13]

To overcome this problem, governments in some of the countries that have tried to create competition between private and public insurance have designed a more complicated subsidy model in which the amount of subsidy to which a person is entitled when he or she chooses a substitute private plan is differentiated according to factors that influence the expected cost of insuring him or her. For example, a larger subsidy is paid for an older person, or for a person who has been diagnosed with certain kinds of chronic illness.

Both the Dutch system and the Medicare Advantage model in the U.S. are based on such "risk-adjusted" subsidies, which can eliminate

---

[13] A detailed exposition of the adverse selection problem is in Cutler and Zeckhauser (2000).

the bias in favor of persons at low risk of illness in the private insurance market, at least partially. But at the same time, designing such a system is not a simple task.[14] To further reduce the tendency for private insurers to discriminate against persons at high risk of illness, governments in both Holland and the U.S. have imposed regulations on private substitute insurance plans under which they must charge the same out-of-pocket premiums to every plan enrollee (although the government subsidy is risk-adjusted). They also are not allowed to deny coverage to any eligible subsidized applicant who is willing to pay the plan's out-of-pocket premium. Once again, these regulations help offset the tendency of private insurers to discriminate against high-risk individuals, but enforcing them effectively may be complicated and costly.

3.4. *Individual vs. group insurance?*

Both the Dutch system and the Medicare Advantage model are based on the idea of allowing competition between government and private plans by allowing each eligible *individual* to choose between them. In many other private health insurance markets, in contrast, the most intense competition among insurers is not for individual enrollees, but instead, for employment-related group insurance contracts under which employers negotiate for coverage that will apply to all or most of their employees collectively. Group insurance contracts often offer coverage on more favorable terms than in the individual market, partly because they have lower administration costs. But another reason is that the issue of risk selection is less significant in the group insurance market. When groups of employees, for example, negotiate insurance collectively, each member of the group will have the same coverage and premium, whether he or she has high or low expected health care costs.

Even though the Dutch and American models focus on insurance markets where individuals choose among plans, a system of mixed public-private coverage can be designed in such a way that it allows

---

[14]A clear exposition of the problems of creating workable risk-adjustment schedules in practice is van de Ven and Schut (2011).

private group insurance plans to compete with the government plans. As an example, under China's current health insurance system, urban firms and their employees jointly contribute to the BHI plans' individual and social pooling accounts. If the system were modified so that the firms and their employees could choose to collectively channel these contributions either to the BHI plan as at present, or to a private group plan, private insurance companies would have an incentive to compete with BHI by developing plans that provided more extensive or better quality coverage. As in other countries, they could do this by negotiating more favorable terms with specific hospitals and other service providers, and use the savings to offer enrollees better coverage (for example, in the form of a wider range of covered drugs or services than in the public plan, or lower patient cost-sharing) if they agree to get their services from the providers with whom the plans have contracts.

In rural areas, townships or villages might be able to obtain better coverage for their residents if they were allowed to channel the health insurance subsidies from higher levels of government either to the local NCMS plan offered by the county Health Bureau, or to an approved private plan with different features. Another way in which private insurance could play a role in rural areas under a mixed public-private system would be for the local Health Bureau to contract with a private insurer to design and manage the local NCMS plan. Although such an arrangement could be interpreted as a form of subcontracting by the local government plan (rather than as competition between a government plan and a private plan), it could also be interpreted as a form of private group insurance under which the local Health Bureau purchased subsidized private insurance on behalf of the local population. By soliciting offers for such contracts from more than one private insurer, the Health Bureau could exploit competition in the private insurance market in order to secure the most favorable terms for its population. Implicitly, the possibility of such an arrangement also creates competition between private insurers and local government plans, since the Health Bureau would retain the option to manage the local plan on its own if it did not find the offers from private insurers sufficiently attractive.

3.5. *Private insurance and consumer information*

In earlier chapters, the information asymmetry between buyers and sellers of health care was identified as one of the main reasons why unregulated competitive markets might not function well in the health care sector. Individual patients cannot be expected to have the technical expertise necessary to decide what services or drugs they would benefit from when they suffer from particular illness conditions, or how the terms offered by a given provider compare with alternative ones.

Clearly, the information asymmetry problem is also present in the market for health *insurance*. Insurance plans are complex contracts whose value depends on the benefits the seller promises in a great variety of future hypothetical situations corresponding to different health problems that the consumers may suffer from. When choosing among insurance plans, individual consumers are handicapped not only by their lack of expertise with respect to what services and drugs will help them deal with different health problems, but also regarding the likelihood that they will experience these problems. The difficulty for individual consumers to make well-informed purchase decisions in the market for health insurance is another reason why private insurance markets in most countries are dominated by group insurance. When insurance is bought on behalf of many individuals at the same time, the cost of the expert advice that is needed to find the best combination of quality and cost will be shared by all the members of the group.

In systems where private substitute insurance plans are allowed to compete with government plans, regulation is typically used to address the problem of information asymmetry in the insurance market. One approach is to specify that the coverage offered under substitute private plans must meet certain minimum standards in order for them to qualify for government subsidies. These standards may be defined in terms of what drugs and types of services must be covered, or in terms of the out-of-pocket costs insured patients must pay, in the form of deductibles or cost-sharing percentages; they may also specify minimum upper limits on benefits payable, or maximum annual consumer out-of-pocket costs. Regulation of this kind clearly might have a useful role to play in China's future health financing system if private insurance were to be allowed an expanded role in supplying substitute coverage.

4. The Role of Private Provision of Health Services

In principle, the question what role the private sector should have in the provision of health *services* can be considered separately from that of the role of private *insurance* in health care. In particular, it is possible to design a system (such as that in Canada) where financing is almost entirely through government plans, but almost all health services are supplied by private hospitals or privately practicing doctors. In the type of financing model that was outlined in Chapter 9, the question whether hospitals or clinics are government-owned or privately owned would in fact be relatively unimportant.

Even if hospitals and clinics were owned by the government, they are supposed to be independently managed and earn the revenues that cover their salaries and other costs under the contracts they negotiate with the purchasing agencies, just as privately owned firms would. And while managers in government-owned firms are not supposed to be under any pressure from their owners to earn a profit, experience in other sectors with TV enterprises and state-owned firms has shown that as long as they are subject to "hard" budget constraints (that is, cannot count on having any losses covered by government) and are allowed to retain at least some of their profits within the firm, managers of government firms can be made to pay as much attention to cost control and making a net profit as managers of private firms. Conversely, the techniques that government purchasing agencies would use in negotiating favorable terms for the supply of health services to their populations from privately owned hospitals or clinics could be very much the same as those they would use in negotiating with government-owned providers in a well-designed model of a purchaser-provider split.

4.1. *Competition in the hospital services market*

With respect to hospital services, current plans for the implementation of Chinese health system reform in the near future foresee an increased role for the private sector. Specifically, the guidelines for the 12th Five-Year Plan anticipate an expansion of the percentage of hospital beds that are in private hospitals from around 8.5% in 2010 to as much as 20% in 2015.[15] It is likely that private hospitals today mostly supply relatively advanced services that are not included in most existing social insurance plans, so that most of their revenue is paid for by well-to-do patients out of their own pockets, or through supplementary private insurance. However, with more beds in private hospitals and as the social insurance system expands and begins to cover an increased range of services, competition among private and government-owned hospitals to supply services to persons in the social insurance system is likely to increase.

In a model under which government-owned hospitals are financed mostly through revenue that they earn from patients under contracts with the local purchasing agencies, and under which they do not receive direct government subsidies, competition between private and government-owned hospitals can take place on reasonably equal terms. However, an issue that becomes important in this context is the treatment of capital costs. Private investment in hospitals can only be justified if their anticipated revenue is large enough to cover not only the cost of salaries and other current inputs, but also the cost of depreciation and a return on the investment in the hospital itself and its equipment. In order for the competition to be on equal terms, the revenue that government-owned hospitals should be required to generate should therefore not just be enough to cover salaries and other current costs, but also depreciation and some return on the government's investment in the hospitals it owns.

4.2. Competition in primary and out-patient care

Regarding primary care, there has so far been relatively little discussion of any future role for the private sector. This is understandable. As discussed in previous chapters, the deterioration in the earlier system of government-funded primary care has been seen as perhaps the main problem in China's health care system since the early 1980s, and

---

[15] Qian (2012a).

strengthening it, rather than supporting privately provided primary care, has been seen by many as a central task of health reform. In the future, however, an expanded role for privately supplied primary care might be a helpful element of the health care sector's evolution. In other countries, provision of primary care through government clinics is the exception rather than the rule. For example, even in the U.K., the GP practices that are the core of its government-financed health care system are privately owned, and at the other end of the spectrum, competition between privately practicing family doctors and hospitals' out-patient departments has been identified as an important reason for the relative efficiency of Japan's health care system.

As in the case of hospital services, competition on equal terms between privately supplied primary care and that provided in government-owned clinics is facilitated if the latter are funded through revenue that they earn under contracts with public purchasing agencies, rather than through direct subsidies from the government. In Chapter 9, we argued that the best way to fund the government clinics that will be at the core of China's future health care system is through a mixed model based primarily on capitation payments for each patient registered with the clinic, perhaps supplemented by payments for specified public health services and some out-of-pocket payments by patients. As for hospital services, the fact that privately owned clinics or individual physician practices must earn enough revenue to pay not just salaries and other current costs, but also depreciation and a return on the investment in the clinic itself and its equipment, is relevant in creating a level playing field. The revenue targets that should be the basis for funding government clinics should include an allowance for capital costs, not just enough to cover operating costs.

A further consideration that is relevant to the possible role of allowing a greater role for provision of primary care (as well as specialist physician care) in private practices and clinics has to do with the high cost of training doctors who are qualified to treat patients using the complex and rapidly changing technology that is used in modern medicine. Again, part of the problems that have affected the Chinese health care system in the last several decades has to do with the relatively small supply of qualified physicians, and as discussed in Chapter 4, an important component of the plans to strengthen primary care in China is to train a large number of new doctors for practice in primary care. Even if the cost of training doctors in China on average may be lower than it is in the U.S. and other advanced countries, it still will be high, and this high cost should be taken into account when making decisions about the mix of doctors and other less expensive personnel in staffing hospitals and clinics.

Since medical students only pay a relatively small share of the total cost of their training, most of that cost is borne by government. In a situation where most doctors work in government clinics and hospitals, this may not be a matter of great concern. When doctors do not pay for their own training, it is possible to attract good students to medical schools even if doctors' salaries are not very high. However, in a system where well-qualified doctors are in relatively short supply, they may be able to earn high incomes by setting themselves up in private practice, if they are allowed to do so. In these circumstances, allowing doctors to practice privately, in competition with government-owned clinics, may either force these clinics to pay doctors higher salaries, thereby raising their costs, or make it difficult for them to retain well-qualified doctors. While this problem can be avoided through regulation that prevents doctors from practicing privately, an alternative solution that retains the opportunity to create public-private competition is to subject the income of doctors in private practice to some form of taxation that reflects the government's past cost in training them.

In the next section, we will argue that in a model in which there is some degree of competition between private substitute insurance and the government social insurance plans, it would be desirable to allow doctors to supply primary care in private practices outside the network of government-owned clinics. However, even in a model where financing of health care is dominated by social insurance, there are advantages in allowing competition between government clinics and privately practicing doctors in primary care. As the supply of qualified doctors coming out of medical schools increases over time, it may be more efficient to let this be reflected in more decentralized production of primary care in private practices, rather than by employing larger numbers of doctors in the existing government clinics. More decentralized production increases the accessibility of primary care as it reduces patients' travel costs, and the model of financing of primary care through capitation under contracts in which the providers have incentives to control drug costs and limit referrals of patients to hospitals can be used both for government clinics and for privately practicing doctors. (Recall that in the U.K., the GPs who supply primary care under capitation contracts are private practitioners.) Moreover, allowing primary-care doctors to practice privately and compete for patients under a capitation model may be more effective in creating an incentive for government clinics to maintain a high quality of care than just allowing competition among government clinics.

4.3. *Private provision and private insurance*

Although it is possible in principle to separate the question of the extent of private provision of health services from that of what role private insurance should have, in practice there are reasons to expect that in a model in which private insurance is allowed to play a more substantial role on the financing side, it would also be easier for private providers to become more prominent in the market for health services. We believe this would be the case both for hospital services, and for the services supplied by primary-care physicians as well as specialists.

If health care financing is predominantly through government plans, private hospitals would have to compete with government-owned hospitals on similar terms, for comparable services. A private hospital that wanted to supply services of a higher quality in some dimension (for example, by offering more comfortable amenities than the public ones, or by employing more highly trained doctors) would find it difficult to do so if the revenue it earned for its services had to be the same as what government hospitals were paid for services of lower quality. If the private hospital chose to charge more and operate outside the government insurance system, its market would be limited mostly to individuals who were willing to pay out of their own pockets, or had duplicate insurance beyond the government plan.

If individuals and firms were allowed to opt for subsidized private insurance as a substitute for the government plans, on the other hand, more of them could opt for private plans that allow them to receive higher-quality services from private hospitals even if they charge higher fees. With a larger role for substitute private insurance, therefore, the outcome might be a more differentiated hospital sector giving individuals and firms a wider range of choice than in a system dominated by government insurance only. If allowed to do so, private hospitals may in fact take the initiative to strengthen their ability to compete with government-owned hospitals by entering into collaborations with private insurers that would require or encourage their clients to get treatment in these hospitals.

Similarly, rules that would allow individuals and firms to substitute private insurance for government plans could indirectly encourage private provision of primary care and independent specialist physician services. Private insurance plans that are designed using the model of "preferred provider networks" that are common in the U.S. follow the principle of directing their patients to providers with whom they have negotiated prior contracts regarding fees and other conditions with respect to the services supplied. Such plans would more likely prefer to direct their patients to privately practicing primary-care providers rather than to government clinics, since they can better control the terms of these contracts when they rely on private practitioners rather than on government clinics who mostly treat patients covered by the social insurance plans. Thus, with more private insurance, there would be a greater demand for privately supplied primary care.

In particular, an expanded role for privately supplied substitute group insurance could contribute to such a trend. In the employment-related system of health care financing that prevailed several decades ago, primary care was supplied to a large extent through clinics that were owned and operated by employers, by doctors and nurses that worked for them. In many cases, this was a convenient and efficient way of organizing the provision of primary care. In a model under which urban firms could substitute private group insurance for the social insurance coverage that their employees would otherwise have (through the basic BHI plan, and their access to subsidized primary care in government clinics), many of them might find it advantageous to do so, and to once again rely on primary care supplied by doctors and nurses that they employed, or with whom they had contracts.[16]

5. Conclusion: Could China Follow the Dutch Model?

In Chapter 9, we briefly considered the question of how China's current system of health care financing might gradually evolve into one modelled on the universal insurance coverage that every U.K. resident enjoys under the NHS in that country. Here we turn to a similar question with respect to the other system that we have identified as a possible model for China's future — that designed and being introduced in the Netherlands.

To recapitulate, the Dutch approach essentially is a universal voucher model in which citizens contribute to a common risk-sharing pool, from which everyone is entitled to a subsidy that must be used to purchase one of many competing approved health insurance plans that are offered in the market, both by the old sickness funds and by private insurers. While the subsidy is risk-adjusted, the government regulates the insurance market in three critical ways. First, every plan must offer a range of benefits that meets a defined standard. Second, while plans can decide what out-of-pocket premium they will charge consumers, the premium for a given plan must be the same for everyone who enrolls in the plan. Third, a plan cannot refuse to enroll anyone who is willing to pay the stated premium. Could China's health financing system evolve along similar lines?

The version of a voucher system that we propose here would build on the existing social insurance system in a way similar to what we discussed in Chapter 9. That is, the present system would gradually be

---

[16]Although the basic principle is that insurance plans in the Dutch system must accept all applicants and charge each one the same premium, there is in fact an exception that allows them to offer discounts (of up to 10%) when a number of individuals enroll as a group (for example, all the employees in a workplace). According to van de Ven and Schut (2008), over 50% of those insured in the Dutch system have enrolled at discounted rates.

modified such that every citizen would be eligible for coverage under either the low-cost social insurance plan (that we referred to as G+ in Chapter 9), or (for urban employees) the local expanded BHI plan. However, while those plans would be similar to what we discussed there, the difference now would be that everyone eligible for coverage under those two plans would also have the option to instead receive a voucher (subsidy) that could be used to enroll in a substitute private insurance plan of his or her choice.

Administration of such a voucher system need not be complicated, and would build on the same purchasing agency model as was discussed in Chapter 9. In urban areas, there would be two types of vouchers: one for those eligible for the G+ social insurance plan, and another for urban employees who are required to contribute to the BHI plan; in rural areas, there would be only one. The voucher amounts in either category would be risk-adjusted, as in the Dutch model, to reflect the fact that individuals in different categories may have vastly different expected health care costs. While construction of an accurate risk adjustment scheme can be an extremely complex task, a simple approach can be used as a starting point. As we discussed in Chapter 9 in the context of funding primary care, adjustments could initially just be based on age, sex, and whether or not a patient has been classified as suffering from one or more of a set of specified chronic conditions.

Under the Dutch approach, the emphasis is to create a more competitive environment in the insurance market by giving *individuals* a wider range of options with respect to the choice of coverage. But as discussed earlier, insurance markets where most transactions are between insurers and individual buyers tend to be inefficient because of the adverse selection problem, and because insurers then have an incentive to devote resources to trying to identify those who are at high risk of illness, rather than to create more cost-effective plans. Moreover, unless the markets are regulated, they will discriminate against high-risk individuals either by charging them higher premiums, or by denying them coverage.

Risk adjustment of the voucher subsidies that individuals are eligible for is intended to reduce the extent of these problems, since they imply that insurers earn more revenue from high-risk individuals than from others. To further reduce the equity and efficiency problems resulting from risk selection, however, the Dutch model also contains two key regulations noted above. First, a plan would have to charge the same out-of-pocket premium to all individual enrollees. Second, the plan is not allowed to refuse coverage to anyone willing to pay this premium. We believe a Chinese version of the Dutch approach should also contain regulations of this kind, but with certain modifications.

First, in urban areas, private plans should be allowed to differentiate their out-of-pocket premiums to reflect the fact that they would receive higher subsidy amounts from those who otherwise would be covered by the BHI plan than from others. Hence, to have the same incentive to enroll individuals in these two categories, private plans should be allowed to charge lower out-of-pocket premiums to those with a higher subsidy, for a plan with a given set of benefits. Second, we believe there is a much better chance to create more competition in insurance markets when there is a strong role for group insurance rather than individual insurance. Thus, we think insurers should be allowed to charge lower premiums when signing up individuals in groups rather than one by one. The rules under which these transactions would be allowed would have to be clearly defined, for example, with respect to the minimum number of individuals who would be required in order for a contract to be classified as group insurance. Also, the case for requiring insurers to offer coverage to all applicants on the same terms is much less strong when coverage is sold as group insurance, so a case can be made for allowing insurers and buyers to freely negotiate the terms of group contracts.

As under the Dutch model, only plans that meet a set of minimum standards in terms of the benefits offered would be eligible under the voucher scheme. These standards would apply not only to provisions such as upper annual or lifetime limits on benefits, deductibles and rates of patient cost-sharing, but also to the range of drugs and types of services that would have to be covered. In keeping with the relatively decentralized approach that China has adopted to health policy in general, local governments could be given some degree of freedom in establishing such rules, but there clearly also is an important role for the state in encouraging the kind of research and data collection that is required for purposes of evaluating the cost-effectiveness of various drugs and intervention techniques that should be required in both the social insurance plans and private substitute plans.

REFERENCES

Asian Development Bank (2002). *People's Republic of China: Toward Establishing a Rural Health Protection System*. Report 090902, by Y. Liu, K. Rao, and S. Hu. Manila: Asian Development Bank.

Baker, George (1992). "Incentive contracts and performance measurement", *Journal of Political Economy*, 100(3), 598–614.

Baker, Laurence (2011). "Managed care", Ch. 18, pp. 405–431 in Glied and Smith, eds.

Banister, Judith (1987). *China's Changing Population*. Stanford University Press.

Barros, Pedro Pita and Pau Olivella (2011). "Hospitals: Teaming up", Ch. 19, pp. 432–462 in Glied and Smith, eds.

Blomqvist, Åke (2001). "International health care models: Sweden". Submitted to the Standing Senate Committee on Social Affairs, Science and Technology, Study on the State of the Health Care System in Canada (The Kirby Committee).

Blomqvist, Åke (2002). *Canadian Health Care in a Global Context*. Toronto: C.D. Howe Institute.

Blomqvist, Åke (2009). "Health system reform in China: What role for private insurance?", *China Economic Review*, 20, 605–612.

Blomqvist, Åke (2011). "Public-sector health care financing", Ch. 12, pp. 257–284 in Glied and Smith, eds.

Blomqvist, Åke and Pierre-Thomas Léger (2005). "Information asymmetry, insurance, and the decision to hospitalize", *Journal of Health Economics*, 24, 775–793.

Blomqvist, Åke and Jiwei Qian (2008). "Health system reform in China: An assessment of recent trends", *Singapore Economic Review*, 53(1), 5–26.

Blomqvist, Åke and Jiwei Qian (2010). "Direct provider subsidies vs. social health insurance: A compromise proposal", in Zhao and Lim, eds.

Blumenthal, D. and W. Hsiao (2005). "Privatization and its discontents — The evolving Chinese health care system", *New England Journal of Medicine*, 353, 1165–1170.

Brereton, Laura and Vilashiny Vasoodaven (2010). "The impact of the NHS market: An overview of the literature". Civitas: Institute for the Study of Civil Society,

available at http://www.civitas.org.uk/nhs/download/Civitas_LiteratureReview_
NHS_ market_ Feb10.pdf.

Bunker, John P., Howard S. Frazier, and Frederick Mosteller (1994). "Improving
health: Measuring effects of medical care", *The Milbank Quarterly*, 72, 225–258.

Cai, S. (2007). "Thoughts on improving the rural public health system", *China State
Finance*, 5, 13–16 (in Chinese).

Canadian Institute for Health Information (CIHI) (2011). *National Health Expenditure Trends, 1975 to 2011*.

Chen, Helen and Yanyan Lin (2012). "Waiting for the boom", *China Economic Review*,
March, pp. 24–25; downloadable from http://www.lek.com/search/node/
private%20health%20insurance.

Cheng, Tsung-Mei (2013). "A pilot project using evidence-based clinical pathways and
payment reform in China's rural hospitals shows early success", *Health Affairs*,
May.

Chernew, Michael E. and Dustin May (2011). "Health care cost growth", Ch. 14,
pp. 308–328 in Glied and Smith, eds.

Chernew, Michael E. and Joseph P. Newhouse (2012). "Health care spending
growth", Ch. 1, pp. 1–44 in Pauly, McGuire, and Barros, eds.

China Development Brief (2003). "The physician will not heal himself".
http://www.chinadevelopmentbrief.com/node/262.

China Reform (2007). "A number of possible arrangements of fiscal system for sub-
province government", 9, 51–53.

Chou, Y.J., *et al.* (2003). "Impact of separating drug prescribing and dispensing
on provider behavior: Taiwan's experience", *Health Policy and Planning*, 18(3),
316–329.

Christianson, Jon B. and Douglas Conrad (2011). "Provider payment and incentives",
Ch. 26, pp. 624–648 in Glied and Smith, eds.

Colombo, Francesca and Nicole Tapay (2003). "Private health insurance in Australia:
A case study", OECD Health Working Papers, No. 8. Paris: OECD.

Colombo, Francesca and Nicole Tapay (2004). "Private health insurance in OECD
countries: The benefits and costs for individuals and health systems", OECD
Health Working Papers, No. 15. Paris: OECD.

Culyer, Anthony J. and Joseph P. Newhouse, eds. (2000). *Handbook of Health
Economics*, Volumes 1A and 1B. Amsterdam: North-Holland.

Currie, Janet, Wanchuan Lin, and Wei Zhang (2011). "Patient knowledge and
antibiotic abuse: Evidence from an audit study in China", *Journal of Health
Economics*, 30, 933–949.

Curry, Natasha and Ruth Thorlby (2007). "Practice-based commissioning", King's
Fund Briefing, November (available at www.kingsfund.org).

Cutler, David M. and Richard J. Zeckhauser (2000). "The anatomy of health
insurance", Ch. 11, pp. 568–576, 580–586 in Culyer and Newhouse, eds.

Cutler, David M., Allison B. Rosen, and Sandeep Vijan (2006). "The value of medical
spending in the United States, 1960–2000", *New England Journal of Medicine*,
355, 920–927.

Danzon, Patricia (2011). "The economics of the biopharmaceutical industry", Ch. 22, pp. 520–554 in Glied and Smith, eds.

Danzon, Patricia M. and Sean Nicholson, eds. (2012). *The Oxford Handbook of the Economics of the Biopharmaceutical Industry*. Oxford University Press.

Dong, Weizhen (2006). "Can health care financing policy be emulated? The Singaporean medical savings accounts model and its Shanghai replica", *Journal of Public Health*, 28, 209–214.

Dong, Weizhen (2008). "Cost containment and access to care: The Shanghai health care financing model", *Singapore Economic Review*, 53(1), 27–42.

Dranove, David (2012). "Health care markets, regulators, and certifiers", Ch. 10, pp. 639–690 in Pauly, McGuire, and Barros, eds.

Du, Lexun and Wenmin Zhang, eds. (2009). *Green Cover Book of Health Care*. China: Social Sciences Academic Press.

Duckett, Jane (2010). *The Chinese State's Retreat from Health: Policy and the Politics of Retrenchment*. Routledge.

Duckett, S. and S. Willcox (2011). *The Australian Health Care System*. Melbourne: Oxford University Press.

Economist Intelligence Unit (1998). *Healthcare in China into the 21st Century*. London: The Economist Intelligence Unit.

Eggleston, Karen, ed. (2009). *Prescribing Cultures and Pharmaceutical Policy in the Asia-Pacific*. The Brookings Institution for the Walter H. Shorenstein Asia-Pacific Research Center, Stanford University.

Enthoven, Alain C. (1993). "The history and principles of managed competition", *Health Affairs*, 12(Supplement 1), 24–48.

Enthoven, Alain C. and Wynand P.M.M. van de Ven (2007). "Going Dutch: Managed-competition health insurance in the Netherlands", *New England Journal of Medicine*, 357, 2421–2423.

European Observatory on Health Systems and Policies (2004). *Health Systems in Transition: Netherlands* (written by André den Exter, Herbert Hermans, Milena Dosljak, and Reinhard Busse). (Also U.K. 1999, Ray Robinson with Anna Dixon; Sweden 2001, Catharina Hjortsberg and Ola Ghatnekar.)

Felder, Stefan (2009). "The variance of length of stay and optimal DRG outlier payments", *International Journal of Health Care Finance and Economics*, 9, 279–289.

Fleisher, Belton M., Åke Blomqvist, and Kerry Tan, eds. (2009). "Special issue — Symposium on health economics issues in China", *China Economic Review*, 20, 587–633.

Flood, Colleen M. (2000). *International Health Care Reform: A Legal, Economic and Political Analysis*. London: Routledge, especially Ch. 3, pp. 41–126.

Folland, Sherman, Allen Goodman, and Miron Stano (2007). *The Economics of Health and Health Care*, 5th edition. Pearson Prentice Hall.

Gao, Jiechun (2009). "Guanyu liangge fengli de kexingxi tantao" ("A feasible discussion over two separations"), *Hospital Director's Forum*, 3, 14–27.

Garber, Alan M. and Mark J. Sculpher (2012). "Cost-effectiveness and payment policy", Ch. 8, pp. 472–497 in Pauly, McGuire, and Barros, eds.

Gaynor, Martin and Robert J. Town (2012). "Competition in health care markets", Ch. 9, pp. 499–638 in Pauly, McGuire, and Barros, eds.

Ge, Yanfeng, *et al.* (2007). *China Healthcare Reform.* Beijing: China Development Press.

Gerdtham, Ulf G. and Bengt Jönsson (2000). "International comparisons of health expenditure", Ch. 1, pp. 11–54 in Culyer and Newhouse, eds.

Glied, S. (2000). "Managed care", pp. 707–753 in Culyer and Newhouse, eds.

Glied, Sherry and Peter C. Smith, eds. (2011). *The Oxford Handbook of Health Economics.* Oxford University Press.

Goddeeris, John H. (1984a). "Insurance and incentives for innovation in medical care", *Southern Economic Journal,* 51, 530–539.

Goddeeris, John H. (1984b). "Medical insurance, technological change, and welfare", *Economic Inquiry,* 22, 56–67.

Goldman, Dana and Darius Lakdawalla (2012). "Intellectual property, information technology, biomedical research, and marketing of patented products", Ch. 13, pp. 825–872 in Pauly, McGuire, and Barros, eds.

Gordon, Roger and Wei Li (2011). "Provincial and local governments in China: Fiscal institutions and government behavior", NBER Working Papers 16694.

Gruber, Jonathan (2009). "Universal health insurance coverage: Progress and issues", Center for Policy Research, Syracuse University (available at http://surfac.syr/edu/cpr/2).

Gu, Xin (2008). "China new round of healthcare reforms", EAI Background Brief, No. 379.

Gu, Xin (2010). "Towards central planning or regulated marketization? China debates on the direction of new healthcare reforms", Ch. 2, pp. 23–40 in Zhao and Lim, eds.

Gu, Xin, *et al.* (2006). *China's Health Care Reforms: A Pathological Analysis.* Beijing: Social Science Academic Press.

Han, Jun and Dan Luo (2007). *Survey on China's Rural Medical & Health Reality.* Shanghai: Shanghai Far East Publishers.

He, Alex Jingwei and Jiwei Qian (2013). "Hospitals' responses to administrative cost-containment policy in urban China: the case of Fujian province", *The China Quarterly,* 216, 946–969.

Ho, Christina S. (2010). "Health reform and de facto federalism in China", *China: An International Journal,* 8, 33–62.

Holmstrom, B. and P. Milgrom (1991). "Multitask principal-agent analyses: Incentive contracts, asset ownership, and job design", *Journal of Law, Economics, and Organization,* 7, 24–52.

Hsiao, William C. (1995). "Medical savings accounts: Lessons from Singapore", *Health Affairs,* 14, 260–266.

Hsiao, William C. (2004). "Disparity in health: The underbelly of China's economic development", *Harvard China Review,* 5, 64–70.

Huang, Yasheng (1996). *Inflation and Investment Controls in China.* Cambridge University Press.

Hurley, Jeremiah and G. Emmanuel Guindon (2008). "Medical savings accounts: Promises and pitfalls", Ch. 6, pp. 125–148 in Mingshan Lu and Egon Jonsson, eds., *Financing Health Care: New Ideas for a Changing Society*. Wiley.

Ikegami, Naoki and Gerard F. Anderson (2012). "In Japan, all-payer rate setting under tight government control has proved to be an effective approach to containing costs", *Health Affairs*, 31, 1049–1056.

Ikegami, Naoki and John Creighton Campbell (1998). *The Art of Balance in Health Policy: Maintaining Japan's Low-Cost, Egalitarian System*. Cambridge University Press.

Kahneman, Daniel (2011). *Thinking, Fast and Slow*. Allen Lane.

Kahneman, Daniel and Amos Tversky (1979). "Prospect theory: An analysis of decision under risk", *Econometrica*, 47, 263–291.

Kahneman, Daniel, Jack Knetsch, and Richard Thaler (1990). "Experimental test of the endowment effect and the Coase theorem", *Journal of Political Economy*, 98, 1325–1348.

Kung, James Kai-Sing and Ting Chen (2013). "Do land revenue windfalls reduce the career incentives of county leaders? Evidence from China", Working Paper, HKUST.

Kwon, S. (2003). "Pharmaceutical reform and physician strikes in Korea: Separation of drug prescribing and dispensing", *Social Science and Medicine*, 57(3), 529–538.

Laffont, J.J. and Jean Tirole (1991). "The politics of government decision-making: A theory of regulatory capture", *Quarterly Journal of Economics*, 106, 1089–1127.

Leu, Robert E., Frans F.H. Rutten, Werner Brouwer, Pius Matter, and Christian Rüschi (2009). "The Swiss and Dutch health insurance systems: Universal coverage and regulated competitive insurance markets". The Commonwealth Fund (available from www.commonwealthfund.org).

Li, H. and L.-A. Zhou (2005). "Political turnover and economic performance: The incentive role of personnel control in China", *Journal of Public Economics*, 89(9–10), 1743–1762.

Li, Liu (2008). "Creating a regulatory framework for managing subnational borrowing", Ch. 9, pp. 171–192 in Lou and Wang, eds.

Lim, Meng-Kin (2004). "Shifting the burden of health care finance: A case study of public-private partnership in Singapore", *Health Policy*, 69, 83–92.

Lin, Justin, Ran Tao, and Mingxing Liu (2003). "Decentralization, Deregulation and Economic Transition in China". Mimeo, London School of Economics.

Lin, Justin, Ran Tao, and Mingxing Liu (2006). "Decentralization and local governance in China's economic transition", in Pranab Bardhan and Dilip Mookherjee, eds., *Decentralization and Local Governance in Developing Countries: A Comparative Perspective*. MIT Press.

Lin, Justin Yifu, Ran Tao, and Mingxing Liu (2013). "Decentralization, deregulation and economic transition in China", in David Kennedy and Joseph Stiglitz, eds., *Law and Economics with Chinese Characteristics: Institutions for Promoting Development in the Twenty-First Century*. Oxford University Online. (First published in 2003 as a China Center for Economic Research working paper.)

Lin, Zhonglin (2007). "Comparison and analysis of new CMS", *China State Finance*, No. 2, pp. 23–24 (in Chinese).

Liu, G., B. Nolan, and C. Wen (2004). "Urban health insurance and financing in China". http://www.worldbank.org.cn/English/content/cr4_ en.pdf.

Liu, Mingxing, Juan Wang, Ran Tao, and Rachel Murphy (2009). "The political economy of earmarked transfers in a state-designated poor county in Western China: Central policies and local responses", *The China Quarterly*, 200, 973–994.

Liu, Yuanli (2002). "Reforming China's urban health insurance system", *Health Policy*, 60, 133–150.

Liu, Yuanli and Keqin Rao (2006). "Providing health insurance in rural China: From research to policy", *Journal of Health Politics, Policy and Law*, 31, 71–92.

Lou, Jiwei and Shulin Wang, eds. (2008). *Public Finance in China: Reform and Growth for a Harmonious Society*. World Bank Publication.

Ma, Yuqin, Lulu Zhang, and Qian Chen (2012). "China's New Cooperative Medical Scheme for rural residents: Popularity of broad coverage poses challenges for costs", *Health Affairs*, 31(5), 1058–1064.

Martin, A.B., *et al.* (2012). "Growth in U.S. health spending remained slow in 2010", *Health Affairs*, 31(1), 208–219.

McGuire, Thomas (2000). "Physician agency", Ch. 9, pp. 461–536 in Culyer and Newhouse, eds.

McGuire, Thomas (2011). "Physician agency and payment for primary medical care", Ch. 25, pp. 602–623 in Glied and Smith, eds.

Medicare Payment Advisory Commission (2012). "The Medicare Advantage Program: Status Report", Ch. 12 in *Report to the Congress: Medicare Payment Policy*. Downloadable from http://www.medpac.gov/chapters/Mar12_Ch12.pdf.

Morton, Fiona Scott and Margaret Kyle (2012). "Markets for pharmaceutical products", Ch. 12, pp. 763–824 in Pauly, McGuire, and Barros, eds.

Nicholson, Sean and Carol Propper (2012). "Medical workforce", Ch. 14, pp. 873–926 in Pauly, McGuire, and Barros, eds.

Nordhaus, William D. (2005). "Irving Fisher and the contribution of improved longevity to living standards", *American Journal of Economics and Sociology*, 64, 367–392.

Oliver, Adam (2005). "The English National Health Service: 1979–2005", *Health Economics*, 14(S1), S75–S99.

Oliver, Adam (2007). "The Veterans Health Administration: An American Success Story?", *The Milbank Quarterly*, 85(1).

Olsen, Jan Abel (2011). "Concepts of equity and fairness in health and health care", Ch. 34, pp. 814–836 in Glied and Smith, eds.

Ostrom, E. (1990). *Governing the Commons*. New York: Cambridge University Press.

Pauly, Mark V. (1980). *Doctors and Their Workshops: Economic Models of Physician Behavior*. University of Chicago Press.

Pauly, Mark V. (2011). "Insurance and the demand for medical care", Ch. 16, pp. 354–379 in Glied and Smith, eds.

Pauly, Mark V., Thomas G. McGuire, and Pedro P. Barros, eds. (2012). *Handbook of Health Economics*, Volume 2. Elsevier.

Porter, Michael E. and Elizabeth Olmstead Teisberg (2006). *Redefining Health Care: Creating Value-Based Competition on Results.* Harvard Business School Press.

Propper, Carol and George Leckie (2011). "Increasing competition between providers in health care markets: The economic evidence", Ch. 28, pp. 671–688 in Glied and Smith, eds.

Propper, C., D. Wilson, and N. Söderlund (1998). "The effects of regulation and competition in the NHS internal market: The case of general practice fundholder prices", *Journal of Health Economics*, 17, 645–674.

Qian, Jiwei (2011a). "Building networks of primary care providers in China", *East Asian Policy*, 3(4), 87–97.

Qian, Jiwei (2011b). "Reforming public hospitals in China", *East Asian Policy*, 3(1), 75–82.

Qian, Jiwei (2012a). "Health reform in China: Three years after", *East Asian Policy*, 4(3), 5–16.

Qian, Jiwei (2012b). "Mental health care in China: Providing services for under-treated patients", *Journal of Mental Health Policy and Economics*, 15(4), 179–186.

Qian, Jiwei (2013a). "Anti-poverty in China: Minimum livelihood guarantee scheme", *East Asian Policy*, 5(3).

Qian, Jiwei (2013b). "Financial sustainability of the basic pension system in China", Background Brief, East Asian Institute.

Qian, Jiwei and Åke Blomqvist (forthcoming). "Reforming China's health care in the Xi era", in Zheng Yongnian and Lance Gore, eds., *China Entering the Xi Era*. Routledge.

Qian, Jiwei and Y. Do (2012). "Regional inequality in healthcare and government health grant in China", Working Paper.

Qian, Jiwei and C. Leong (2012). "Better treatment for hospital violence", *China Daily*, March 29.

Ren, Bo, *et al.* (2007). "Start of 'Urban Resident Health Insurance Plan'", *Caijing*, April 16, pp. 78–80 (website: www.caijing.com.cn).

Rothschild, Michael and Joseph E. Stiglitz (1976). "Equilibrium in competitive insurance markets: An essay on the economics of imperfect information", *Quarterly Journal of Economics*, 90(4), 630–649.

Schelling, Thomas (1968). "The life you save may be your own", pp. 127–162 in Samuel B. Chase, ed., *Problems in Public Expenditure Analysis*. Washington, DC: The Brookings Institution.

Schreyögg, Jonas, Tom Stargardt, Oliver Tiemann, and Reinhard Busse (2006). "Methods to determine reimbursement rates for diagnosis-related groups (DRG): A comparison of nine European countries", *Health Care Management Science*, 9(Special Issue), 215–223.

Scott, Anthony and Stephen Jan (2011). "Primary care", Ch. 20, pp. 463–485 in Glied and Smith, eds.

Shih, V., C. Adolph, and M. Liu (2012). "Getting ahead in the Communist Party: Explaining the advancement of Central Committee members in China", *American Political Science Review*, 106(1), 166–187.

Song, Zheng, Kjetil Storesletten, Yikai Wang, and Fabrizio Zilibotti (2012). "Sharing high growth across generations: Pensions and demographic transition in China", available at http://faculty.chicagobooth.edu/zheng.song.

Stigler, George (1971). "The theory of economic regulation", *Bell Journal of Economics and Management Science*, 2, 3–21.

Sun, Qiang, *et al.* (2008). "Pharmaceutical policy in China", *Health Affairs*, 27, 1042–1050.

Talbot-Smith, Alison and Allyson M. Pollock (2006). *The New NHS: A Guide.* Abingdon, Oxon: Routledge, especially Ch. 5, pp. 78–103.

Tang, Shenglan, *et al.* (2007). "Pharmaceutical policy in China: Issues and problems", World Health Organization Chinese Pharmaceutical Policy Studies, English background document, downloaded from http://archives.who.int/tbs/Chinese PharmaceuticalPolicy/BackgroundENGdefault.htm.

Tao, Ran and Dali Yang (2008). "The revenue imperative and the role of local government in China's transition and growth". Paper presented at conference on China's Reforms, University of Chicago.

Tarn, Yen-Huei, *et al.* (2008). "Health care systems and pharmacoeconomics research in Asia-Pacific region", *Value in Health*, Special Issue: Pharmacoeconomics and Outcomes Research in Asia, S137–S155.

Tatara, K. and E. Okamoto (2009). *Japan: Health System Review*, Health Systems in Transition Series. European Observatory on Health Systems and Policies.

Taylor, A.K., P.F. Short, and C.M. Horgan (1988). "Medigap insurance: Friend or foe in reducing deficits?", in H.E. Frech, ed., *Health Care in America*. San Francisco: Pacific Institute for Public Policy.

Tong, S. and J. Yao (2011). "China's local government debts: How serious?", EAI Background Brief, No. 559.

Trinh, Hahn Q., James W. Begun, and Roice D. Luke (2008). "Hospital service duplication: Evidence on the medical arms race", *Health Care Management Review*, 33, 192–202.

Triplett, Jack E. (2011). "Health system productivity", Ch. 30, pp. 707–732 in Glied and Smith, eds.

Tsui, Kai-Yuen and Yongqiang Wang (2008). "Decentralization with political trump: Vertical control, local accountability and regional disparities in China", *China Economic Review*, 19, 18–31.

Tuohy, Carolyn Hughes (1999). *Accidental Logics: The Dynamics of Change in the Health Care Arena in the United States, Britain, and Canada.* New York: Oxford University Press.

Tuohy, Carolyn Hughes and Sherry Glied (2011). "The political economy of health care", Ch. 4, pp. 58–77 in Glied and Smith, eds.

Usher, Dan (1973). "An imputation to the measurement of economic growth for changes in life expectancy", pp. 193–232 in Milton Moss, ed., *The Measurement of Economic and Social Performance*. New York: Columbia University Press.

van de Ven, Wynand P.M.M. and Frederik T. Schut (2008). "Universal mandatory health insurance in the Netherlands: A model for the United States?", *Health Affairs*, 27, 771–781.

van de Ven, Wynand P.M.M. and Frederik T. Schut (2011). "Guaranteed access to affordable coverage in individual health insurance markets", Ch. 17, pp. 380–404 in Glied and Smith, eds.

van Doorslaer, Eddy and Tom van Ourti (2011). "Measuring inequality and inequity in health and health care", Ch. 35, pp. 837–869 in Glied and Smith, eds.

Vogel, Ezra F. (2011). *Deng Xiaoping and the Transformation of China.* Harvard University Press.

Wagstaff, Adam (2007). "Social health insurance reexamined", World Bank Policy Research Working Paper 4111.

Wagstaff, Adam and Magnus Lindelow (2008). "Can insurance increase financial risk? The curious case of health insurance in China", *Journal of Health Economics,* 27, 990–1005.

Wagstaff, Adam, Magnus Lindelow, Shiyong Wang, and Shuo Zhang (2009). *Reforming China's Rural Health System.* The World Bank.

Walker, Simon, Mark Sculpher, and Mike Drummond (2011). "The methods of cost-effectiveness analysis to inform decisions about the use of health care interventions and programs", Ch. 31, pp. 733–758 in Glied and Smith, eds.

Whiting, Susan (2007). *Central-Local Fiscal Relations in China.* National Committee on U.S.-China Relations and Renmin University of China.

WHO (2010). "Cuba answers the call for doctors", *WHO Bulletin,* 88(5), downloaded from http://www.who.int/bulletin/volumes/88/5/10-010510/en/index.html (accessed June 15, 2013).

Wong, Christine and Richard Bird (2008). "China's public finance, a work in progress", in Loren Brandt and Thomas Rawski, eds., *China's Great Economic Transformation.* New York: Cambridge University Press.

Wong, C.K., K.L. Tang, and V.I. Lo (2007). "Unaffordable healthcare amid phenomenal growth: The case of healthcare protection in reform China", *International Journal of Social Welfare,* 16(2), 140–149.

World Bank (2002). *China: National Development and Subnational Finance, a Review of Provincial Expenditures.* Washington, DC.

World Bank (2009). *From Poor Areas to Poor People: China's Evolving Poverty Alleviation Agenda, an Assessment of Poverty and Inequality in China.* Washington, DC.

Xu, C. (2011). "The fundamental institutions of China's reforms and development", *Journal of Economic Literature,* 49(4), 1076–1151.

Yang, Dali (2009). "Regulatory learning and its discontents in China: Promise and tragedy at the State Food and Drug Administration", in John Gillespie and Randall Peerenboom, eds., *Regulation in Asia: Pushing Back Globalization.* Routledge.

Yip, W. and K. Eggleston (2004). "Addressing government and market failures with payment incentives: The case of hospital reimbursement in Hainan, China", *Social Science and Medicine,* 58, 267–277.

Yip, Winnie and William C. Hsiao (2008). "The Chinese health system at a crossroads", *Health Affairs,* 27, 460–468.

Yip, Winnie and William C. Hsiao (2009). "China's health care reform: A tentative assessment", *China Economic Review*, 20, 613–619.

Yip, W., H. Wang, and W. Hsiao (2008). "The impact of Rural Mutual Health Care on access to care: Evaluation of a social experiment in rural China", Working Paper, Harvard School of Public Health.

Yip, Winnie, Adam Wagstaff, and William C. Hsiao, eds. (2009). "China's health care system", *Health Economics*, 18(2), Special Issue, S1–S156.

Zhao, Litao and Tin Seng Lim, eds. (2010). *China's New Social Policy: Initiatives for a Harmonious Society*. World Scientific.

Zhou, Qingzhi (2004). *County-Level Government Organization and Operation in China — a Sociological Study of County W*. Guiyang: Guizhou People's Press.

Zhu, Hengpeng (2007). "Problems of health systems and distortion of pricing drugs", *Social Sciences in China*, 4, 89–103.

INDEX

township and village enterprises, 259
township hospitals and health centers,
87, 113, 129, 164
training doctors, *see* medical education
travel costs of patients, 164, 330
treatment protocols, 88, 90
TRIPS, 187

U.K. Department for International
Development (DFID), 116
U.K. health care system, 30–32, 273,
277, 278, 308
unemployment insurance, 222
unitary states vs. federations, 243
universal health insurance coverage, 57,
217
in China, 9, 93, 99, 302–304
in other countries, 70, 71, 76,
102, 236, 304, 309, 315, 332
through single or multiple plans,
236
Urban Resident Basic Medical
Insurance (URBMI), 91–93, 221,
281, 320

U.S. Food and Drug Administration
(FDA), 201
U.S. health care system, 36–38, 273,
276, 280
federal vs. state responsibilities,
243, 244

value added tax, 257
vested interests, 26, 38, 42, 178
Veterans Health Administration (VHA),
250

Wen Jiabao, 98, 238
work units, 111
World Bank, 88
World Health Organization (WHO),
88, 116
World Trade Organization (WTO),
186

Xi Jinping, 238

Printed in the United States
By Bookmasters